This book is a

From
....

To
....

Date
....

21/40 NIGHTS OF DECREES AND
YOUR ENEMIES WILL SURRENDER

21/40 NIGHTS OF DECREES
AND YOUR ENEMIES WILL SURRENDER

PRAYER M. MADUEKE

PRAYER PUBLICATIONS
1 Babatunde close, Off Olaitan Street,
Surulere, Lagos, Nigeria
+234 803 353 0599

21/41 Nights of Decrees And Your Enemies Will Surrender

Copyright © 2013 Prayer M. Madueke

Revised Edition

ISBN: 978-9780-7209-4-0

Prayer Publications

All rights reserved. No part of this work may be reproduced or transmitted in any form or by any means without written permission from the publisher.

Unless otherwise indicated, all Scripture quotations are taken from the King James Version of the Bible, and used by permission. All emphasis within quotations is the author's additions.

First Edition, 2006

For further information of permission

1 Babatunde close, off Olaitan Street,
Surulere, Lagos, Nigeria

Table of Contents

21 DAYS DECREES

Acknowledgment	viii
How to start your program	ix
Understanding the meaning of decree	1

Decree 1 -	For a new beginning	53
Decree 2 -	Against evil alliance for your sake	57
Decree 3 -	Against household wickedness	62
Decree 4 -	Against uncompromising enemies	67
Decree 5 -	Against evil verdicts	72
Decree 6 -	Against evil foundations	76
Decree 7 -	For immediate solutions	80
Decree 8 -	Against collective captivity	84
Decree 9 -	For financial breakthroughs	88
Decree 10 -	For divine promotion	92
Decree 11 -	Against satanic oppositions	96
Decree 12 -	Against hidden curses	100
Decree 13 -	Against evil soul ties	104
Decree 14 -	For supernatural abilities	108
Decree 15 -	Against sexual perversion	112
Decree 16 -	Against evil lateness to good things	116
Decree 17 -	Against unrepentant oppositions	120
Decree 18 -	Against evil growths and invisible sickness	124
Decree 19 -	Against satanic network	128

Decree 20 -	Against the spirit of fear	132
Decree 21 -	Against water spirits attack	136

40 DAYS DECREES

Decree 1 -	To kill uncompromising Haman	141
Decree 2 -	For spiritual cleansing	146
Decree 3 -	To intimidate your enemies	151
Decree 4 -	For sound decisions	156
Decree 5 -	Against satanic traps	161
Decree 6 -	Against the spirit of antichrist	166
Decree 7 -	To Stand against the devil	171
Decree 8 -	For resurrection power	177
Decree 9 -	To laugh last	182
Decree 10 -	For a new opening	188
Decree 11 -	Against witchcraft powers	193
Decree 12 -	To get wealth	198
Decree 13 -	Against the spirit of the tail	203
Decree 14 -	Against iron-like problems	207
Decree 15 -	Against stagnancy	212
Decree 16 -	For God's support	217
Decree 17 -	Against evil inheritance	221
Decree 18 -	For divine increase	226
Decree 19 -	Against Jezebel	231
Decree 20 -	For uncommon elevation	238
Decree 21 -	To enter the third heaven	244
Decree 22 -	For divine opportunities	249
Decree 23 -	Against little foxes	254
Decree 24 -	Against the god of gold	258

Decree 25 -	Against evil group	264
Decree 26 -	Against household witchcraft	270
Decree 27 -	For divine presence	275
Decree 28 -	For freedom and victory	280
Decree 29 -	To Be preferred above others	287
Decree 30 -	Against debt and death	294
Decree 31 -	To Stop weeping forever	299
Decree 32 -	Against destructive curses	304
Decree 33 -	For holiness everywhere	309
Decree 34 -	Against stubborn enemies	315
Decree 35 -	To frustrate the enemies' plans	320
Decree 36 -	Against evil accusations	325
Decree 37 -	For a better end	330
Decree 38 -	Against the coming shame	335
Decree 39 -	To destroy death	342
Decree 40 -	For open doors	347

Acknowledgment

I would like to acknowledge the immeasurable and unquantifiable encouragement of my general overseer, Dr. Daniel Olukoya, who supported me spiritually in my ministry over the years. Without his vision, this book would have not seen the light of the day.

HOW TO START YOUR PROGRAM

1. This book is a precious guide and help in your prayers of decree and fasting.

2. Choose a suitable method of fasting that suits you, as directed by the Holy Spirit.

3. It is best to handle prayers of decree at nights or early mornings, as the Holy Spirit directs you.

4. You can start your fast at 6:00 am and break off at 2:00 pm, or 3:00 pm, or 4:00 pm, or 6:00 pm; as you consider most suitable.

5. Please note that it is compulsory for you to pass your decrees between 12 midnight and 2:00 am every night.

6. You can repeat your decrees as many times as you could, both day and night. Again, decrees are effective at nights, between 12 and 2:00 am.

   May God Almighty hear your prayers - Amen

UNDERSTANDING THE MEANING OF DECREE

Decree is a strong and unshakeable utterance, or exercise of power through word and command, which is more of certainty. A decree can also be an order that has force equal to a law. It can be defined also as a religious ordinance, enacted by a council or a particular head.

Decree is force that ordains a will, like a judicial decision of a Roman emperor. When we talk of decree, we mean to give or issue a command, or to enjoin, as if by decree or to determine to order a judicial punishment. It is like pronouncing a law to be enacted by the legislature.

In every democratic government, the executive, legislative and judiciary share power and run the government. However, in God's kingdom and government, it is not so.

God the Father, Son and Holy Ghost are one God, and God operates with absolute power. His government is theocratic. He has all powers at His disposal, to do or undo anything He likes. He has absolute power to kill and give life. His Words are final and His rule reaches the heavens and earth. His decree is powerful and can change any situation, no matter who is involved.

God's absolutism can be seen throughout the ages, even to the end of this age. My God is not obligated by any government and cannot report to any authority. Instead, all governments on earth, powers and dominions are bound to report or bow down to Him.

God can take the form of executive, legislature or the judiciary, but He will not take the form of a servant. No human can question God. However, God's character is abounding. He is a faithful God, great in mercies, and all-powerful. Nevertheless, He is also a consuming fire. He does not use *'apology'* in His actions. Right from the beginning of time, He took decisions and the heavens and earth came into being.

God is not obligated to consult anyone or seek approval before taking any action. His Words are decree for He is omnipotent.

> *"Thou shalt bring them in, and plant them in the mountain of thine inheritance, in the place, O LORD, which thou hast made for thee to dwell in, in the Sanctuary, O Lord, which thy hands have established"* (Exodus 15:17).

> *"O Lord GOD, thou hast begun to shew thy servant thy greatness, and thy mighty hand: for what God is there in heaven or in earth, that can do according to thy works, and according to thy might?"* (Deuteronomy 3:24).

Among the gods that other powers and authority serve and fear, our God is greater. He is greatly to be feared above other gods. God can do everything, doable and undoable, that is beyond the scope of man and man-made gods that men serve, worship and fear. Even when hope is withdrawn from men, God appears without fear or consultation with any power and brings hope. When the devil and men that serve him conclude that nothing else can be done outside the realm of their power, God intervenes and works wonders.

> *"I know that thou canst do every thing, and that no thought can be withholding from thee"* (Job 42:2).

Without assistance from anywhere, God alone decreed and the heaven and the earth appeared by the great power of God.

> *"Ah Lord GOD! Behold, thou hast made the heaven and the earth by thy great power and stretched out arm, and there is nothing too hard for thee"* (Jeremiah 32:17).

God is so powerful that He can just decree anything and it will be exactly as He decreed it. No matter the claims of earthly wise men and numerous scientists through their groundbreaking discoveries, God created and allowed it all. The activities of dark powers, all their works and mysteries amount to nothing before God's decree. The armies of God in heaven are ready at all times to back up God's decree no matter who is involved as an opposition.

In His administration of justice, no one, not even the combined forces of all the creation, can stand to oppose God. The armies of heaven are trained and well equipped to deal with any opposing force to God's decree. There are no rooms for questions as soon as God passes His decree for none can stay His hands or Words of decree.

> *"And all the inhabitants of the earth are reputed as nothing: and he doeth according to his will in the army of heaven, and among the inhabitants of the earth: and none can stay his hand, or say unto him, What doest thou?"* (Daniel 4:35).

Heavenly angels are ever ready to enforce, with an overwhelming energy, any decree that comes from God. No power can constrain, compel, or bribe the angels of God from carrying out required actions to establish God's decree. At God's decree, heavenly enforcers are released in full force and in all aggressiveness, with divine hit men ready to carry out details of God's Words of decree.

The first decree that God decreed against the language of the world still stands today. All the wise men of the world together with all the universities have not been able to restore one language to mankind.

> *"And the whole earth was of one language, and of one speech"* (Genesis 11:1).
>
> *"And the LORD said, Behold, the people is one, and they have all one language; and this they begin to do: and now nothing will be restrained from them, which they have imagined to do"* (Genesis 11:6).
>
> *"Go to, let us go down, and there confound their language, that they may not understand one another's speech"* (Genesis 11:7).

The terrible and unsolved language barriers all over the world today are as a result of God's decree against men's resolve and evil agreement.

When God wants to stop any determined and united evil force, He passes a decree against their speech.

In the decree of God against evil men, no one can change the decree of God against evil men. There were once people in cities called Sodom and Gomorrah, who were gays and lesbians. They committed homosexuality without restriction, even by the government of their day. They were beyond the control of men, not even the righteous could persuade them to stop. They were evil and determined homosexuals, who could go into any house and defile even the righteous. The cry of the people they forced into homosexuality was so great. Their sins were so terrible that God had to come down because of the cries of the people they defiled.

> *"And the LORD said, because the cry of Sodom and Gomorrah is great, and because their sin is very grievous"* (Genesis 18:20).

Their sins rose up to God to the extent that they were ready to commit sexual immorality at all cost. Even when they saw angels of God, they still wanted to have sexual relationship with them.

> *"And there came two angels to Sodom at even; and Lot sat in the gate of Sodom: and Lot seeing them rose up to meet them; and he bowed himself with his face toward the ground; And he said, Behold now, my lords, turn in, I pray you, into your servant's house, and tarry all night, and wash your feet, and ye shall rise up early, and go on your ways. And they said, nay; but we will abide in the street all night. And he pressed upon them greatly; and they turned in unto him, and entered into his house; and he made them a feast, and did bake unleavened bread, and they did eat"* (Genesis 19:1-3).

In those days, Lot was a child of God but he did not use any word of decree against the evil men of his generation. These evil men of Sodom were committing sins without fear, even wanting to enter into the house of the righteous Lot.

> *"But before they lay down, the men of the city, even the men of Sodom, compassed the house round, both old and young, all the people from every quarter: And they called unto Lot, and said unto him, Where are the men which came in to thee this night? bring them out unto us, that we may know them. And Lot went out at the door unto them, and shut the door after him, And said, I pray you, brethren, do not so wickedly. Behold now, I have two daughters which have not known man; let me, I pray you, bring them out unto you, and do ye to them as is good in your eyes: only unto these men do nothing; for therefore came they under the shadow of my roof. And they said, Stand back. And they said again, this one fellow came in to sojourn, and he will needs be a judge: now will we deal worse with thee, than with them. And they pressed sore upon the man, even Lot, and came near to break the door"* (Genesis 19:4-9).

The angels waited for Lot to decree but he chose to offer homosexuals his daughters. The days of Lot have returned like Jesus Christ rightly told us. Believers should rise up and decree against the wickedness of these days or else many shall be wasted.

There are many evil groups that are rising up, all over the world, with supports of governments of the nations. Many laws have been passed contrary to God's law and His people. The bible is being confronted by many constitutions all over the world. It is time true believers rise up and decree against all these evil taking place in the world today.

> *"Likewise also as it was in the days of Lot; they did eat, they drank, they bought, they sold, they planted, they*

builded; But the same day that Lot went out of Sodom it rained fire and brimstone from heaven, and destroyed them all" (Luke 17:28-29).

Some determined and unrepentant sinners need to be decreed against so that God's fear will spread all over the earth and people who are under captivities will be delivered.

"But the men put forth their hand, and pulled Lot into the house to them, and shut to the door. And they smote the men that were at the door of the house with blindness, both small and great: so that they wearied themselves to find the door" (Genesis 19:10-11).

Our God is a God of decree and all His decrees surely stand firm. Abraham was a great man of God but he was afraid of a man called King Abimelech. Abimelech took the wife of Abraham from him and at God's decree, the wombs of the house of Abimelech were closed up.

"And Abraham said of Sarah his wife, she is my sister: and Abimelech king of Gerar sent, and took Sarah. But God came to Abimelech in a dream by night, and said to him, Behold; thou art but a dead man, for the woman which thou hast taken; for she is a man's wife" (Genesis 20:2-3).

"So Abraham prayed unto God: and God healed Abimelech, and his wife, and his maidservants; and they bare children. For the LORD had fast closed up all the wombs of the house of Abimelech, because of Sarah Abraham's wife" (Genesis 20:17-18).

The decree of God can affect anyone no matter his or her ranks. The decree of men can fail but God's decree can never fail. By God's decree, all flesh that was filthy and evil died.

> *"And all flesh died that moved upon the earth, both of fowl, and of cattle, and of beast, and of every creeping thing that creepeth upon the earth, and every man: All in whose nostrils was the breath of life, of all that was in the dry land, died. And every living substance was destroyed which was upon the face of the ground, both man, and cattle, and the creeping things, and the fowl of the heaven; and they were destroyed from the earth: and Noah only remained alive, and they that were with him in the ark. And the waters prevailed upon the earth an hundred and fifty days"* (Genesis 7:21-24).

By God's decree there was a rain of fire like brimstones from heaven and all the people living in Sodom and Gomorrah died. By God's decree, the wife of Lot was converted to a useless pillar of salt. By God's decree, Er, the first son of Judah died in his wickedness.

When a man called Onan displeased God, God decreed his death and he died instantly. By God's decree the king of Egypt died together with all the men who sought after the life of Moses. When will you start your own decree? God, the heaven, the earth and all creatures are waiting for your decrees.

> *"And the LORD said unto Moses in Midian, Go, return into Egypt: for all the men are dead which sought thy life"* (Exodus 4:19).

By God's decree also, hail came down from heaven to smite many people in the land of Egypt.

> *"And the hails smote throughout all the land of Egypt all that was in the field, both man and beast; and the hail smote every herb of the field, and break every tree of the field"* (Exodus 9:25).

By God's decree, all trained hosts of Egyptian's army died and God disciplined and overthrew them at Red Sea.

> *"And the children of Israel went into the midst of the sea upon the dry ground: and the waters were a wall unto them on their right hand, and on their left. And the Egyptians pursued, and went in after them to the midst of the sea, even all Pharaoh's horses, his chariots, and his horsemen. And it came to pass, that in the morning watch the LORD looked unto the host of the Egyptians through the pillar of fire and of the cloud, and troubled the host of the Egyptians, And took off their chariot wheels, that they heavily: so that the Egyptians said, Let us flee from the face of Israel; for the LORD fighteth for them against the Egyptians. And the LORD said unto Moses, Stretch out thine hand over the sea, that the waters may come again upon the Egyptians, upon their chariots, and upon their horsemen. And Moses stretched forth his hand over the sea, and the sea returned to his strength when the morning appeared; and the Egyptians fled against it; and the LORD overthrew the Egyptians in the midst of the sea. And the waters returned, and covered the chariots, and the horsemen, and all the host of Pharaohs that came into the sea after them; there remained not so much as one of them. But the children of Israel walked upon dry land in the midst of the sea; and the waters were a wall unto them on their right hand, and on their left. Thus the LORD saved Israel that day out of the*

hand of the Egyptians; and Israel saw the Egyptians dead upon the seashore. And Israel saw that great work which the LORD did upon the Egyptians: and the people feared the LORD, and believed the LORD, and his servant Moses" (Exodus 14:22-32).

By the decree of God, Joshua arose in battle and discomfited the Amalekites, who came to the battlefield with the edge of the sword.

"And it came to pass, when Moses held up his hand, that Israel prevailed: and when he let down his hand, Amalek prevailed. But Moses' hands were heavy; and they took a stone, and put it under him, and he sat thereon; and Aaron and Hur stayed up his hands, the one on the one side, and the other on the other side; and his hands were steady until the going down of the sun. And Joshua discomfited Amalek and his people with the edge of the sword" (Exodus 17:11-13).

By God's decree, Nadab and Abihu, who were called of God as minister and priest, died inside the temple of God by the fire of God's judgment.

"And Nadab and Abihu, the sons of Aaron, took either of them his censer, and put fire therein, and put incense thereon, and offered strange fire before the LORD, which he commanded them not. And there went out fire from the LORD, and devoured them, and they died before the LORD" (Leviticus 10:1-2).

By God's decree, a particular blasphemer was stoned to death.

> *"And Moses spake to the children of Israel, that they should bring forth him that had cursed out of the camp, and stone him with stones. And the children of Israel did as the LORD commanded Moses"* (Leviticus 24:23).

By God's decree, the host of the children of Israel who lusted in the wilderness were smitten with a very great plague.

> *"And while the flesh was yet between their teeth, ere it was chewed, the wrath of the LORD was kindled against the people, and the LORD smote the people with a very great plague. And he called the name of that place Kibroth–hattaavah: because there they buried the people that lusted"* (Numbers 11:33-34).

By God's decree, Korah, Dathan and Abiram were buried alive as the ground opened and swallowed them with the members of their families and all that belonged to them.

> *"And it came to pass, as he had made an end of speaking all these words, that the ground clave asunder that was under them: And the earth opened her mouth, and swallowed them up, and their houses, and all the men that appertained unto Korah, and all their goods. They, and all that appertained to them, went down alive into the pit, and the earth closed upon them: and they perished from among the congregation. And all Israel that were round about them fled at the cry of them: for they said, Lest the earth swallow us up also"* (Numbers 16:31-34).

By God's decree, 250 men in Israel were consumed by fire for standing against Moses and his ministry.

> *"And there came out a fire from the LORD, and consumed the two hundred and fifty men that offered incense"* (Numbers 16:35).

By God's decree, Miriam, the elder sister of Moses, became a leper for daring to talk against his brother, Moses. By God's decree, idolatrous and immoral people numbering 24,000 died instantly. By God's decree, the entire males in the nation of Midian were slain in one day together with their king.

> *"And the LORD spake unto Moses, saying, [17]Vex the Midianites, and smite them: For they vex you with their wiles, wherewith they have beguiled you in the matter of Peor, and in the matter of Cozbi, the daughter of a prince of Midian, their sister, which was slain in the day of the plague for Peor's sake"* (Numbers 25:16-18).

> *"And the LORD spake unto Moses, saying, Avenge the children of Israel of the Midianites: afterward shalt thou be gathered unto thy people… they warred against the Midianites, as the LORD commanded Moses; and they slew all the males"* (Numbers 31:1-2, 7).

> *"And he went after the man of Israel into the tent, and thrust both of them through, the man of Israel, and the woman through her belly. So the plague was stayed from the children of Israel"* (Numbers 25:8).

By God's decree, Balaam, a great prophet, who could see well, was killed by the sword.

> *""And he went after the man of Israel into the tent, and thrust both of them through, the man of Israel, and the*

woman through her belly. So the plague was stayed from the children of Israel"" ([Numbers 25:8](#)).

No matter your status, who or what is protecting you, once God decrees against you, no mortal can deliver you. There was a day that God decreed against all immoral girls and boys in a particular place. And they all died that very day.

> *"And Moses, and Eleazar the priest, and all the princes of the congregation, went forth to meet them without the camp. And Moses was wroth with the officers of the host, with the captains over thousands, and captains over hundreds, which came from the battle. And Moses said unto them, Have ye saved all the women alive? Behold, these caused the children of Israel, through the counsel of Balaam, to commit trespass against the LORD in the matter of Peor, and there was a plague among the congregation of the LORD. Now therefore kill every male among the little ones, and kill every woman that hath known man by lying with him. But all the women children, that have not known a man by lying with him, keep alive for yourselves. And do ye abide without the camp seven days: whosoever hath killed any person, and whosoever hath touched any slain, purify both yourselves and your captives on the third day, and on the seventh day. And purify all your raiment, and all that is made of skins, and all work of goats' hair, and all things made of wood. And Eleazar the priest said unto the men of war which went to the battle, This is the ordinance of the law which the LORD commanded Moses; Only the gold, and the silver, the brass, the iron, the tin, and the lead, Every thing that may abide the fire, ye shall make it go through the fire, and it shall be clean: nevertheless it shall be purified*

with the water of separation: and all that abideth not the fire ye shall make go through the water. And ye shall wash your clothes on the seventh day, and ye shall be clean, and afterward ye shall come into the camp" (Numbers 31:13-24).

Once, there were people born by giants and they grew up as giants. They had never suffered defeat. They all had intimidating sizes and people were very much afraid of them. But one day, at the decree of God, the sons of Lot arose and killed all of them with swords.

"And I sent messengers out of the wilderness of Kedemoth unto Sihon king of Heshbon with words of peace, saying, Let me pass through thy land: I will go along by the high way, I will neither turn unto the right hand nor to the left. ²⁸Thou shalt sell me meat for money, that I may eat; and give me water for money, that I may drink: only I will pass through on my feet; (As the children of Esau which dwell in Seir, and the Moabites which dwell in Ar, did unto me;) until I shall pass over Jordan into the land which the LORD our God giveth us. But Sihon king of Heshbon would not let us pass by him: for the LORD thy God hardened his spirit, and made his heart obstinate, that he might deliver him into thy hand, as appeareth this day. And the LORD said unto me, Behold, I have begun to give Sihon and his land before thee: begin to possess, that thou mayest inherit his land. ³²Then Sihon came out against us, he and all his people, to fight at Jahaz. And the LORD our God delivered him before us; and we smote him, and his sons, and all his people. And we took all his cities at that time, and utterly destroyed the men, and the women, and the little ones, of every city,

> *we left none to remain: Only the cattle we took for a prey unto ourselves, and the spoil of the cities which we took. From Aroer, which is by the brink of the river of Arnon, and from the city that is by the river, even unto Gilead, there was not one city too strong for us: the LORD our God delivered all unto us: Only unto the land of the children of Ammon thou camest not, nor unto any place of the river Jabbok, nor unto the cities in the mountains, nor unto whatsoever the LORD our God forbad us"* (<u>Deuteronomy 2:26-37</u>).

> *"And we utterly destroyed them, as we did unto Sihon king of Heshbon, utterly destroying the men, women, and children, of every city"* (<u>Deuteronomy 3:6</u>).

There was once a city called Jericho, and the walls surrounding it was too tall and strongly built that no scientific method and human can destroy the walls. They enjoyed perfect protection from their enemies because of those walls. They went to bed without closing their doors because they trusted the city security walls.

But one day at the decree of God, that walls suddenly collapsed and fell flat. The children of Israel entered into the city and at God's decree, they destroyed all the inhabitants, both old and young, with the edge of the sword except a harlot called Rehab.

> *"And they utterly destroyed all that was in the city, both man and woman, young and old, and ox, and sheep, and ass, with the edge of the sword. But Joshua had said unto the two men that had spied out the country, Go into the harlot's house, and bring out thence the woman, and all that she hath, as ye sware unto her. And the young men that were spies went in,*

and brought out Rehab, and her father, and her mother, and her brethren, and all that she had; and they brought out all her kindred, and left them without the camp of Israel. And they burnt the city with fire, and all that was therein: only the silver, and the gold, and the vessels of brass and of iron, they put into the treasury of the house of the LORD. And Joshua saved Rehab the harlot alive, and her father's household, and all that she had; and she dwelleth in Israel even unto this day; because she hid the messengers, which Joshua sent to spy out Jericho." (Joshua 6:21-25).

No one, not even all nations of the world put together, can successfully oppose the decree of God. At God's decree, a man popularly known and called Achan in the army of Israel died in one day with all the members of his family.

"So Joshua sent messengers, and they ran unto the tent; and, behold, it was hid in his tent, and the silver under it. And they took them out of the midst of the tent, and brought them unto Joshua, and unto all the children of Israel, and laid them out before the LORD and Joshua, and all Israel with him, took Achan the son of Zerah, and the silver, and the garment, and the wedge of gold, and his sons, and his daughters, and his oxen, and his asses, and his sheep, and his tent, and all that he had: and they brought them unto the valley of Achor and Joshua said, Why hast thou troubled us? the LORD shall trouble thee this day. And all Israel stoned him with stones, and burned them with fire, after they had stoned them with stones And they raised over him a great heap of stones unto this day. So the LORD turned from the fierceness of his anger. Wherefore the name of

that place was called, The valley of Achor, unto this day" (Joshua 7:22-26).

At God's decree, all the inhabitants of Canaan, the Perizzites and others, who vowed never to vacate the land of promise for the children of Israel, died together with all their kings.

> "And Judah went up; and the LORD delivered the Canaanites and the Perizzites into their hand: and they slew of them in Bezek ten thousand men And they found Adonibezek in Bezek: and they fought against him, and they slew the Canaanites and the Perizzites. But Adonibezek fled; and they pursued after him, and caught him, and cut off his thumbs and his great toes. And Adonibezek said, Threescore and ten kings, having their thumbs and their great toes cut off, gathered their meat under my table: as I have done, so God hath requited me. And they brought him to Jerusalem, and there he died. Now the children of Judah had fought against Jerusalem, and had taken it, and smitten it with the edge of the sword, and set the city on fire" (Judges 1:4-8).

When God decreed against His own people for their sins, it also brought destruction because up to 70,000 men died from Dan to Beersheba.

> "So the LORD sent a pestilence upon Israel from the morning even to the time appointed: and there died of the people from Dan even to Beer–sheba seventy thousand men. And when the angel stretched out his hand upon Jerusalem to destroy it, the LORD repented him of the evil, and said to the angel that destroyed the people, It is enough: stay now thine hand. And the angel of the LORD was by the threshing place of

Araunah the Jebusite. And David spake unto the LORD when he saw the angel that smote the people, and said, Lo, I have sinned, and I have done wickedly: but these sheep, what have they done? let thine hand, I pray thee, be against me, and against my father's house" (2 Samuel 24:15-17).

"And God was displeased with this thing; therefore he smote Israel o the LORD sent pestilence upon Israel: and there fell of Israel seventy thousand men. ¹⁵And God sent an angel unto Jerusalem to destroy it: and as he was destroying, the LORD beheld, and he repented him of the evil, and said to the angel that destroyed, It is enough, stay now thine hand. And the angel of the LORD stood by the threshing floor of Ornan the Jebusite And David lifted up his eyes, and saw the angel of the LORD stand between the earth and the heaven, having a drawn sword in his hand stretched out over Jerusalem. Then David and the elders of Israel, who were clothed in sackcloth, fell upon their faces.
And David said unto God, Is it not I that commanded the people to be numbered? even I it is that have sinned and done evil indeed; but as for these sheep, what have they done? let thine hand, I pray thee, O LORD my God, be on me, and on my father's house; but not on thy people, that they should be plagued" (1 Chronicle 21:7, 14-17).

There was once a terrible king called Azariah. He even imprisoned some prophets of God. But one day, God arose and decreed against him. By that decree, he became a leper and died a leper.

> *"And the LORD smote the king, so that he was a leper unto the day of his death, and dwelt in a several house. And Jotham the king's son was over the house, judging the people of the land. And the rest of the acts of Azariah, and all that he did, are they not written in the book of the chronicles of the kings of Judah? So Azariah slept with his fathers; and they buried him with his fathers in the city of David: and Jotham his son reigned in his stead"* (2 Kings 15:5-7).

There was a city called Samaria where people of God also lived. It happened that the king of Assyria defeated the children of Israel and imported other people into that land. When no one could defeat them in that land, God decreed and lions entered into the cities and by that decree, most of the people were eaten by lions.

> *"And the king of Assyria brought men from Babylon, and from Cuthah, and from Ava, and from Hamath, and from Sepharvaim, and placed them in the cities of Samaria instead of the children of Israel: and they possessed Samaria, and dwelt in the cities thereof. And so it was at the beginning of their dwelling there, that they feared not the LORD: therefore the LORD sent lions among them, which slew some of them"* (2 Kings 17:24-25).

At God's decree, even nations fought for God. At God's decree, even your best friend or children can be used to bring judgment upon your head. The nature can arise and fight for God at His express decree.

> *"So Sennacherib king of Assyria departed, and went and returned, and dwelt at Nineveh. And it came to pass, as he was worshipping in the house of Nisroch his*

> *god, that Adrammelech and Sharezer his sons smote him with the sword; and they escaped into the land of Armenia: and Esarhaddon his son reigned in his stead"* (Isaiah 37:37- 38).

Anything can happen to make God's decree a reality. At God's decree, victims are helpless.

At God's decree, nations can be wiped out, seas can rage, mountains can melt and stones can come down from heaven to fight. At God's decrees, conspirators can be raised against God's enemies. At God's decrees, mass death can take place in the presence of the most qualified physicians. Children can be killed helplessly before their own parents.

> *"So they took the king, and brought him up to the king of Babylon to Riblah; and they gave judgment upon him. And they slew the sons of Zedekiah before his eyes, and put out the eyes of Zedekiah, and bound him with fetters of brass, and carried him to Babylon"* (2 Kings 25:6-7).

At God's decree, great men and women can die childless. At God's decree, experienced soldiers, who had fought and won many battles, can be defeated and killed in minor battles.

> *"And Abijah and his people slew them with a great slaughter: so there fell down slain of Israel five hundred thousand chosen men. Thus the children of Israel were brought under at that time, and the children of Judah prevailed, because they relied upon the LORD God of their fathers. And Abijah pursued after Jeroboam, and took cities from him, Bethel with the towns thereof, and Jeshanah with the towns thereof and Ephraim with the*

towns thereof. Neither did Jeroboam recover strength again in the days of Abijah: and the LORD struck him, and he died" (2 Chronicles 13:17-20).

At God's decree, when men of war can no more fight, God can mobilize soldiers from heaven to defend His decree.

> "And the LORD sent an angel, which cut off all the mighty men of valor, and the leaders and captains in the camp of the king of Assyria. So he returned with shame of face to his own land. And when he was come into the house of his god, they that came forth of his own bowels slew him there with the sword. Thus the LORD saved Hezekiah and the inhabitants of Jerusalem from the hand of Sennacherib the king of Assyria, and from the hand of all other, and guided them on every side. And many brought gifts unto the LORD to Jerusalem, and presents to Hezekiah king of Judah: so that he was magnified in the sight of all nations from thenceforth" (2 Chronicles 32:21-23).

> "Then the angel of the LORD went forth, and smote in the camp of the Assyrians a hundred and fourscore and five thousand: and when they arose early in the morning, behold, they were all dead corpses" (Isaiah 37:36).

At God's decree, flames on enemies' fire can loose power over God's children and burn to ashes all enemies of God.

> "Then was Nebuchadnezzar full of fury, and the form of his visage was changed against Shadrach, Meshach, and Abed-nego: therefore he spake, and commanded that they should heat the furnace one seven times more than it was won't to be heated. And he commanded the

> *most mighty men that were in his army to bind Shadrach, Meshach, and Abed-nego, and to cast them into the burning fiery furnace. Then these men were bound in their coats, their hosen, and their hats, and their other garments, and were cast into the midst of the burning fiery furnace. Therefore because the king's commandment was urgent, and the furnace exceeding hot, the flame of the fire slew those men that took up Shadrach, Meshach, and Abed-nego"* (Daniel 3:19-22).

At God's decree, lions can be rendered impotent before a true child of God. But the same lion can waste lives of God's enemies at His decree.

> *"And the king commanded, and they brought those men which had accused Daniel, and they cast them into the den of lions, them, their children, and their wives; and the lions had the mastery of them, and brake all their bones in pieces or ever they came at the bottom of the den"* (Daniel 6:24).

Nothing can be impossible before the decree of the Almighty God. The decree of God can set captives free. The decree of God can bring curses upon unrepentant sinners. It can also bring a curse upon the land.

> *"And the LORD said unto Cain, Where is Abel thy brother? And he said, I know not: Am I my brother's keeper? And he said, what hast thou done? the voice of thy brother's blood crieth unto me from the ground. And now art thou cursed from the earth, which hath opened her mouth to receive thy brother's blood from thy hand; When thou tillest the ground, it shall not henceforth yield unto thee her strength; a fugitive and a vagabond shalt thou be in the earth. And Cain said*

unto the LORD, My punishment is greater than I can bear. Behold, thou hast driven me out this day from the face of the earth; and from thy face shall I be hid; and I shall be a fugitive and a vagabond in the earth; and it shall come to pass, that every one that findeth me shall slay me" (Genesis 4:9-14).

God's decree can bring water of destruction upon the earth. It can bring confusion and scatter nations or groups that are united. It can separate evil group and place judgment upon them for life. It can bring plagues and great famine into a prosperous life, family or nation. God's decree can activate angels to enter the world to bless or curse people, to defend or oppose people.

The decree of God can promote or demote, destroy or save lives, kill or give abundant life. The decree of God can bring negative or positive messages on earth. It can come down to accept the offering of Abel and reject Cain's offering.

By God's decree, a ram can appear before Abraham to save the life of Isaac and make Abraham a mighty prince and a man of favor. By God's decree, a runaway and lovely boy called Jacob can be comforted with a promise of blessings and protection from his enemies. By God's decree, closed wombs can be opened to bear many children.

At the point of God's decree, prosperity can emerge out of nothing. At God's decree a forgotten person can be remembered, rewarded and promoted by force. At God's decree, your dreams can come true and all enemies can bow. At God's decree, a condemned person can be set free and commissioned to deliver others from bondage. At God's decree, divine favor can manifest to set captives free.

THE DECREE OF KINGS

Kings' decrees are honored and respected by their subjects. Hezekiah once commanded that all Israel should come together in the house of the Lord, which was at Jerusalem, to keep the Passover unto the Lord. In order to make it hold, he established a decree to make the proclamation throughout all Israel and every one obeyed.

> *"So they established a decree to make proclamation throughout all Israel, from Beersheba even to Dan, that they should come to keep the Passover unto the LORD God of Israel at Jerusalem: for they had not done it of a long time in such sort as it was written"* (2 Chronicles 30:5).

Likewise, in the days of Ezra, the priest, King Cyrus of Persia made a decree to build the house of God at Jerusalem after about 70 years of its destruction and his words of decree were carried out.

> *"But in the first year of Cyrus the king of Babylon the same king Cyrus made a decree to build this house of God"* (Ezekiel 5:13).

> *"Now therefore, if it seem good to the king, let there be search made in the king's treasure house, which is there at Babylon, whether it be so, that a decree was made of Cyrus the king to build this house of God at Jerusalem, and let the king send his pleasure to us concerning this matter"* (Ezekiel 5:17).

> *"Then Darius the king made a decree, and search was made in the house of the rolls, where the treasures were laid up in Babylon"* (Ezekiel 6:1).

A decree can be made to build a house; it can also be made to search for records. A king's decree cannot be joked with. Decrees can describe how things should be done. It can lay strong foundation.

Decrees can compel people, and even their enemies, to spend their money and time to do anything to see that orders are carried out. The consequence of altering a king's decree is disastrous. At times, such victims may lose their houses, while some may lose their lives. To some, their houses may be made a dunghill. If no one could play with kings' decrees, can any mortal play with God's decree then?

> "In the first year of Cyrus the king the same Cyrus the king made a decree concerning the house of God at Jerusalem, Let the house be builded, the place where they offered sacrifices, and let the foundations thereof be strongly laid; the height thereof threescore cubits, and the breadth thereof threescore cubits" (Ezra 6:3).

> "Moreover I make a decree what ye shall do to the elders of these Jews for the building of this house of God: that of the king's goods, even of the tribute beyond the river, forthwith expenses be given unto these men, that they be not hindered" (Ezra 6:8).

> "That they may offer sacrifices of sweet savors unto the God of heaven, and pray for the life of the king, and of his sons" (Ezra 6:11).

> "Also I have made a decree, that whosoever shall alter this word, let timber be pulled down from his house, and being set up, let him be hanged thereon; and let his house be made a dunghill for this. And the God that hath caused his name to dwell there destroy all kings

> *and people that shall put to their hand to alter and to destroy this house of God, which is at Jerusalem. I Darius have made a decree; let it be done with speed"* (Ezra 6:11-12).

Kings' decrees are very dangerous and must be carried out to the letter. Kings' decrees can also force you to help your enemies.

> *"And I, even I Artaxerxes the king, do make a decree to all the treasurers which are beyond the river, that whatsoever Ezra the priest, the scribe of the law of the God of heaven, shall require of you, it be done speedily"* (Ezra 7:21).

Prayers of decree are not said apologetically. It carries a lot of force that is capable of destroying yokes. It is an urge that must be carried out by force of power. No matter your status, once you are under an empire, you are bound to obey the decree of any king ruling that empire.

> *"And when the king's decree which he shall make shall be published throughout all his empire, (for it is great,) all the wives shall give to their husband's honor, both to great and small"* (Esther 1:20).

Any decree that comes from the king's palace must be hastened to get to the people in his empire. Otherwise, people who are left in ignorance would suffer.

> *"Then Esther bade them return Mordecai this answer"* (Esther 4:15).

The entire province, village, city, towns and nations under the realm of the king that passed a decree must be made to be aware of the king's decree. The people that kings' decrees affect negatively are always in great mourning, weeping and wailing because kings' decrees cannot be changed once they are passed and sealed with the kings' seals. Likewise, the people that decree favor are always rejoicing because they know that by and by, the decree cannot be changed.

> *"And in every province, whithersoever the king's commandment and his decree came, there was great mourning among the Jews, and fasting, and weeping, and wailing; and many lay in sackcloth and ashes"* (Esther 4:3).

> *"Also he gave him the copy of the writing of the decree that was given at Shushan to destroy them, to shew it unto Esther, and to declare it unto her, and to charge her that she should go in unto the king, to make supplication unto him, and to make request before him for her people"* (Esther 4:8)

King's decree can condemn a healthy person to die. King's decree can cause people to die before their actual time of death. Unborn children in the womb can be condemned just by a king's decree. As it can bring sorrow to some people, it can also bring joy, gladness and feast to others.

> *"So the posts that rode upon mules and camels went out, being hastened and pressed on by the king's commandment. And the decree was given at Shushan the palace"* (Esther 8:14).

> *"And in every province, and in every city, whithersoever the king's commandment and his decree came; the Jews had joy and gladness, a feast and a good day. And many of the people of the land became Jews; for the fear of the Jews fell upon them"* (Esther 8:17).

Decrees can cause execution. It can give you power over your enemies. It can turn your enemies' hope upside down. It can make you have rule over your enemies that hate you with perfect hatred. It can hang your enemies in the gallows, which they have prepared for your sake. It can convert your enemies' joy to sorrows.

> *"On that day the number of those that were slain in Shushan the palace was brought before the king"* (Esther 9:11).

> *"Then said Esther, If it please the king, let it be granted to the Jews which are in Shushan to do to morrow also according unto this day's decree, and let Haman's ten sons be hanged upon the gallows. And the king commanded it so to be done: and the decree was given at Shushan; and they hanged Haman's ten sons"* (Esther 9:13-14).

When a king determines to make a decree, people that would be affected negatively are troubled.

> *"But if ye will not make known unto me the dream, there is but one decree for you: for ye have prepared lying and corrupt words to speak before me, till the time be changed: therefore tell me the dream, and I shall know that ye can shew me the interpretation thereof"* (Daniel 2:9).

No matter how important you may be, or how powerful you are, once a king decrees against you, you are in trouble.

> *"And the decree went forth that the wise men should be slain; and they sought Daniel and his fellows to be slain"* (Daniel 2:13).

"He answered and said to Arioch the king's captain, why is the decree so hasty from the king? Then Arioch made the thing known to Daniel" (Daniel 2:15).

Even the righteous suffers at kings' decrees, especially when they remain quiet and choose to do nothing. When the righteous fail to oppose kings' decrees that are evil, such decrees would likely prevail over them and waste their lives.

"Thou, O king, hast made a decree, that every man that shall hear the sound of the cornet, flute, harp, sackbut, psaltery, and dulcimer, and all kinds of music, shall fall down and worship the golden image" (Daniel 3:10).

"Therefore I make a decree, That every people, nation, and language, which speak any thing amiss against the God of Shadrach, Meshach, and Abednego, shall be cut in pieces, and their houses shall be made a dunghill: because there is no other God that can deliver after this sort" (Daniel 3:29).

The decree of the king affected Daniel and later sent him into the lion's den. But thank God he went into prayers of decree to counter the king's decree.

"All the presidents of the kingdom, the governors, and the princes, the counselors, and the captains, have consulted together to establish a royal statute, and to make a firm decree, that whosoever shall ask a petition of any God or man for thirty days, save of thee, O king, he shall be cast into the den of lions. {Decree: or, interdict} Now, O king, establish the decree, and sign the writing, that it be not changed, according to the law of the Medes and Persians, which altereth not.

Wherefore king Darius signed the writing and the decree" (Daniel 6:7-9).

"Then they came near, and spake before the king concerning the king's decree; Hast thou not signed a decree, that every man that shall ask a petition of any God or man within thirty days, save of thee, O king, shall be cast into the den of lions? The king answered and said, the thing is true, according to the law of the Medes and Persians, which altereth not. Then answered they and said before the king, That Daniel, which is of the children of the captivity of Judah, regardeth not thee, O king, nor the decree that thou hast signed, but maketh his petition three times a day" (Daniel 6:12-13).

"Then these men assembled unto the king, and said unto the king, Know, O king, that the law of the Medes and Persians is, That no decree nor statute which the king establisheth may be changed" (Daniel 6:15).

"I make a decree, That in every dominion of my kingdom men tremble and fear before the God of Daniel: for he is the living God, and stedfast for ever, and his kingdom that which shall not be destroyed, and his dominion shall be even unto the end" (Daniel 6:26).

The decree of kings is very effective because God is aware of their kingdom. But believers, who are God's children, can overrule kings' decrees when they contradict God's law and His people.

"By me king's reign, and princes decree justice" (Proverbs 8:15).

> "When he gave to the sea his decree, that the waters should not pass his commandment: when he appointed the foundations of the earth" (Proverbs 8:29).

A king's decree can only affect God's children if they keep quiet or get out of God's protection and covering. Any occult personality, king or evil power that makes evil decree that is affecting any believer is only alive because that believer does not know his or her rights.

Any king, nation or leader that passes a law or decree that contradicts the Bible and Christians is surely under a curse. A simple decree from the least believer can deal with such people and their decrees. The wicked is prevailing in many places today because true believers don't make decrees against their activities.

> "Woe unto them that decree unrighteous decrees and that write grievousness which they have prescribed" (Isaiah 10:1).

Kings reign by God's permission, therefore, true believers can talk to God and remove any wicked king who is making unrighteous decrees.

> "By me king's reign, and princes decree justice" (Proverbs 8:15).

A simple prayer of decree coming from a true and righteous Christian can deal with any evil personality at any level of authority. Tribal prayer warriors and church leaders, who follow tribal sentiments or race at the expense of allowing evil kings to reign may not decree effectively when wicked leaders emerge from other tribes or race.

Even when a king or leader is not corrupt, true Christians can decree for a change if they want and God can honor their prayers of decree.

> *"Then all the elders of Israel gathered themselves together, and came to Samuel unto Ramah, And said unto him, Behold, thou art old, and thy sons walk not in thy ways: now make us a king to judge us like all the nations. But the thing displeased Samuel, when they said; Give us a king to judge us. And Samuel prayed unto the LORD. And the LORD said unto Samuel, Hearken unto the voice of the people in all that they say unto thee: for they have not rejected thee, but they have rejected me, that I should not reign over them. According to all the works which they have done since the day that I brought them up out of Egypt even unto this day, wherewith they have forsaken me, and served other gods, so do they also unto thee. Now therefore hearken unto their voice: howbeit yet protest solemnly unto them and shew them the manner of the king that shall reign over them"*(1 Samuel 8:4-9).

However, believers must be united irrespective of their tribes or races before they can decree against evil kings.

THE DECREE OF THE UNRIGHTEOUS

Unrighteous people make unrighteous decrees that are often directed towards God or His people. An evil decree is an evil utterance made by evil men. Pharaoh made an evil decree against all male Hebrew children in Egypt. He charged the midwives to kill all Hebrew male children.

> *"And he said, When ye do the office of a midwife to the Hebrew women, and see them upon the stools; if it be a son, then ye shall kill him: but if it be a daughter, then she shall live"* (Exodus 1:16).

> *"And Pharaoh charged all his people, saying, every son that is born ye shall cast into the river, and every daughter ye shall save alive"* (Exodus 1:22).

Today, there are many Pharaohs who are in forms of qualified medical personnel. Their primary duty is to kill or destroy the destinies of children born in their hospitals and clinics. They use occult powers to discover and destroy greatly destined babies born in their clinics. They transmit evil loads to children born in their hospitals, while some of these hospitals are specialists in aborting pregnancies. Such evil and unrighteous people are obviously working for Satan. Those who decree unrighteous decrees are already under divine judgment.

> *"Woe unto them that decree unrighteous decrees, and that write grievousness which they have prescribed; To turn aside the needy from judgment, and to take away the right from the poor of my people, that widows may be their prey, and that they may rob the fatherless! And*

> *what will ye do in the day of visitation, and in the desolation, which shall come from far? To whom will ye flee for help? and where will ye leave your glory?"*
> (Isaiah 10:1-3)

Pharaoh made an unrighteous decree and he died a shameful death with all the people that gave him support. Evil powers backup decrees of evil men. Surprisingly, there are people in every city who come out every morning to utter unrighteous decrees.

Some years ago, there was a woman from my village, who used to wake up every morning and walked around completely naked to decree evil things against peoples' lives. Initially, we thought that she was mad but we later discovered that she was very wicked. She came in contact with some of our brethren, who woke up early to pray and preach in the morning. That was how people discovered she was a very wicked woman.

There is another young man, who used to wake up very early in the morning, to talk to the moon, the sun, the stars, and the powers in the heavenlies. Once he started looking up to speak to the heavens, he never looked down to know what was going on, even if you touched him, until he finished his incantations.

As young believers in those days, we never understood the implications of what he was doing. We have come in contact with people who carried sacrifices very early in the morning and once they are on their mission, they never talk to any one. So many things are really happening in this world.

There are also people who wake up very early in the morning to pour drinks in libation around their neighborhood to take charge of what happens in that area. These wicked personalities wake up very early to address lights in the firmament of the heaven that give light upon the earth. They defile the light that shines upon the earth, while others are sleeping. They speak to the moon at night to control the night and speak to the sun very early to control the day. They speak to these heavenly bodies to carry out wicked functions for the day in order to rob people of their rights, benefits and entitlements.

One day, after preaching on a topic titled *Evil Altars* at Enugu State, eastern part of Nigeria, a woman, who was then living in Lagos, approached me. Her daughter who came from riverine area invited her for a deliverance program. So she asked me, *"How do you, young boys, know about all these altars you teach people?"*

She told me that she has an altar inside her room at her house in Lagos and another one in her state of origin. She told me many things about powers in the heavenlies. She said that when her husband was alive, she scarcely had sex with him. She said that at times, her husband would insist on having sexual relationship with her at night. But before the man would start, she would quickly look at the moon from the windows right from her bed, and immediately, a snake would emerge from the moon and the husband would fall asleep.

The woman went ahead to reveal that while the snake slept between her husband and her, the husband would not wake up till the next morning and that even when he woke up, he would not have strength to do anything. Because of that, she had only one daughter for the man.

There are powers residing in the heavenlies and evil men invoke such powers to control other human beings. Some people have married and lived with half-human half-snake beings all through their lives. Many people are going through horrible experiences that they don't have the courage to tell people because of fear of those powers from the bodies of waters and the heavenlies. Many evil people plant evil altars in the moon, sun and stars to control other people's lives. They speak to the sun, moon and stars to tell them what they wanted these heavenly bodies to do for them.

The woman I talked about told me that every morning she talked to the sun, moon and other heavenly powers and that all that she told them to do, they never disappointed her. People come out early morning to talk to the sun and tell the sun what she would bring out. And in the evening, they also speak to the sun and commanded the sun to go with some things, like lives, money, businesses of some people and they happen just as they said it. The sun, moon and stars are created by God to serve men but evil men use them against their fellow human beings.

> *"Hast thou commanded the morning since thy days; and caused the dayspring to know his place; that it might take hold of the ends of the earth, that the wicked might be shaken out of it?"* (Job 38:12-13).

It is our responsibility to talk to the morning to tell them what we want. Evil men understand these things very well and that is why they control people's lives and destinies.

The wicked hold on to the day and control it. They program wicked things into the day to waste people's lives. They heap evil into the day by rising up early to say what and how they wanted things to be.

> *"Have respect unto the covenant: for the dark places of the earth are full of the habitations of cruelty"* (Psalms 74:20).

They come out every morning to speak to the day springs, in order to control everything in the land, even churches. They talk against men of God, ministers and the whole congregation of the body of Christ.

> *"Lift up thy feet unto the perpetual desolations; even all that the enemy hath done wickedly in the sanctuary"* (Psalms 74:3).

They rose up early to program desolations and wickedness in the moon, sun and stars against the church of Christ called sanctuary.

These evil people, who use the heavenlies against men, have destroyed the world with a lot of evil things they program in the heavenlies. The medical science of our day has failed. The government has equally failed. People who are helpless have ran into churches for deliverance and protection but unfortunately, these wicked people have come also into the sanctuaries of God. Their focus has shifted on the church of Jesus Christ.

Our generation is possessed, demonized and is being oppressed by these wicked powers. Many have been taken captive, enslaved and spellbound by some evil powers. Many are under night dreams attacks, placed under curses, spirit of hatred, rejection, jealousy, worry, sexual immorality, drug abuse, barrenness, poverty, premature deaths, mental problems, and other incurable diseases.

The government, medicines and the entire world are defeated by the means of evil decrees of men, who employ the powers of the heavenlies. The battle is now carried to the church and many churches are gone already.

> *"Thine enemies roar in the midst of thy congregations; they set up their ensigns for signs"* (Psalms 74:4).

> *"They have cast fire into thy sanctuary, they have defiled by casting down the dwelling place of thy name to the ground"* (Psalms 74:7).

Signs that follow believers no longer follow them. What we are seeing in churches today is worst than what was obtainable in the world. Believers have allowed wicked people around them to use evil decrees against them. The wicked people of the world are making it, and are becoming more famous for destroying gifted believers and ministries that they received from the Lord.

Eventually, Satan has programmed evil fires and problems into the heavenlies and fires are already burning in the sanctuaries of God. Many great ministers and their God-given ministries are already destroyed, burned and cast down. True miracles that the church of old is used to are no more obtainable.

Many ministers and ministries are sleeping while agents of Satan wakes up every morning and night to take control of the day and nights with evil decrees.

> *"They said in their hearts, Let us destroy them together: they have burned up all the synagogues of God in the*

land. We see not our signs: there is no more any prophet: neither is there among us any that knoweth how long" (Psalms 74:8-9).

People, who know how to use the sun and the moon, control the days and the nights of their generation. The wicked people are using forces of the nature to destroy people's destinies. Believers should not worship the sun and the moon like the heathen but we can command them to obey us. Believers should exercise dominion over evil men, evil spirits and forces of nature.

The first and second heavens above us before the third heaven are the abode of evil forces of darkness that are very wicked. That is where you get devil's headquarters and the head office of wicked principalities like the queen of heaven, leviathan and the rest of other wicked powers. In satanic kingdom, principalities, like the queen of heaven, are usually more wicked and destructive than Satan.

> *"Then all the men which knew that their wives had burned incense unto other gods, and all the women that stood by, a great multitude, even all the people that dwelt in the land of Egypt, in Pathros, answered Jeremiah, saying, As for the word that thou hast spoken unto us in the name of the LORD, we will not hearken unto thee. But we will certainly do whatsoever thing goeth forth out of our own mouth, to burn incense unto the queen of heaven, and to pour out drink offerings unto her, as we have done, we, and our fathers, our kings, and our princes, in the cities of Judah, and in the streets of Jerusalem: for then had we plenty of victuals, and were well, and saw no evil. But since we left off to burn incense to the queen of heaven, and to pour out*

drink offerings unto her, we have wanted all things, and have been consumed by the sword and by the famine" (Jeremiah 44:15-18).

There is a serious competition going on among wicked actors in the heavenlies. They give powers to wicked men on earth to waste lives. The beast called leviathan has been in serious disagreement with the queen of heaven that is being supported by Satan to sit upon the (beast) leviathan. The queen of heaven has found favor with other powers in the heavenlies and she has usurped the position of the leviathan now.

"So he carried me away in the spirit into the wilderness: and I saw a woman sit upon a scarlet colored beast, full of names of blasphemy, having seven heads and ten horns" (Revelation 17:3).

"Because of the multitude of the whoredoms of the well-favored harlot, the mistress of witchcrafts, that selleth nations through her whoredoms, and families through her witchcrafts" (Nahum 3:4).

People who know how to contact evil powers in the first and second heavens are very wicked. The highest occult people talk to the sun, moon, and get powers from wicked spirits that invest powers in the heavenlies.

"For we wrestle not against flesh and blood, but against principalities, against powers, against the rulers of the darkness of this world, against spiritual wickedness in high places" (Ephesians 6:12).

These wicked agents of darkness are empowered by the devil to decree anything they wanted, using the sun, moon and the stars. But unfortunately, believers who are empowered by God only sit and watch while evil prevail on earth.

Evil men wake up early to program blessings into their day and curses into other peoples' lives. In Moses' day, people woke up to talk to their evil altars until God consumed them with fire.

> *"And Moses was very wroth, and said unto the LORD, Respect not thou their offering: I have not taken one ass from them, neither have I hurt one of them"* (Numbers 16:15).

> *"And there came out a fire from the LORD, and consumed the two hundred and fifty men that offered incense"* (Numbers 16:35).

> *"Now they that died in the plague were fourteen thousand and seven hundred, beside them that died about the matter of Korah"* (Numbers 16:49).

If we keep quiet, evil and enemies will prevail over us. The wicked people around us are taking evil decisions against us everyday. We need to challenge their decrees with opposing decrees. We need to go to God concerning any decision, action or manifestation that does not favor us.

Abraham, even though he was righteous, took a decision to remove his son Ishmael but when Ishmael saw that the decision of his own father didn't favor him, he cried to the same God of Abraham and God answered him and showed his mother Hagar a moving stream.

> *"And God said unto Abraham, Let it not be grievous in thy sight because of the lad, and because of thy*

bondwoman; in all that Sarah hath said unto thee, hearken unto her voice; for in Isaac shall thy seed be called. And also of the son of the bondwoman will I make a nation, because he is thy seed. And Abraham rose up early in the morning, and took bread, and a bottle of water, and gave it unto Hagar, putting it on her shoulder, and the child, and sent her away: and she departed, and wandered in the wilderness of Beersheba. And the water was spent in the bottle, and she cast the child under one of the shrubs. And she went, and sat her down over against him a good way off, as it were a bowshot: for she said, let me not see the death of the child. And she sat over against him, and lift up her voice, and wept. And God heard the voice of the lad; and the angel of God called to Hagar out of heaven, and said unto her, what aileth thee, Hagar? Fear not; for God hath heard the voice of the lad where he is. Arise, lift up the lad, and hold him in thine hand; for I will make him a great nation. And God opened her eyes, and she saw a well of water; and she went, and filled the bottle with water, and gave the lad drink. And God was with the lad; and he grew, and dwelt in the wilderness, and became an archer. And he dwelt in the wilderness of Paran: and his mother took him a wife out of the land of Egypt" (Genesis 21:12-21).

When Isaac saw that a decision was taken against his wife because her womb was closed, he took a decision to go to God in prayers and God opened the womb of his wife, Rebecca. When Hannah saw that her womb was shut, and her husband unperturbed, she went to the altar of God alone, and God opened her womb. Don't watch evil prosper in your life. It is not the will of God for you to die in ugly situations. Pass a decree against every works of the wicked against your life.

There was a king called Nahash, who was also an occult. He demanded the right eye of all the people in a whole nation for an evil sacrifice. He mobilized evil soldiers against the people of God but his army was scattered and defeated.

> *"Then Nahash the Ammonite came up, and encamped against Jabeshgilead: and all the men of Jabesh said unto Nahash, Make a covenant with us, and we will serve thee. And Nahash the Ammonite answered them, on this condition will I make a covenant with you, that I may thrust out all your right eyes, and lay it for a reproach upon all Israel. And the elders of Jabesh said unto him, Give us seven days' respite, that we may send messengers unto all the coasts of Israel: and then, if there be no man to save us, we will come out to thee"* (1 Samuel 11:1-3).

There are many people who cannot see spiritually, though they have physical eyes, because evil men around them have decreed against their spiritual eyes.

There was a man of God who was posted to pastor a particular church. He was the Zonal Pastor in that community having 5 churches under him. The first pastor he met in another church, who was very vibrant when he first came to that town, was arrested because he committed adultery and arranged for an abortion. The wicked occult people he challenged decreed against him and watched him fall out of faith.

The second pastor, who was a sectional leader in another church, was afflicted by a mysterious sickness. By the time he was leaving that community because of the sickness, twenty-one occult pins came out of his body. Few ministers survived in that community.

So, this man of God who was posted to that church called for a combined service of the five churches under him. After the service, he made an altar call for people who will join him for three days prayers. He planned for a 3 days crusade after the fasting program. The fasting started on Monday morning with 51 people in attendance. On Thursday evening, the crusade team could not come. On Friday there was a heavy rain. By the next Monday morning, when the crusade team was going back, they had an accident and the driver died and others were badly wounded and rushed to the Hospital.

The interpretation we gave to the series of event was that three days dry fast was a provocation to the powers of darkness in that town. So in response, we planned for days and nights of prayers of decrees, and so we started a relay praying and fasting program.

In that particular community, there was a man called doctor Onu, who had bewitched many people in that community. He was a very powerful native doctor. People came to him from far and near for consultation. As we started our prayers, each group prayed from morning till the next morning. This prayers of decree lasted for fifty-six days and fifty-six nights.

During this period, all other native doctors, who accused Dr. Onu of taking away their customers, planned and killed him. The community in turn arrested all the native doctors around that community and killed them. The prayers of decree for fifty-six days and nights caused a lot of confusion in that community that made many people to start coming to the church uninvited. It became evident that believers need to come out boldly with prayers of decree to counter all evil decrees opposing God and His children in these last days.

Believers can talk to the elements and the elemental powers will obey. We can destroy what evil men have programmed on their evil altars and the heavenlies. We can control what happens in the day by commanding the early hours of every day. You can direct your day to favor you by the words of decree

As a Christian, whatever you say happens and no power can successfully stop your words of decrees. Every creature can hear, even nature carries out the instructions of true believers.

> *"Then spake Joshua to the LORD in the day when the LORD delivered up the Amorites before the children of Israel, and he said in the sight of Israel, Sun, stand thou still upon Gibeon; and thou, Moon, in the valley of Ajalon. And the sun stood still, and the moon stayed, until the people had avenged themselves upon their enemies. Is not this written in the book of Jasher? So the sun stood still in the midst of heaven, and hasted not to go down about a whole day. And there was no day like that before it or after it that the LORD hearkened unto the voice of a man: for the LORD fought for Israel"* (Joshua 10:12-14).

WHAT IS A DECREE OF THE RIGHTEOUS?

1. It is a decision, or an order that has a force from someone, who is really born again. (John 3:1-3).

2. It is a word of command given by someone, who is living above sin.

3. It is a decree made by someone, who bears fruits of the spirit.

4. It is a decree made in agreement with the Word of God.

5. It is a decree made by someone, who abides by the God's Word.

6. It is a decree said by faith and in humility with a holy force.

7. It is an utterance said violently in faith in Christ Jesus.

8. It is a decree made with a purity of heart, and without fear or doubts.

9. It is a direct and targeted specific words.

10. It is a decree that stands without wavering at any opposition or forces.

11. It is a command that brings order to earth, as it is in heaven.

12. It is a decree through which God's children demonstrate their rights to govern their Father's kingdom in truth and in righteousness.

Whenever a true believer decrees anything, it would be established.

> *"Thou shalt also decree a thing, and it shall be established unto thee: and the light shall shine upon thy ways. When men are cast down, then thou shalt say, There is lifting up; and he shall save the humble person"* (Job 22:28-29).

Believer's decrees are not limited by impossibilities. When men are confronted with imminent defeats, decrees can overturn every manner of hopeless situation, no matter what powers are involved.

> *"Wherefore God also hath highly exalted him, and given him a name which is above every name: That at the name of Jesus every knee should bow, of things in heaven, and things in earth, and things under the earth; And that every tongue should confess that Jesus Christ is Lord, to the glory of God the Father"* (Philippians 2:9-11).

No power can overcome a believer's decree. This is because the Godhead gets involved to see that every believer's decree is carried out to the letter. Samson said, *"O Lord God, remember me, that I may avenge the Philistines,"* and God heard him. He decreed again and said, *"Let me die with the Philistines,"* and God equally answered him instantly."

> *"Now the house was full of men and women; and all the lords of the Philistines were there; and there were upon the roof about three thousand men and women that beheld while Samson made sport. And Samson called unto the LORD, and said, O Lord GOD, remember me, I pray thee, and strengthen me, I pray thee, only this*

> *once, O God, that I may be at once avenged of the Philistines for my two eyes. And Samson took hold of the two middle pillars upon which the house stood, and on which it was borne up, of the one with his right hand, and of the other with his left. And Samson said; Let me die with the Philistines. And he bowed himself with all his might; and the house fell upon the lords, and upon all the people that were therein. So the dead which he slew at his death were more than they which he slew in his life"* (Judges 16:27-30).

David said to the champion of the Philistines, "*This day will the Lord deliver thee into mine hand and I will smite thee and take thine head from thee,*" and God granted his decree to him that very day.

> *"Then said David to the Philistine, Thou comest to me with a sword, and with a spear, and with a shield: but I come to thee in the name of the LORD of hosts, the God of the armies of Israel, whom thou hast defied. This day will the LORD deliver thee into mine hand; and I will smite thee, and take thine head from thee; and I will give the carcasses of the host of the Philistines this day unto the fowls of the air, and to the wild beasts of the earth; that all the earth may know that there is a God in Israel"* (1 Samuel 17:45-46)

When kings of powers that be say, "*kill,*" soldiers waste no time in carrying out such assignments, no matter who is or was involved.

> *"And King Solomon sent by the hand of Benaiah the son of Jehoiada; and he fell upon him that he died"* (1 Kings 2:25).

Whenever prophets of the old decreed a thing, no power opposed their words and succeeded. Their words were decrees that even death carried out assignments within their decrees. When they said *'death* or *kill,'* death obeyed them.

> *"Then Elisha said, Hear ye the word of the LORD; Thus saith the LORD, To morrow about this time shall a measure of fine flour be sold for a shekel, and two measures of barley for a shekel, in the gate of Samaria. Then a lord on whose hand the king leaned answered the man of God, and said, Behold, if the LORD would make windows in heaven, might this thing be? And he said, Behold, thou shalt see it with thine eyes, but shalt not eat thereof"* (2 Kings 7:1-2).

> *"And the king appointed the lord on whose hand he leaned to have the charge of the gate: and the people trode upon him in the gate, and he died, as the man of God had said, who spake when the king came down to him. And it came to pass as the man of God had spoken to the king, saying, Two measures of barley for a shekel, and a measure of fine flour for a shekel, shall be to morrow about this time in the gate of Samaria: And that lord answered the man of God, and said, Now, behold, if the LORD should make windows in heaven, might such a thing be? And he said, Behold, thou shalt see it with thine eyes, but shalt not eat thereof. And so it fell out unto him: for the people trode upon him in the gate, and he died"* (2 Kings 7:17-20).

When true believers talk, even the waters obey their words. If they decreed and said, *'Water* or *heal,'* water obeys their words of decree by force. Powers from the waters cannot resist the decree of a true child of God.

> *"And Elisha sent a messenger unto him, saying, Go and wash in Jordan seven times, and thy flesh shall come again to thee, and thou shalt be clean"* (2 Kings 5:10).

> *"Then went he down, and dipped himself seven times in Jordan, according to the saying of the man of God: and his flesh came again like unto the flesh of a little child, and he was clean"* (2 Kings 5:14).

Once, there was a captain in Israeli army, who opened his mouth and decreed against a whole nation and his words affected the lives of all the people in that nation, born and unborn at that time.

> *"And Joshua made them that day hewers of wood and drawers of water for the congregation, and for the altar of the LORD, even unto this day, in the place which he should choose"* (Joshua 9:27).

You may be a true Christian and yet decrees of evil men and women is still ruling your life. It shouldn't be so. Most bad conditions you find yourself in today could be as results of negative words that people spoke against you or your ancestors. But you can change such situations by ordinary words of decree.

> *"And afterward when David heard it, he said, I and my kingdom are guiltless before the LORD for ever from the blood of Abner the son of Ner: Let it rest on the head of Joab, and on all his father's house; and let there not fail from the house of Joab one that hath an issue, or that is a leper, or that leaneth on a staff, or that falleth on the sword, or that lacketh bread"* (2 Samuel 3:28-29).

You can re-direct evil decrees directed towards you, your family, business and health. People have lived and died by dictates of evil men and women, who spoke evil words against them. Cain decreed that everybody around him must sacrifice to God the way he approved, but his younger brother, Abel, said 'no' and stood by his decision unto death and God defended him.

In Enoch's day, people decreed against holy living, but Enoch lived and walked with God and God honored him. Everybody in the days of Noah bowed to evil decrees of unrighteous living, but Noah remained a holy man in that generation.

Evil men in Abraham's day decreed that no one should answer the call of God, but Abraham revolted and answered God's call and God blessed him. Laban decreed against the freedom of Jacob but he rejected it and escaped from bondage of perpetual slavery. All the brothers of Joseph decreed for his death and even announced it to their father, but Joseph overcame their evil decrees and lived longer than many of them, even in prosperity.

The wife of Potiphar decreed and vowed to defile Joseph, but Joseph decreed against being defiled. The ten spies sent to spy the land of Canaan brought back evil report, but Joshua and Caleb brought good report. When Israel decided to live immoral life before God, Phinehas vowed to fight against immorality in the congregation of the righteous.

All the relations of Jabez bowed to the decrees of poverty but Jabez decreed and prayed against it and God honored His decisions. Nebuchadnezzar decreed against the worship of true God, but three Hebrew children called Shedrack,

Meshack and Abednego stood against his decree and changed it.

The powers of darkness in the heavenlies decreed against the prayers of the children of Israel and prevented it from entering into the third heaven but Daniel went into the prayers of decrees for 21 days (*See* Daniel 10:12-13).

The wicked people of Jesus' day decreed and many people were afflicted with all manners of sicknesses, diseases and some of them were mad, while others are possessed with evil spirits, but Jesus used gospel teachings and preaching of the kingdom to set them free.

> *"And Jesus went about all Galilee, teaching in their synagogues, and preaching the gospel of the kingdom, and healing all manner of sickness and all manner of disease among the people. And his fame went throughout all Syria: and they brought unto him all sick people that were taken with divers diseases and torments, and those which were possessed with devils, and those which were lunatick, and those that had the palsy; and he healed them. And there followed him great multitudes of people from Galilee, and from Decapolis, and from Jerusalem, and from Judaea, and from beyond Jordan"* (Matthew 4:23-25).

Sicknesses they decreed unto people include leprosy, fever, blindness, withered hands, hunger, fear, grievous problems, lameness, dumbness, unclean spirits, plaques, great storm, evil chains, deaths, issue of blood, toiling without achievements, infirmities, dropsy, impotency, etc. But Jesus appeared in the scene and broke the chains of all these evil decrees and set all captives free.

> *"How God anointed Jesus of Nazareth with the Holy Ghost and with power: who went about doing good, and healing all that were oppressed of the devil; for God was with him"* (Acts 10:38).

Jesus Christ, in His parting Words to His disciples, said that all power is given unto Him both the powers in heaven and the ones on the earth. The decreed work has been transferred from God the Father to God the Son. God the Son has given the same to true believers today.

> *"Verily I say unto you, whatsoever ye shall bind on earth shall be bound in heaven: and whatsoever ye shall loose on earth shall be loosed in heaven"* (Matthew 18:18).

Believers are given the power to decree anything on earth and be sure that heavenly angels will enforce it. Believers, who know Christ, know very well that he created all things, both things in heaven and on earth. All visible and invisible things, thrones, dominions, principalities and powers were all created by Him and for Him. Any decree against Christ or God's Word should be confronted and opposed by believer's decrees.

> *"And I baptized also the household of Stephanas: besides, I know not whether I baptized any other. For Christ sent me not to baptize, but to preach the gospel: not with wisdom of words, lest the cross of Christ should be made of none effect"* (Colossians 1:16-17).

Having delegated all powers to true believers, Christ Himself is no more in full business of passing decrees because He has committed it into the hands of believers.

> *"Then he called his twelve disciples together, and gave them power and authority over all devils, and to cure diseases"* (Luke 9:1).

Believers may enter into evil situations and die in it as a result of failing to pass a decree against such conditions. It is our right to challenge evil decrees and they will bow. Jesus does not expect that we expect Him to come down from heaven to decree against our problems. It is the duty of all believers to do it themselves. The early believers, who tried it in the past, succeeded.

> *"And they did eat, and were all filled: and there was taken up of fragments that remained to them twelve baskets. And it came to pass, as he was alone praying, his disciples were with him: and he asked them, saying, who say the people that I am? They answering said, John the Baptist; but some say, Elias; and others say, that one of the old prophets is risen again"* (Luke 10:17-19).

God backs up decrees passed in the name of Christ because with God all things are possible. Believers who know how to decree any thing win their battles.

> *"I can do all things through Christ which strengthens me"* (Philippians 4:13).

The heavenly invisible enforcers are anxiously waiting for believers to make a decree so that they will rise and take control of every situation in our lives.

Our God is not happy that His own legitimate children are suffering under the decrees of evil men. We have the power of God at our disposal to decree anything and it will be established. When the early believers decreed a thing, they don't compromise. Likewise, the Old Testament believers did the same. No matter who is involved, believer's decree can affect or touch them.

> *"And Pharaoh called unto Moses, and said, Go ye, serve the LORD; only let your flocks and your herds be stayed: let your little ones also go with you. And Moses said, Thou must give us also sacrifices and burnt offerings, that we may sacrifice unto the LORD our God. Our cattle also shall go with us; there shall not an hoof be left behind; for thereof must we take to serve the LORD our God; and we know not with what we must serve the LORD, until we come thither"* (Exodus 10:24-26).

In job's afflictions, he prayed but did not pray the prayers of decree. He spent much time shifting blames and finding faults. He thought that living a holy life is enough without the prayers of decree. By the time God confronted him with some questions, he realized that he was to be blamed and not God or the day he was born. Satan was busy every morning decreeing against Job, but Job was busy decreeing death to the day he was born and the night he was conceived. He said so many things against the day he was born, the night he was conceived and the stars of the twilight. Instead of decreeing against his enemy's decree, he was busy decreeing against himself.

> *"After this opened Job his mouth, and cursed his day. And Job spake, and said, let the day perish wherein I was born, and the night in which it was said, there is a man-child conceived. Let that day be darkness; let not God regard it from above, neither let the light shine*

upon it. Let darkness and the shadow of death stain it; let a cloud dwell upon it; let the blackness of the day terrify it. As for that night, let darkness seize upon it; let it not be joined unto the days of the year, let it not come into the number of the months. Lo, let that night be solitary, let no joyful voice come therein. Let them curse it that curse the day, who are ready to raise up their mourning. Let the stars of the twilight thereof be dark; let it look for light, but have none; neither let it see the dawning of the day: Because it shut not up the doors of my mother's womb, nor hid sorrow from mine eyes. Why died I not from the womb? Why did I not give up the ghost when I came out of the belly?" (Job 3:1-11).

There was an evil decree against job but he only woke up to decree in support of evil decrees that were already against him. By the time God appeared in his situation, he was almost dead.

"Then the LORD answered Job out of the whirlwind, and said, who is this that darkeneth counsel by words without knowledge?" (Job 38:1-2).

"Hast thou commanded the morning since thy days; and caused the dayspring to know his place; that it might take hold of the ends of the earth, that the wicked might be shaken out of it?" (Job 38:12-13).

God told job that morning decrees of believers can save the righteous. He let Job know that morning can be commanded with words of decree to favor him. He assured him that the day can be directed with decrees of true believers. He told him that the wicked can be shaken out of the day in this earth. The wicked can be prevented from functioning. The wicked can be put out of work.

Jesus stopped the work of the wicked in the life of the centurion's servant, who was suffering from palsy. He stopped the wicked in the life of Peter's mother-in-law by touching her hand and the fever left her. You can touch the day with your prayers of decrees and the day will be directed to favor you. Paul stopped wicked works by praying with Silas before the day broke.

> *"And at midnight Paul and Silas prayed, and sang praises unto God: and the prisoners heard them. And suddenly there was a great earthquake, so that the foundations of the prison were shaken: and immediately all the doors were opened, and every one's bands were loosed"* (Acts 16:25-26).

You can decide to decree a thing and it will be established unto you. Jesus, even though He was God, rose up to pray very early to command the morning. He knew the secret of victory and He never joked with that. He confronted the powers of darkness and took the mornings from them. That was the secret of His victory over all the powers of darkness.

> *"And in the morning, rising up a great while before day, he went out, and departed into a solitary place, and there prayed"* (Mark 1:35).

If you are a believer and you fail in life, you have nobody to blame because everything you need to succeed is made available. You can divide your Red Sea. You can decree anything and it will be established.

> *"Thou shalt also decree a thing, and it shall be established unto thee: and the light shall shine upon thy ways"* (Job 22:28).

Heavenly soldiers are waiting for you to decree a thing. You put God's angels out of work when you are not praying the prayers of decree. This is sad.

> *"Then Moab rebelled against Israel after the death of Ahab. And Ahaziah fell down through a lattice in his upper chamber that was in Samaria, and was sick: and he sent messengers, and said unto them, Go, enquire of Beelzebub the god of Ekron whether I shall recover of this disease. But the angel of the LORD said to Elijah the Tishbite, Arise, go up to meet the messengers of the king of Samaria, and say unto them, Is it not because there is not a God in Israel, that ye go to enquire of Beelzebub the god of Ekron? Now therefore thus saith the LORD, Thou shalt not come down from that bed on which thou art gone up, but shalt surely die. And Elijah departed"* (2 Kings 1:1-4).

> *"So he died according to the word of the LORD which Elijah had spoken. And Jehoram reigned in his stead in the second year of Jehoram the son of Jehoshaphat king of Judah; because he had no son"* (2 Kings 1:17).

You can open and shut heaven if you are really born again. All power belongs to God, and His children can decree anything to happen anywhere.

> *"And Elijah answered and said to the captain of fifty, if I be a man of God, then let fire come down from heaven, and consume thee and thy fifty. And there came down*

fire from heaven, and consumed him and his fifty" (2 Kings. 1:10).

"And Elijah answered and said unto them, if I be a man of God, let fire come down from heaven, and consume thee and thy fifty. And the fire of God came down from heaven, and consumed him and his fifty. And he sent again a captain of the third fifty with his fifty. And the third captain of fifty went up, and came and fell on his knees before Elijah, and besought him, and said unto him, O man of God, I pray thee, let my life, and the life of these fifty thy servants, be precious in thy sight. Behold, there came fire down from heaven, and burnt up the two captains of the former fifties with their fifties: therefore let my life now be precious in thy sight. And the angel of the LORD said unto Elijah, Go down with him: be not afraid of him. And he arose, and went down with him unto the king" (2 Kings. 1:12-15).

By faith, you can decree and subdue kingdoms. You can quench fire, and you can stop the mouths of evil lions. You can obtain the promises of God the your decrees. You can touch heaven with a prayer of decree.

"Elias was a man subject to like passions as we are and he prayed earnestly that it might not rain: and it rained not on the earth by the space of three years and six months. And he prayed again, and the heaven gave rain, and the earth brought forth her fruit" (James 5:17-18).

In spiritual positioning, New Testament saints have better benefits than Old Testament believers. We have been given the power to do greater things than Elijah.

21 DECREES

"Thou shalt also decree a thing, and it shall be established unto

DECREE 1

FOR A NEW BEGINNING

> *"In the beginning God created the heaven and the earth"* (Genesis 1:1).

I command everything about me to embrace the divine spirit of new beginnings. Let God of new beginnings be honored by everything within and around me.

Any power that opposes God in my life this year shall die and be buried. I decree that forces of heaven shall stand by my side throughout this year to oppose, destroy and kill every evil force, voice, actions and powers of darkness that will be mobilized against me this year. Any power that will stand against God in my life this year shall be wasted immediately. I decree against the spirit that fights against new beginnings.

I decree that every spirit against prosperity power in my life shall die and be buried for my sake this year. I decree that witchcraft powers assigned to bewitch good things I intend to start off this year shall die, just as they are about to start their evil works. I decree that heavenly forces will not spare any evil power that will add, promote, or support evil in my life this year. Right from now, any good thing I intend to start shall prosper and be perfected by God of new beginnings.

> *"Behold, they shall surely gather together, but not by me: whosoever shall gather together against thee shall fall for thy sake. Behold, I have created the smith that*

> *bloweth the coals in the fire, and that bringeth forth an instrument for his work; and I have created the waster to destroy. No weapon that is formed against thee shall prosper; and every tongue that shall rise against thee in judgment thou shalt condemn. This is the heritage of the servants of the LORD, and their righteousness is of me, saith the LORD"* (Isaiah 54:15-17).

> *"Remember ye not the former things, neither consider the things of old. Behold, I will do a new thing; now it shall spring forth; shall ye not know it? I will even make a way in the wilderness, and rivers in the desert"* (Isaiah 43:18-19).

I decree against powers of darkness that are in charge of stopping my advancement. Satan, listen to me very well, it is written, *"In the beginning, God created the heaven and the earth."* Therefore, because I have the image of God, you cannot stop me from starting any good thing this year. I decree for immediate manifestation of God's power of creation upon my life now. I must have more than enough power, courage to start and finish every good thing this year.

All the hosts of hell that are prepared to fight me this year shall all die and perish, in the mighty name of Jesus. Amen.

> *"Now Jericho was straightly shut up because of the children of Israel: none went out, and none came in"* (Joshua 6:1).

> *"So the people shouted when the priests blew with the trumpets: and it came to pass, when the people heard the sound of the trumpet, and the people shouted with a great shout, that the wall fell down flat, so that the*

people went up into the city, every man straight before him, and they took the city" (Joshua 6:20).

I issue an order against every evil power assigned to attack my new beginning this year. Let the hand of God take away every evil invested in my original destiny from the beginning, in the mighty name of Jesus.

PRAYERS FOR A NEW BEGINNING

1. As I start this program, O Lord, empower me to bring it to a perfect end, in the name of Jesus.

2. Blood of Jesus, arise and fight for me until the last enemy of my destiny is dead, in the name of Jesus.

3. Any power that has vowed to hinder me from starting well, fall down and die, in the name of Jesus.

4. I pour the blood of Jesus into my foundation, in the name of Jesus.

5. Any power assigned to hinder me from the beginning, die, in the name of Jesus.

6. Spirit of the living God, move upon my life and perfect the works of my hands, in the name of Jesus.

7. Every altar of my father's house working against my destiny, be uprooted by thunder, in the name of Jesus.

8. Any evil power polluting my foundation, fall down and die, in the name of Jesus.

9. Every arrow of my family idol that is working against my life, backfire, in the name of Jesus.

10. Any power designed to spoil my present efforts, collapse and die, in the name of Jesus.

11. Let all demonic terrors that are working against my present efforts die, in the name of Jesus.

12. Any evil power of my father's house that has vowed I will never start any good thing, die, in the name of Jesus.

13. Holy Ghost fire, purge my foundation and start a new thing in my life, in the name of Jesus.

14. Every witchcraft attack against my new beginning, be frustrated, in the name of Jesus.

15. Every circle of hardship that is preventing me from starting a new thing, break, in the name of Jesus.

16. Every voice of the enemy that is speaking against my new beginning, be silenced, in the name of Jesus.

17. Every seed of fear that is planted into my foundation, die, in the name of Jesus.

18. Any power, assigned to stand against new projects in my life, die, in the name of Jesus.

19. Any marine spirit problem that is fighting against my new beginning, die, in the name of Jesus.

20. Any power, pursuing me up and down from the place of my blessings, die, in the name of Jesus.

21. Every evil sacrifice that was offered to hinder me from making progress, expire, in the name of Jesus.

22. Power to start a new thing, possess me by force, in the name of Jesus.

Go back to the words of decree and pass your decree again.

DECREE 2

AGAINST EVIL ALLIANCE FOR YOUR SAKE

> *"And the whole earth was of one language, and of one speech. And the LORD said, Behold, the people is one, and they have all one language; and this they begin to do: and now nothing will be restrained from them, which they have imagined to do"* (Genesis 11:1).

I stand against every demonic speech spoken against my destiny to turn back now and rush back to those speakers. I decree that evil people gathering against me anywhere shall be scattered by the angels of God.

Blood of Jesus, speak destruction to every evil alliance gathering against me in the spirit world. I decree against evil languages being used against my family, ministry and I all over the world. Evil men and women gathering against me in any evil group, begin to destroy your own works with your own hands. Every occult language released by any wicked personality for my sake, backfire without delay. Any evil that enemies of my destiny have started against me shall not prosper.

> *"Now Korah, the son of Izhar, the son of Koath, the son of Levi, and Dathan and Abiram, the sons of Eliab, and On, the son of Peleth, sons of Reuben, took men: And they rose up before Moses, with certain of the children of Israel, two hundred and fifty princes of the assembly, famous in the congregation, men of renown: And they*

> gathered themselves together against Moses and against Aaron, and said unto them, Ye take too much upon you, seeing all the congregation are holy, every one of them, and the LORD is among them: wherefore then lift ye up yourselves above the congregation of the LORD" (Numbers 16:1-3).

> "And Korah gathered the entire congregation against them unto the door of the tabernacle of the congregation: and the glory of the LORD appeared unto the entire congregation" (Numbers 16:19).

I decree against every evil imagination from the hearts of the wicked. Evil decree against me, scatter by thunder. Let the power of God arise in anger and restrain all dark forces rising up against my destiny.

Every evil alliance with an evil vow to execute evil projects in the land, be disgraced and confounded. Blood of Jesus, flow into the camps of evil forces and decree against their evil works by force.

> "And Pharaoh said who is the LORD that I should obey his voice to let Israel go? I know not the LORD; neither will I let Israel go" (Exodus 5:2).

> "And the king of Egypt said unto them, wherefore do ye, Moses and Aaron, let the people from their works? get you unto your burdens. And Pharaoh said, Behold, the people of the land now are many, and ye make them rest from their burdens. And Pharaoh commanded the same day the taskmasters of the people, and their officers, saying, Ye shall no more give the people straw to make brick, as heretofore: let them go and gather straw for themselves. And the tale of the bricks, which

they did make heretofore, ye shall lay upon them; ye shall not diminish ought thereof: for they be idle; therefore they cry, saying, Let us go and sacrifice to our God. Let there more work be laid upon the men, that they may labor therein; and let them not regard vain words" (Exodus 5:4-9).

"And the taskmasters hasted them, saying, Fulfill your works, your daily tasks, as when there was straw. And the officers of the children of Israel, which Pharaoh's taskmasters had set over them, were beaten, and demanded, Wherefore have ye not fulfilled your task in making brick both yesterday and to day, as heretofore?" (Exodus 5:13-14).

"But he said, ye are idle, ye are idle: therefore ye say, Let us go and do sacrifice to the LORD. Go therefore now, and work; for there shall no straw be given you, yet shall ye deliver the tale of bricks. And the officers of the children of Israel did see that they were in evil case, after it was said, ye shall not minish ought from your bricks of your daily task" (Exodus 5:17-19).

Heavenly soldiers on divine assignments, arise to work now and confound evil alliances in the world. I decree against every evil wisdom, knowledge and understanding of the wicked now.

Lord Jesus, send Your destroying speech into the camp of all united evil forces of darkness.

I decree confusing speeches into the residence and conference halls of evil associations.

PRAYERS AGAINST EVIL UNION

1. Father Lord, arise and scatter every evil coalition gathering against my destiny, in the name of Jesus.

2. Blood of Jesus, flow into the camp of evil organization and put them to shame, in the name of Jesus.

3. You, agents of demonic gang-up against my life, be frustrated by fire, in the name of Jesus.

4. I break the powers of evil coalition forces assigned to waste my destiny, in the name of Jesus.

5. Every evil thing done against me by evil coalition forces of marine powers, die, in the name of Jesus.

6. I blind every ancestral spirit, gathering evil powers against me and I command them to scatter, in the name of Jesus.

7. Every stubborn power that has vowed to waste my life, be wasted, in the name of Jesus.

8. O Lord, deliver me from strong enemies and put them to shame, in the name of Jesus.

9. I release myself from the grip of unknown enemies, in the name of Jesus.

10. Let the blood of Jesus be transfused into my blood to scatter all my secret enemies, in the name of Jesus.

11. Every arrow of enemies that is fired into my life from any evil group, backfire, in the name of Jesus.

12. Any evil association that is assigned to destroy me, scatter and die, in the name of Jesus.

13. All adversaries of my breakthrough, gathering against me, scatter, in the name of Jesus.

14. Father Lord, in the movement of Your power, confront and conquer all evil groups that are against me, in the name of Jesus.

15. Let all scorpions and serpents of darkness gathering against me die, in the name of Jesus.

16. Let every enemy of my soul be put to shame wherever they are gathered, in the name of Jesus.

17. Let angels of God roll stones of fire on the heads of every evil personality gathered against me, in the name of Jesus.

18. Every decision of evil people against me, be rendered null and void, in the name of Jesus.

19. My name, become too hot to be discussed by marine powers, in the name of Jesus.

20. Any evil discussions that are going on against my promotion, be terminated to my favor, in the name of Jesus.

21. Let all drinkers of blood and eaters of flesh eat their own flesh and drink their own blood, in the name of Jesus.

22. Every evil cloud that is gathering against me, scatter, in the name of Jesus.

23. Any power that is gathered to mock me, scatter in shame and die, in the name of Jesus.

24. O Lord, promote me before all my enemies, who have gathered to laugh at me, in the name of Jesus.

Go back to the words of decree and pass your decree again.

DECREE 3

AGAINST HOUSEHOLD WICKEDNESS

The scriptures said that if I decree a thing, it would be established unto me and that the light shall shine upon my way. Based on that statement made by the Word of God, I decree that all the unrepentant *Cain* personalities that are pursuing my life shall stumble and die. You that *Cain* personality, wherever you are now surrender or die by fire. I decree that any *Cain* personality operating in my family's that has vowed to expand my problems shall not see the light of the day. Let the *Cain* personality against my destiny, marriage and finance be oppressed to death now. You, *Cain* personality in my life, I command you to commit suicide by force.

> *"And Cain talked with Abel his brother: and it came to pass, when they were in the field, that Cain rose up against Abel his brother, and slew him"* (Genesis 4:8).

> *"He answered and said unto them, well hath Esaias prophesied of you hypocrites, as it is written, this people honoreth me with their lips, but their heart is far from me"* (Mark 7:6).

> *"Howbeit in vain do they worship me, teaching for doctrines the commandments of men"* (Mark 7:7).

> *"And a man's foes shall be they of his own household"* (Matthew 10:36).

I decree that curses in my life from my family's *Cain* shall expire forever. Blood of Jesus, destroy every peace of the *Cain* personality by fire. Let the *Cain* after my life be paralyzed with weapons he is using against me.

> *"And, behold, there came a man of God out of Judah by the word of the LORD unto Bethel: and Jeroboam stood by the altar to burn incense. And he cried against the altar in the word of the LORD, and said, O altar, altar, thus saith the LORD; Behold, a child shall be born unto the house of David, Josiah by name; and upon thee shall he offer the priests of the high places that burn incense upon thee, and men's bones shall be burnt upon thee. And he gave a sign the same day, saying, this is the sign, which the LORD hath spoken; Behold, the altar shall be rent, and the ashes that are upon it shall be poured out. And it came to pass, when king Jeroboam heard the saying of the man of God, which had cried against the altar in Bethel, that he put forth his hand from the altar, saying, Lay hold on him. And his hand, which he put forth against him, dried up, so that he could not pull it in again to him. The altar also was rent, and the ashes poured out from the altar, according to the sign, which the man of God had given by the word of the LORD. And the king answered and said unto the man of God, Entreat now the face of the LORD thy God, and pray for me, that my hand may be restored me again. And the man of God besought the LORD, and the king's hand was restored him again, and became as it was before"* (1 Kings 13:1-6).

Let evil powers supporting any *Cain* personality in my life turn against him now. I decree that the *Cain* person shall not kill me. You that *Cain*, die in the field of shame. Any evil power that wants to turn members of my family against me, I decree failure unto your plans. I decree death unto the spirit of enmity raised against me in my own house. I convert hatred and wars fashioned against me in my own house to divine love.

> *"And Jacob lifted up his eyes, and looked, and, behold, Esau came, and with him four hundred men. And he divided the children unto Leah, and unto Rachel, and unto the two handmaids. And he put the handmaids and their children foremost, and Leah and her children after, and Rachel and Joseph hindermost. And he passed over before them, and bowed himself to the ground seven times, until he came near to his brother. And Esau ran to meet him, and embraced him, and fell on his neck, and kissed him: and they wept"* (Genesis 33:1-4).

Any power that is blocking the God of deliverance from my house, I decree your death immediately. I decree the death of every evil sacrifice offered against my home. Evil statement said against my household by anyone living or dead, I decree against you now, perish, die and be buried by force.

You, enemies of my home, by the decree of the Almighty God, drink poison, eat your flesh and confess unto death immediately.

> *"And he took Agag the king of the Amalekites alive, and utterly destroyed all the people with the edge of the sword. But Saul and the people spared Agag, and the best of the sheep, and of the oxen, and of the fatlings, and the lambs, and all that was good, and would not*

utterly destroy them: but every thing that was vile and refuse, that they destroyed utterly " (1 Samuel 15:8-9).

"Then said Samuel, Bring ye hither to me Agag the king of the Amalekites. And Agag came unto him delicately. And Agag said, surely the bitterness of death is past. And Samuel said, as thy sword hath made women childless, so shall thy mother be childless among women. And Samuel hewed Agag in pieces before the LORD in Gilgal" (1 Samuel 15:32-33).

By the power in the name of Jesus, I challenge every weapon of household wickedness assigned to render me useless, in the name of Jesus. Let the wind of the Holy Ghost dry up every evil river from my place of birth flowing into my life, in the name of Jesus.

PRAYERS AGAINST HOUSEHOLD WICKEDNESS

1. Heavenly father, deliver me from the grip of household wickedness, in the name of Jesus.

2. Every evil force assigned to destroy me from my ancestral altars, fall down and die, in the name of Jesus.

3. Every angel of darkness assisting my household enemies, fall down and die, in the name of Jesus.

4. Every evil covenant that is promoting curses in my life, break, in the name of Jesus.

5. Every evil gang-up in my place of birth that is set up against my life, scatter in shame, in the name of Jesus.

6. Every wicked strongman of my father's house, fall down and die, in the name of Jesus.

7. Every spirit of Cain, assigned to waste my destiny, be wasted, in the name of Jesus.

8. Any power that is outside my family, sponsoring attacks against my life, be exposed unto death, in the name of Jesus.

9. Every evil arrow that is fired into my life from my place of birth, backfire, in the name of Jesus.

10. O Lord, arise in Your anger and deliver me from household wickedness, in the name of Jesus.

11. Every curse placed upon my life from my blood relations, die immediately, in the name of Jesus.

12. I cut myself off from any communal bondage, in the name of Jesus.

13. Any evil power in my family, prospering with my destiny, die, in the name of Jesus.

14. Heavenly Father, deliver me completely from enemies that are very close to me, in the name of Jesus.

15. Any evil personality in my family that has vowed to destroy me, fail woefully in shame, in the name of Jesus.

16. Every enchantment, curse and spell that is working against me, backfire, in the name of Jesus.

17. Let the *Goliath* of my father's house fall down and die now, in the name of Jesus.

18. Every evil tongue that is speaking against my life, be silenced forever, in the name of Jesus.

19. Let every devourer in my family be devoured by force, in the name of Jesus.

20. I shall not bow down to powers of darkness in my household, in the name of Jesus.

21. I break and loose myself from all attacks of my household powers, in the name of Jesus.

22. Every evil utterance said against me by evil powers of my father's house, die, in the name of Jesus.

Go back to the words of decree and pass your decree again.

DECREE 4

AGAINST UNCOMPROMISING ENEMIES

"Then the earth shook and trembled; the foundations also of the hills moved and were shaken, because he was wroth" (Psalms 18:7).

You my uncompromising enemies, I decree that confusion will fall upon you now. Begin to oppress yourselves without a break. See yourself as worst enemies. Block all your ways of blessings with your own hands. I decree that you will be so confused to the extent that you will stripe yourselves naked in public. Begin to behave abnormal before your own helpers.

"And David put his hand in his bag, and took thence a stone, and slang it, and smote the Philistine in his forehead that the stone sunk into his forehead; and he fell upon his face to the earth. So David prevailed over the Philistine with a sling and with a stone, and smote the Philistine, and slew him; but there was no sword in the hand of David. Therefore David ran, and stood upon the Philistine, and took his sword, and drew it out of the sheath thereof, and slew him, and cut off his head therewith. And when the Philistines saw their champion was dead, they fled. And the men of Israel and of Judah arose, and shouted, and pursued the Philistines, until thou come to the valley, and to the gates of Ekron. And the wounded of the Philistines fell down by the way to Shaaraim, even unto Gath, and

unto Ekron. And the children of Israel returned from chasing after the Philistines, and they spoiled their tents. And David took the head of the Philistine, and brought it to Jerusalem; but he put his armor in his tent" (1 Samuel 17:49-54).

I decree that unless you repent, you shall continue to attack yourselves until you finish yourselves off.

You my uncompromising enemies, by the decree of God, come together mysteriously and use every weapon that is available against yourselves. I decree by the anointing that cannot be turned back, you my uncompromising enemies will walk into the camp of your own enemies and open your own mouth and tell lies, give wrong reports and use your own mouth to destroy yourselves.

You my uncompromising enemies, I decree against you, arise on your feet and walk straight into danger that will finish your evil works. As Paul in Acts 13:9-12 decreed against Elymas, the sorcerer, who withstood him, I degree that the hand of the Lord will be upon all my uncompromising enemies. They shall all be blind and will not see the sun until they repent. Every uncompromising enemy of my destiny, enough is enough; let your strengths be confiscated completely by force. I decree that your problems will increase, explode and swallow you. I decree that your mental storehouse will fail you. Begin to announce your own failings with your own mouth unto death.

"And the children of Israel went into the midst of the sea upon the dry ground: and the waters were a wall unto them on their right hand, and on their left. And the Egyptians pursued, and went in after them to the midst of the sea, even all Pharaoh's horses, his chariots,

and his horsemen. And it came to pass, that in the morning watch the LORD looked unto the host of the Egyptians through the pillar of fire and of the cloud, and troubled the host of the Egyptians, And took off their chariot wheels, that they drave them heavily: so that the Egyptians said, Let us flee from the face of Israel; for the LORD fighteth for them against the Egyptians And the LORD said unto Moses, Stretch out thine hand over the sea, that the waters may come again upon the Egyptians, upon their chariots, and upon their horsemen. And Moses stretched forth his hand over the sea, and the sea returned to his strength when the morning appeared; and the Egyptians fled against it; and the LORD overthrew the Egyptians in the midst of the sea. And the waters returned, and covered the chariots, and the horsemen, and all the host of Pharaoh that came into the sea after them; there remained not so much as one of them. But the children of Israel walked upon dry land in the midst of the sea; and the waters were a wall unto them on their right hand, and on their left. Thus the LORD saved Israel that day out of the hand of the Egyptians; and Israel saw the Egyptians dead upon the seashore. And Israel saw that great work which the LORD did upon the Egyptians: and the people feared the LORD, and believed the LORD, and his servant Moses" (Exodus 14:22-31).

Whatever you have done against me, receive it back double.

PRAYERS AGAINST UNCOMPROMISING ENEMIES

1. Blood of Jesus, speak destruction unto all my uncompromising enemies, in the name of Jesus.

2. Every enemy of my destiny, attacking me in my dreams, be exposed unto death, in the name of Jesus.

3. I cut off heads of my uncompromising enemies, in the name of Jesus.

4. Any foreign hand that has vowed to poison my life, catch fire and wither, in the name of Jesus.

5. I poison the brain of my unrepentant enemy and I command them to be wasted, in the name of Jesus.

6. I bind and render to uselessness every evil hand raised against my life, in the name of Jesus.

7. Any pollution that entered into my blood from the marine kingdom, receive deliverance, in the name of Jesus.

8. I command all evil powers standing against me to fall down and die, in the name of Jesus.

9. Every strongman delegated against my progress, fall down and die, in the name of Jesus.

10. Lord Jesus, cause my enemies to bow down their heads in shame, in the name of Jesus.

11. I receive divine anointing to excel above all stubborn enemies, in the name of Jesus.

12. Every spirit of the tail that has vowed to keep me behind, die, in the name of Jesus.

13. Father Lord, dispatch Your angels to kill every uncompromising enemy, in the name of Jesus.

14. Let the backbone of my strong enemy be broken to pieces, in the name of Jesus.

15. Every Stubborn adversary in my life, fall down and die, in the name of Jesus.

16. I bind every Stubborn agent of Satan assigned to confuse my life to become frustrated, in the name of Jesus.

17. Every success of my uncompromising enemy, be wasted, in the name of Jesus.

18. Every evil network of devil and his agents to destroy me, be shattered, in the name of Jesus.

19. Every collaborators, working hard to disgrace me, be disgraced, in the name of Jesus.

20. Stubborn evil followers from hell, assigned to frustrate all my efforts, scatter, in the name of Jesus.

21. Lord Jesus, identify my unrepentant enemies and destroy them, in the name of Jesus.

22. Let my enemies make great mistakes that will terminate their lives, in the name of Jesus.

23. I reject every unprofitable controversy that is ignited to destroy me, in the name of Jesus.

24. Every vow of my enemy that is working against me, be nullified by the blood of Jesus, in the name of Jesus.

Go back to the words of decree and pass your decree again.

DECREE 5

AGAINST EVIL VERDICTS

> *"Blotting out the handwriting of ordinances that was against us, which was contrary to us, and took it out of the way, nailing it to his cross; And having spoiled principalities and powers, he made a shew of them openly, triumphing over them in it"* (Colossians 2:14-15).

I decree against every evil verdict made against my life by anyone, living or dead. Every evil verdict said against me by wicked relatives and unfriendly friends, I stand and decree now, go back to your senders. Any hand that has written evil against me, you will never write any good thing again for your owner. Any evil hand that is writing evil against me, wither by the decree of God now. Any evil hand that would be assigned to write evil verdicts against me shall receive stroke. Let every oral verdict said against me return to their owners forever. Let the blood of Jesus blot out any evil writing that is working against me.

> *"And the king arising from the banquet of wine in his wrath went into the palace garden: and Haman stood up to make request for his life to Esther the queen; for he saw that there was evil determined against him by the king. Then the king returned out of the palace garden into the place of the banquet of wine; and Haman was fallen upon the bed whereon Esther was. Then said the king, Will he force the queen also before me in the house? As the word went out of the king's*

> *mouth, they covered Haman's face. And Harbonah, one of the chamberlains, said before the king, Behold also, the gallows fifty cubits high, which Haman had made for Mordecai, who had spoken good for the king, standeth in the house of Haman. Then the king said, Hang him thereon so they hanged Haman on the gallows that he had prepared for Mordecai. Then was the king's wrath pacified"* (Esther 7:7-10).

Any evil statement said by my ancestors, spirits or anyone dead or alive, I nail you to the cross. Let every evil agreement by devil himself, principalities and powers or any evil with any human being against me be spoiled by my God. I decree that enough is enough and I command woes upon woes upon all unrepentant enemies of my destiny. You my stubborn enemies, I have kept quiet too long and you have treacherously dealt with me without a challenge. So I challenge you now, begin to meet with treacherous people from now. I decree that you must be spoiled the same way you have spoilt others. Any evil verdict that has wasted my life by evil verdicts of the wicked, backfire.

> *"Woe to thee that spoilest, and thou wast not spoiled; and dealest treacherously, and they dealt not treacherously with thee! when thou shalt cease to spoil, thou shalt be spoiled; and when thou shalt make an end to deal treacherously, they shall deal treacherously with thee"* (Isaiah 33:1).

I decree immediate destruction against every evil verdict made against my business, marriage, academic career, etc. Blood of Jesus, flow into every part of my life and frustrate every evil verdict made against my destiny.

PRAYERS AGAINST EVIL VERDICTS

1. Any evil pronouncement that is made against my life, be reversed by force, in the name of Jesus.

2. Great God, arise and change my situation, in the name of Jesus.

3. Blood of Jesus, flow into my life and neutralize every evil deposit by Your power, in the name of Jesus.

4. Heavenly father, let Your words rule and reign over my life, in the name of Jesus.

5. Every witchcraft verdict in my life, backfire, in the name of Jesus.

6. Let the words of the wicked over my life return to them double fold , in the name of Jesus.

7. You my life, reject every evil verdict said against you, in the name of Jesus.

8. Every inherited evil verdict in my life, your time is up, die, in the name of Jesus.

9. It is written, no weapon that is formed against me shall prosper, in the name of Jesus.

10. Every marine spirit curse in that is affecting my life, receive double destruction, in the name of Jesus.

11. Blood of Jesus, speak termination to every evil verdict made against me, in the name of Jesus.

12. Let divine verdicts rule over my destiny forever, in the name of Jesus.

13. I anoint myself against evil utterances said against me, in the name of Jesus.

14. Any evil agreement that is made against me shall not prosper, in the name of Jesus.

15. Let the grace of God be sufficient for me, in the name of Jesus.

16. Every incantation of witchcraft that is working against me, backfire, in the name of Jesus.

17. O Lord, convert every evil speech that is made against me into my favor, in the name of Jesus.

18. By the power in the blood of Jesus, I separate myself from every demonic word, in the name of Jesus.

19. Let the divination of the wicked made against me return to their heads, in the name of Jesus.

20. Every enchantment that is said against my breakthrough shall not stand, in the name of Jesus.

21. By the power in the words of God, I reject every evil verdict made against me, in the name of Jesus.

22. Let every conscious or unconscious speech I have said against myself die, in the name of Jesus.

23. Let my words confront and conquer every evil word of the wicked against me, in the name of Jesus.

24. Every yoke of the wicked standing against me, go back to your sender, in the name of Jesus.

Go back to the words of decree and pass your decree again.

DECREE 6

AGAINST EVIL FOUNDATION

> *"If the foundations be destroyed, what can the righteous do?"* (Psalms 11:3).

I decree in the name of Jesus that evil foundations in my life must collapse, in the name of Jesus. Blood of Jesus Christ of Nazareth, flow into the root of every evil foundation in my destiny and let it lose its strength and fall flat by force now. I command my life to slip out from every faulty foundation by fire. Any evil power, supporting any evil foundation in my life, I decree against you now, die by force immediately.

> *"According to the grace of God which is given unto me, as a wise master builder, I have laid the foundation, and another buildeth thereon. But let every man take heed how he buildeth thereupon. For other foundation can no man lay than that is laid, which is Jesus Christ. Now if any man build upon this foundation gold, silver, precious stones, wood, hay, stubble"* (1 Corinthians 3:10-12).

Heavenly Father, release forces from the third heaven against every evil spirit assigned to mess up my life, in the name of Jesus. Evil powers in my foundation, I force you to break your yoke in my life and finish yourselves.

I decree that angels of God will arise and pull down every evil foundation in my life. Let the power in the name of Christ begin to destroy every evil foundation in my life by fire. Any power that has vowed to keep me under evil shall not see the light of the day. O Lord, let Your unchangeable decree be released against all evil foundations affecting my destiny, in the name of Jesus.

It is written, *"For other foundation can no man lay than that is laid, which is Jesus Christ."* Based on these scripture, I command immediate demolition of any evil foundation laid for my sake, in Jesus name. O Lord, by the power in the blood of Your Son, Lord Jesus, I put the fire of destruction under every evil foundation in my life. Let the fire of judgment begin to attack all demons living inside foundations built by enemies of Christ, in the name of Jesus. Any problem hiding inside my foundation, begin to come out now and die by force, in the name of Jesus. O Lord, search my foundation by fire and cleanse it, in the name of Jesus.

PRAYERS AGAINST EVIL FOUNDATION

1. Every evil thing in my foundation, come out and die immediately, in the name of Jesus.

2. Let the glory of God begin to manifest in my foundation, in the name of Jesus.

3. By the anointing that breaks every yoke of devil, I break every evil yoke in my foundation, in the name of Jesus.

4. Heavenly father, arise and clear my foundation from every evil pollution, in the name of Jesus.

5. Every bad spirit in my foundation, come out and die, in the name of Jesus.

6. Lord Jesus, speak peace into my foundation, in the name of Jesus.

7. Any evil seed planted into my foundation, wither and die, in the name of Jesus.

8. Heavenly father, take away every evil in my foundation, in the name of Jesus.

9. Let the anointing of God arise and waste the wasters in my life, in the name of Jesus.

10. Any serpent of darkness in my foundation, come out and die, in the name of Jesus.

11. Every evil character that has arrested my destiny, die, in the name of Jesus.

12. Blood of Jesus, flow into my foundation and deliver me, in the name of Jesus.

13. Angels of the living God, arise and deliver my foundation from devil, in the name of Jesus.

14. Any power that has refused to set my foundation free, die, in the name of Jesus.

15. Holy Ghost fire, purge my life of evil deposits, in the name of Jesus.

16. Let my breakthrough begin to manifest, in the name of Jesus.

17. O Lord, visit my foundation and deliver me from destruction, in the name of Jesus.

18. Lion of Judah, destroy every fake lion in my foundation, in the name of Jesus.

19. Every demonic worm that is in my root, come out and die, in the name of Jesus.

20. My foundation, receive fire, in the name of Jesus.

21. Every stranger that is in my foundation, come out and die, in the name of Jesus.

22. Every darkness hiding in my foundation, disappear by force, in the name of Jesus.

23. Every evil arrest of my foundation, be frustrated by fire, in the name of Jesus.

24. Every evil inheritance existing in my foundation, I reject you by force, in the name of Jesus.

25. Wind of deliverance, enter into my foundation, in the name of Jesus.

Go back to the words of decree and pass your decree again.

DECREE 7

FOR IMMEDIATE SOLUTIONS

"And they were all filled with the Holy Ghost, and began to speak with other tongues, as the Spirit gave them utterance" (Acts 2:4).

By the power in the blood of Jesus, I decree against every problem in my life. Without remedy, you, problems that are assigned to waste my life, be wasted immediately, in the name of Jesus. Any sickness in my life that is mocking medical science and drugs, your time is up, die and die again by fire, in the name of Jesus. I pass a decree against every enemy of my destiny and I command perfect freedom from every evil hold of the enemy. Let the angry soldiers of darkness militating against my life be scattered in shame and disgrace, in the name of Jesus.

Every stubborn witchcraft problem in my life that has refused to let me go, receive immediate solution and come back no more into my life forever and ever. I decree that my brain shall carry holy fire, soundness, and power to marshal out facts that will make me great. Based on this statement, I decree that I shall make it and by my reasoning power, I receive immediate solution to my problems forever, in the name of Jesus.

Blood of Jesus, conduct a search, trace every root of my problem and bring immediate solutions that would set me free forever, in the name of Jesus.

Lord Jesus, You appeared before the grave of Lazarus, and he received immediate solution to his problem. When You declared, *"Lazarus, come forth,"* there was immediate solution. In my own situation, please arise and declare that all goods things in my life that are dead should come forth, in the name of Jesus.

You had an encounter with a certain man who was suffering from dropsy, and You healed him and let him go. The same way You did it for that man, talk to my situation now and let me leave here without any problem following me, in the name of Jesus.

In a marriage at Cana of Galilee, You decreed and commanded Your disciples to fill water pots with ordinary water and immediately, they turned into sweet wine. Please, Jesus, decree now that every bitterness in my life shall be turned into sweetness. Let there be immediate solution to every problem in my life now, in the name of Jesus.

PRAYERS FOR IMMEDIATE SOLUTIONS

1. Lord Jesus, appear in my case and give me immediate solution, in the name of Jesus.

2. Every stubborn yoke that has remained in my life, break immediately, in the name of Jesus.

3. Any power that is assigned to prolong my bondage, die, in the name of Jesus.

4. Let God intervene and deliver me from every evil power, in the name of Jesus.

5. Heavenly Father, by Your power, move me away from destruction, in the name of Jesus.

6. Where is the Lord God of Elijah? Appear in my situation, in the name of Jesus.

7. Angry soldiers from heaven, appear in the battlefield for my sake, in the name of Jesus.

8. Blood of Jesus, flow into my life and solve all my problems, in the name of Jesus.

9. You, Goliath in the battlefield of my life, fall down and die, in the name of Jesus.

10. Every decree of the wicked that is made against my life, be reversed, in the name of Jesus.

11. My destiny, move forward by fire and by force, in the name of Jesus.

12. Heavenly Father, take me away from every evil authority, in the name of Jesus.

13. Every good thing that refused to take place in my life, manifest now, in the name of Jesus.

14. Let my greatness suddenly manifest, in the name of Jesus.

15. Holy Ghost Fire, burn to ashes every demonic hindrance in my life, in the name of Jesus.

16. Let God that answers by fire be my God in every situation, in the name of Jesus.

17. Let every demonic delay in my life die, in the name of Jesus.

18. Anything that enemies have done in my life, die by force, in the name of Jesus.

19. Ancient of days, appear and set me free from captivity, in the name of Jesus.

20. Every witchcraft problem in my life, your time is up, die, in the name of Jesus.

21. Evil powers that have vowed to waste my life shall be wasted, in the name of Jesus.

22. Every evil gathering against me, scatter, in the name of Jesus.

23. Father Lord, let Your deliverance for my life be perfected, in the name of Jesus.

24. Angels of the living God, work day and night until my deliverance is perfected, in the name of Jesus.

25. Heavenly Father, arise and fight for me, in the name of Jesus.

Go back to the words of decree and pass your decree again.

DECREE 8

AGAINST INSTITUTIONAL CAPTIVITY AND BONDAGE

"But upon mount Zion shall be deliverance, and there shall be holiness; and the house of Jacob shall possess their possessions" (Obadiah 1:17).

"And that they may recover themselves out of the snare of the devil, who are taken captive by him at his will" (2 Timothy 2:26).

By the sin of one man, all humanity was captured by Satan, and by the righteousness of one man, freedom came. I decree that every yoke of institutional captivity in my life should break now, in the name of Jesus.

I command every remnant of forbidden fruit in my life to die and let my deliverance appear by force.

I decree that all forms of bondage in my life shall break by the powers that set men free at the cross of Calvary, in the name of Jesus.

Lord Jesus, You broke the bondage of fornication and immorality in the tribe of Judah. This similar bondage humiliated king David, frustrated and disgraced Solomon, wasted Adonijah, killed Amnon and defiled Tarma. But you came into the tribe of Judah as the lion of Judah and destroyed, wasted, and eliminated, not only fornication and immorality, but the sins of all mankind.

Based on this, I command all stubborn bondage in my life to be broken. Any power of sin of fornication in my life, break, in the name of Jesus. Let the power of sin that captured Potiphar's wife and that is now militating against me break, in the name of Jesus. Any Pharaoh that has imposed taskmasters on me, die and die forever. Every bondage of fear in my family line, break by fire now, in the name of Jesus.

Yoke of careless visitations in my life, yoke of anger and all manner of bondage, break and set me free by fire. Lord Jesus, decree into my life and let me go and sin no more, be sick no more, suffer no more and fear no more.

PRAYERS AGAINST INSTITUTIONAL CAPTIVITY AND BONDAGE

1. Any evil power that is holding me in captive, release me and die, in the name of Jesus.

2. Let the chain of institutional captivity in my life break to pieces, in the name of Jesus.

3. By the anointing that breaks every yoke, I break the yoke of bondage in my life, in the name of Jesus.

4. Every family bondage in my life, break by fire, in the name of Jesus.

5. O Lord my God, arise and deliver me from every evil power, in the name of Jesus.

6. Every common problem in my family that is working against me, die, in the name of Jesus.

7. Blood of Jesus, flow into my life and deliver me from every evil, in the name of Jesus.

8. Heavenly father, deliver me from inherited bondage, in the name of Jesus.

9. Let the yoke of environmental powers that is against me break, in the name of Jesus.

10. Every uncompromising problem, assigned to waste my life, be wasted, in the name of Jesus.

11. Blood of Jesus, speak against every problem in my foundation, in the name of Jesus.

12. Let the anger of God pull down every wall that is standing against my life, in the name of Jesus.

13. Every common evil event that is approaching me for destruction, turn back now, in the name of Jesus.

14. Ancient of days, destroy all ancient problems in my life, in the name of Jesus.

15. Powers of my place of birth that are working hard to destroy me, die, in the name of Jesus.

16. Any evil altar, supplying problems in my life, catch fire, in the name of Jesus.

17. Every yoke of poverty in my family, be broken by fire, in the name of Jesus.

18. Evil circle of untimely death in my family, scatter now, in the name of Jesus.

19. Every problem, visiting people one after the other in my family, die, in the name of Jesus.

20. Blood of Jesus, speak against evil cycles in my life, in the name of Jesus.

21. Every common evil character in my family, I reject you, in the name of Jesus.

22. Lord Jesus, arise and deliver me from all manner of captivity, in the name of Jesus.

Go back to the words of decree and pass your decree again.

DECREE 9

FOR FINANCIAL BREAKTHROUGH

> *"And I will rebuke the devourer for your sakes, and he shall not destroy the fruits of your ground; neither shall your vine cast her fruit before the time in the field, saith the LORD of hosts. And all nations shall call you blessed: for ye shall be a delightsome land, saith the LORD of hosts"* (Malachi 3:11).

> *"Hear me speedily, O LORD: my spirit faileth: hide not thy face from me, lest I be like unto them that go down into the pit. Cause me to hear thy loving-kindness in the morning; for in thee do I trust: cause me to know the way wherein I should walk; for I lift up my soul unto thee. Deliver me, O LORD, from mine enemies: I flee unto thee to hide me"* (Psalms 143:7).

I do not rob my God, I pay my tithes and give my offerings, therefore, I shall be blessed financially, and I decree that I shall not lack money. I stand against any curse placed upon my life. Any power that takes God's portion in my life, you are wicked, I command you to release them and die immediately, in the name of Jesus.

By the decree of God, I command the windows of heaven to open by force now, in the name of Jesus. By the command of God, let royal angels from heaven pour unhindered blessings into my life. Heavenly blessings, begin to come down directly into my account until there are no rooms to contain you.

I decree against all devourers in my life. I rebuke you wasters of my financial blessings, in the name of Jesus. Any evil power assigned to destroy fruits of my labor, I decree against you, die immediately now, in the name of Jesus. Any evil power, assigned by devil to destroy my young vines before the time, die premature now, in the name of Jesus. I decree against every satanic embargo on my financial breakthrough.

Let heavenly angels arrest the spirit of financial lack in my life, in the name of Jesus. Financial demons, assigned to paralyze my potentials, enough is enough, die by thunder in Jesus' name. I sow a seed of faith (*mention the amount and be sure to fulfill it*) against demons of my financial breakthrough. The power that God has given me to make wealth, which the enemy has arrested, be released by force.

The goodness of God over my destiny, arise and shine forever in my life. I decree death over evil spirits against prosperity in my life. Let all hindrances to my financial breakthroughs die by the judgment fire of God. By the means of my decree against financial breakthroughs, I loose angels of my breakthrough by force. I command money to begin to look for me, run after me, serve me and plead to stay with me. By the decree of God, I shall be blessed abundantly beyond human imagination.

PRAYERS FOR FINANCIAL BREAKTHROUGH

1. I climb up to the top ladder of financial breakthroughs, in the name of Jesus.

2. Every evil plantation of poverty that is in my life, wither and die by fire, in the name of Jesus.

3. Every evil covenant of financial set back, break to pieces and loose your hold, in the name of Jesus.

4. Arrows of death fired towards my financial breakthrough, backfire, in the name of Jesus.

5. Father Lord, release divine finances into my life that will prosper me, in the name of Jesus.

6. Any power from the waters that is attacking my financial life, die by force, in the name of Jesus.

7. I command immediate flow of money into my business, in the name of Jesus.

8. Every marine spirit bank that has confiscated my finance, release it by force, in the name of Jesus.

9. From today, wherever I go, people shall bless me financially, in the name of Jesus.

10. Every enemy of my financial breakthrough, be exposed and disgraced, in the name of Jesus.

11. Holy Spirit, baptize me with the spirit of financial favors, in the name of Jesus.

12. Let t Holy Ghost fire surround my financial life, in the name of Jesus.

13. Father Lord, in Your power, arise and maximize my financial life to greatness, in the name of Jesus.

14. Lord Jesus, activate my dead finances by Your power, in the name of Jesus.

15. Every good thing that enemies have stolen from me, I recover you double, in the name of Jesus.

16. Every demonic devourer in my business, receive fire and die by force, in the name of Jesus.

17. Blood of Jesus, give me financial breakthrough this year, in the name of Jesus.

18. Let inner voices that are speaking against my finance be silenced forever, in the name of Jesus.

19. Let fire and thunder of God burn every spirit of financial losses in my life to ashes, in the name of Jesus.

20. Heavenly Father, arise and give me financial breakthrough this year, in the name of Jesus.

21. I paralyze the activities of evil spirits against my financial breakthrough, in the name of Jesus.

22. Every strange money in my finance, catch fire and burn to ashes, in the name of Jesus.

23. O Lord, walk back into my foundation and plant in me financial breakthrough, in the name of Jesus.

Go back to the words of decree and pass your decree again.

DECREE 10

FOR DIVINE PROMOTION

"And now shall mine head be lifted up above mine enemies round about me: therefore will I offer in his tabernacle sacrifices of joy; I will sing, yea, I will sing praises unto the LORD" (Psalms 27:6).

By the power in the name of Jesus, I decree dumbfounding and unmerited promotions, unmerited favors and unimaginable elevations by fire. Any power that is standing against my promotion, I decree your death.

I decree that God that raises the poor out of the dust and lifts the needy out of the dunghill shall appear for my sake and promote me. Whether my enemies like it or not, I decree that my God shall link me with princes of His people out of His divine mercies, in the name of Jesus.

The Lord that is not a respecter of person, who is also God that raises the lowly, shall promote me today by force in His mercy. He did it to the woman of Moab called Ruth. He also promoted Rehab who was also a harlot; an undeserved candidate. He took Joseph out of prison to the throne and changed Mordecai's reproach.

I decree the death of any evil pronouncement and outstanding reproach standing against my promotion this year, in the name of Jesus. I cut every evil spirit against my promotion and I climb the ladder of promotion. I walk out from people on the grand floor of life. I move away from gatherings of the defeated ones. Let owners of evil loads of poverty in my life appear and carry their loads for I am promoted under the decree of Lord Jesus Christ, in the name of Jesus.

I decree against every evil authority standing against me and I command it to scatter into shame, in the name of Jesus.

Great God of heaven, by the power in the name of Your Son, Lord Jesus, I decree that my head shall be lifted up in promotion above all enemies surrounding me. O ye evil heads that are raised against my promotion, I decree now, be lowered immediately. I command every everlasting door closed against me to open by fire and by force, in the name of Jesus.

PRAYERS FOR DIVINE PROMOTION

1. Father Lord, give me Your blessings that make one rich without sorrows, in the name of Jesus.

2. My promotion, wherever you are now, appear now by force, in the name of Jesus.

3. My promotion, you shall not be aborted, in the name of Jesus.

4. O Lord my God, promote me beyond my equals, in the name of Jesus.

5. Heavenly Father, arise and give me unimaginable promotion, in the name of Jesus.

6. Any power that is sitting upon my promotion, be unseated by death, in the name of Jesus.

7. Every curse in my life delaying my promotion, die by fire, in the name of Jesus.

8. By the power of God, I destroy every evil spirit against my promotion, in the name of Jesus.

9. Any witchcraft pot, cooking my promotion, break by thunder, in the name of Jesus.

10. Arrows of backwardness that are fired at my promotion, backfire, in the name of Jesus.

11. Any unfriendly friend that is working against my promotion, be disgraced, in the name of Jesus.

12. Fire of God, burn every evil hindrance in my life to ashes, in the name of Jesus.

13. Every covenant of backwardness in my life, disappear, in the name of Jesus.

14. Let witchcraft powers that are behind my backwardness die now, in the name of Jesus.

15. I write my name among people that will be promoted this year, in the name of Jesus.

16. Any power that is fighting against my promotion, die, in the name of Jesus.

17. You, powers that waste opportunities in people's lives, be wasted, in the name of Jesus.

18. Lord Jesus, let my promotion manifest before others, in the name of Jesus.

19. Blood of Jesus, speak promotion into my life, in the name of Jesus.

20. Any marine altar, holding my promotions, release them now, in the name of Jesus.

21. Every yoke of stagnation in my life, break, in the name of Jesus.

22. Fire of God, burn every evil in my life to ashes, in the name of Jesus.

23. Any witch or wizard standing against my promotion, fall down and die, in the name of Jesus.

Go back to the words of decree and pass your decree again.

DECREE 11

AGAINST SATANIC OPPOSITIONS

"Lift up your heads, O ye gates; and be ye lifted up, ye everlasting doors; and the King of glory shall come in. Who is this King of glory? The LORD strong and mighty, the LORD mighty in battle. Lift up your heads, O ye gates; even lift them up, ye everlasting doors; and the King of glory shall come in" (Psalms 24:7-9).

By the power in the blood of Jesus, I decree against every satanic oppression in my life. Let the rain of affliction fall upon all satanic oppositions in my life, in the name of Jesus. I command every oppositions in my life to scatter and never to gather together again forever and ever. Blood of Jesus, arise and decree death to every opposition that is against me. I bind and cast out of my destiny every strange bullet that has entered into my life.

Every spiritual thief that is opposed to my freedom, receive immediate death now by force. Let all evil things that devil and his agents have planted into my life be destroyed by divine judgment. No power from the pit of hell can triumph over me. Therefore, I pass immediate judgment against every satanic opposition in my life, in the name of Jesus. I send arrows of confusion, death and destruction into the camps of all stubborn enemies, in the name of Jesus.

Angels of the living God, arise in your power and put the works of devil and his agents working against my destiny to an end. I decree death to the root of my problems now. Let all weapons of Satan that are working against my life begin to destroy themselves without mercy, in the name of Jesus.

O Lord, mobilize Your warring angels to frustrate and terminate all that are opposing Your will from manifesting in my life. Let every opened mouth of my enemies be close by fire and be opened no more against me.

I forbid devil from attacking my life from henceforth. I command every witchcraft attack from devil against me to backfire forever and ever. Let all opponents of my life receive divine opposition from the third heaven. Any power that will try to revoke my decree against satanic oppositions in my life shall fail and die without negotiation. I seal my decree against satanic oppositions with the blood of Jesus.

PRAYERS AGAINST SATANIC OPPOSITIONS

1. I stand against every satanic opposition in my life, in the name of Jesus.

2. Every dream of backwardness in my life, die by fire, in the name of Jesus.

3. Any power from my village's altar that is standing against my life, scatter, in the name of Jesus.

4. Every satanic stronghold that is standing against my advancement, I pull you down, in the name of Jesus.

5. Let stumbling blocks of witchcraft be removed, in the name of Jesus.

6. Blood of Jesus, deliver me from every demonic opposition, in the name of Jesus.

7. Any evil personality standing on my way, fall down and die, in the name of Jesus.

8. Heavenly Father, bulldoze my way into supernatural breakthrough, in the name of Jesus.

9. Every evil trap of the enemy against me, catch your owners, in the name of Jesus.

10. Any marine power, pulling me backward, collapse and die, in the name of Jesus.

11. I break and loose myself from the grip of evil powers, in the name of Jesus.

12. Every evil conspiracy from my place of birth, scatter, in the name of Jesus.

13. Let the spirit of the tail in my life die and release me, in the name of Jesus.

14. Blood of Jesus, deliver me from every satanic opposition, in the name of Jesus.

15. Power of God to move forward, possess me by fire, in the name of Jesus.

16. From today henceforth, my life shall move forward, in the name of Jesus.

17. Every seed against progress in my life, wither and die by fire, in the name of Jesus.

18. Divine aircraft, take me to where you want me to be, in the name of Jesus.

19. Every witchcraft broom, sweeping away my progress, catch fire, in the name of Jesus.

20. Let the spirit of hindrance in my life be converted to favor, in the name of Jesus.

21. Any agent of Satan, standing against my breakthrough, be cleared away, in the name of Jesus.

22. Let the thunder of God arise for my sake and destroy every satanic opposition, in the name of Jesus.

Go back to the words of decree and pass your decree again.

DECREE 12

AGAINST HIDDEN CURSES

> *"And when they came again to him, (for he tarried at Jericho,) he said unto them, did I not say unto you, Go not? And the men of the city said unto Elisha, Behold, I pray thee, the situation of this city is pleasant, as my lord seeth: but the water is naught, and the ground barren. And he said, bring me a new cruse, and put salt therein. And they brought it to him. And he went forth unto the spring of the waters, and cast the salt in there, and said, thus saith the LORD, I have healed these waters; there shall not be from thence any more death or barren land. So the waters were healed unto this day, according to the saying of Elisha which he spake"* (2 Kings 2:18-22).

In the name of the Father, Son and the Holy Ghost, I decree that all hidden curses in my life shall not see the light of the day in my life, in the name of Jesus. I decree for the death of all unknown curses that are assigned to waste my life, in the name of Jesus. My life will not be ground for hidden curses. Every evil accomplishment that hidden curses had done in my life, I command them to be overturned immediately, in the name of Jesus.

The secret behind all hidden curses in my life, be exposed by divine revelation, vision and dreams, in the name of Jesus. I command all hidden agents or curses in my life to be exposed and be disgraced by force, in the name of Jesus.

Any evil king installed to promote hidden curses in my life, fall down and die, in the name of Jesus.

Let all the handwritings of hidden curses that are written against me be erased by the blood of Jesus, in the name of Jesus. Let the secrets of hidden curses in my life be exposed, in the name of Jesus. I decree by the power in the blood of Jesus that all evil covenant supporting hidden curses in my life must break immediately, in the name of Jesus. I command the destruction of all unknown evil covenants that are supporting hidden curses in my life, in the name of Jesus. Blood of Jesus, confront and conquer all hidden curses that are warring against my destiny, in the name of Jesus.

Every satanic agent, prospering because of the hidden curses in my life shall be exposed by the decree of God, in the name of Jesus. By the decree of my God, I destroy every impurity in my life that is assisting hidden curses in my life, in the name of Jesus. Let evil angels on guard to protect any hidden curse in my life be paralyzed by the stroke of the Lord, in the name of Jesus.

Any evil traffic warden that is diverting good things away from my life because of hidden curses and covenants, die, in the name of Jesus. Any known and unknown covenant in my life that is promoting hidden covenant and curses, break forever, in the name of Jesus. Power in the blood of Jesus, arise and disgrace all hidden curses in my life by power above all powers, in the name of Jesus.

PRAYERS AGAINST HIDDEN CURSES

1. Let hidden curses in my life that are causing me to suffer be exposed and be disgraced, in the name of Jesus.

2. Every hidden curse in my life, your time is up, die, in the name of Jesus.

3. Blood of Jesus, speak destruction unto every spell in my life, in the name of Jesus.

4. By the power in the name of Jesus, I cancel every evil handwriting that is against me, in the name of Jesus.

5. Every stubborn curse that is placed upon my life when I was a baby, die, in the name of Jesus.

6. Every hidden curse that I inherited from my parents, receive Holy Ghost termination, in the name of Jesus.

7. Every curse of spiritual marriage that is standing in my life, be divorced, in the name of Jesus.

8. Holy Ghost fire, burn every hidden curse in my life to ashes, in the name of Jesus.

9. Every inherited curse of poverty in my life, die, in the name of Jesus.

10. Every inherited curse of untimely death in my life, die, in the name of Jesus.

11. Every inherited evil covenant in my life, be broken, in the name of Jesus.

12. Any strongman, following me about because of ancestral curses, fall down and die, in the name of Jesus.

13. Any inherited curse from my parents, assigned to waste me, my life is not available, die, in the name of Jesus.

14. Any hidden curse that is placed upon me in the dream, die, in the name of Jesus.

15. O Lord, reveal to me all my hidden problems and destroy them, in the name of Jesus.

16. I break and loose my destiny from destruction caused by hidden curses, in the name of Jesus.

17. Every witchcraft curse that is attacking me from the dark, be exposed unto death, in the name of Jesus.

18. Heavenly Father, deliver me from all manner of hidden curses, in the name of Jesus.

19. Any strange sickness or problem in my life as a result of hidden curses, die with your curse, in the name of Jesus.

20. You, yoke of hidden curses in my life, break and loose your hold, in the name of Jesus.

21. Every agent of hidden curses in my life, be exposed unto death, in the name of Jesus.

Go back to the words of decree and pass your decree again.

DECREE 13

AGAINST EVIL SOUL-TIES

"And they that are Christ's have crucified the flesh with the affections and lusts" (Galatians 5:24).

I decree the breaking of evil soul-ties holding me in bondage, in the name of Jesus. By the power in the name of Jesus, I command immediate freedom upon my life against any manner of evil relationship, in the name of Jesus. Let arrows of confusion, fired into my life, to keep me under the bondage of evil soul-tie be completely broken now, in the name of Jesus. By the authority given to me as a child of God, let every yoke of evil soul-tie in my life be broken by force, in the name of Jesus.

O Lord, arise in Your anger and break every bondage of evil soul-tie militating against my destiny. I decree that every part of my life must be set free whether enemies like it or not, in the name of Jesus. Blood of Jesus, flow into every evil relationship that has been assigned to waste my destiny and deliver me by force, in the name of Jesus. Every evil link and satanic label of oppression that is keeping me in bondage of sin, break by fire now, in the name of Jesus. Let all curses placed upon my life to manipulate my decisions be erased by the blood of Jesus, in the name of Jesus.

I decree against any power that has ordained me to die through evil soul-tie. Let such powers be destroyed by death. Any evil personality using charm to keep me in any relationship, be disgraced and be frustrated, in the name of

Jesus. Let evil altars that are keeping me in bondage of evil soul-tie scatter by fire, in the name of Jesus.

Let any marine power that is controlling my mind against the will of God, to remain and die in evil relationship die. O Lord, arise and deliver me from every evil relationship assigned to harvest my destiny, in the name of Jesus. Blood of Jesus, flow into my life and break any evil agreement that does not honor You, in the name of Jesus. Let the spirit of death and hell that has vowed to keep me in evil soul-tie begin to break by force. Let the spirit of slavery holding me in bondage of evil soul-tie break by force, in the name of Jesus.

Father Lord, anoint me for spiritual knowledge to understand the end of any relationship in my life, in the name of Jesus. I decree death against any demonic fear keeping me in any evil soul-tie, in the name of Jesus. Let evil manipulators of my destiny that are assigned to manipulate me into evil relationships die, in the name of Jesus. I command my deliverance from every evil soul-tie to manifest immediately, in the name of Jesus.

PRAYERS AGAINST EVIL SOUL-TIES

1. Any covenant that I entered into with any wrong person, I break you immediately, in the name of Jesus.

2. I break and release myself from the evil effects of evil soul-ties, in the name of Jesus.

3. Every marine spirit that is manipulating of my life, be nullified, in the name of Jesus.

4. Any form of evil soul-tie that is assigned to destroy me, break by force, in the name of Jesus.

5. Let every known and unknown evil soul-ties in my life break by force, in the name of Jesus.

6. Every garment of shame that is upon my life from evil soul-ties, catch fire, in the name of Jesus.

7. I command fire to burn down every altar of evil soul-tie in my life, in the name of Jesus.

8. Any wicked personality that has yoked me to evil persons or thing, release me by force, in the name of Jesus.

9. Every covenant of evil soul-tie in my life, break by fire, in the name of Jesus.

10. By the fire of the Holy Ghost, I set myself free from every evil soul-tie, in the name of Jesus.

11. Every bondage of evil soul-tie in my life, break to pieces, in the name of Jesus.

12. O Lord my God, deliver me from evil soul-ties, in the name of Jesus.

13. Let any power assigned to destroy me through evil relationships be destroyed, in the name of Jesus.

14. Every curse of evil soul-ties that is issued against my life, break, in the name of Jesus.

15. Let the covenant of evil soul-tie in my life break by thunder, in the name of Jesus.

16. Every confusion in my life, your time is up, be terminated, in the name of Jesus.

17. Every power that has arrested my mental storehouse, release it and die, in the name of Jesus.

18. Any generational curse of evil soul-tie, scatter to pieces, in the name of Jesus.

19. Every sin promoting evil soul-tie in my life, die perfectly, in the name of Jesus.

20. Every Stubborn evil partner in my life, loose your hold over my life, in the name of Jesus.

21. Blood of Jesus, speak death to all evil soul-ties in my life, in the name of Jesus.

Go back to the words of decree and pass your decree again.

DECREE 14

FOR SUPERNATURAL ABILITIES

> *"How God anointed Jesus of Nazareth with the Holy Ghost and with power: who went about doing good, and healing all that were oppressed of the devil; for God was with him"* (Acts 10:38).

By the power in the name of Jesus, I decree that I shall be strong. I command every weakness in my life to disappear and die forever in the name of Jesus. Let the power in the blood of Jesus appear and empower me to be filled with all manner of supernatural powers in the name of Jesus. I receive divine ability to do supernatural works for God wherever I go, in the name of Jesus. Father Lord, arise and anoint me with Your Holy Ghost and power.

With the anointing of God in my life, I decree and receive power to disgrace every evil thing that is programmed into my life, in the name of Jesus. I decree that sickness will never prosper in my life, in the name of Jesus. I command every infirmity in my life to perish forever, in the name of Jesus. Let the fire of God enter into my blood and burn every sickness to ashes and destroy evil powers that oppose divine powers in my life, in the name of Jesus. O Lord, arise in Your power and give me Your supernatural ability to do exploits, in the name of Jesus.

Holy Ghost fire, enter into dark rooms of my life and lighten me up, and also purge me of every marine power, in the name of Jesus. Father Lord, arise and quicken me for greatness. I refuse to remain without divine power. O Lord, empower me to defeat every weakness of the Spirit. Any power that wants me to live without supernatural ability must die. With the anointing of divine ability in my life, I will begin to go about from today doing good works and not evil works. I decree that dark powers must bow down to supernatural power of God in my life.

With divine supernatural ability in my life, I receive faith to heal every sickness and to destroy diseases. The divine ability in my life will oppress oppressors anywhere they are now. By the supernatural power of God in my life, I command every work of the devil to bow down by fire, in the name of Jesus. By the supernatural power of God in my life, let divine presence rule over my life, in the name of Jesus.

PRAYERS FOR SUPERNATURAL ABILITIES

1. Father Lord, empower me supernaturally, in the name of Jesus.

2. Power to confront and conquer impossibilities, possess me, in the name of Jesus.

3. Heavenly Father, arise in Your supernatural power and move me forward, in the name of Jesus.

4. Every stronghold of the enemy, working against my life, be pulled down, in the name of Jesus.

5. Every wall of Jericho that is standing against my life, collapse by thunder, in the name of Jesus.

6. I receive supernatural powers to perform signs and wonders, in the name of Jesus.

7. Power to destroy evil work anywhere and at anytime necessary, possess me by fire, in the name of Jesus.

8. O Lord, empower me with diverse kinds of divine abilities to move mountains, in the name of Jesus.

9. Right from this moment, no evil power will overcome me, in the name of Jesus.

10. Blood of Jesus, grant me supernatural abilities to live above sin, in the name of Jesus.

11. Power to close speaking mouths of evil lions, fall upon me now, in the name of Jesus.

12. Let the power of the spirit of wisdom begin to operate in my life, in the name of Jesus.

13. O Lord, give me grace to manifest Your supernatural gift of wisdom and knowledge, in the name of Jesus.

14. Ability to speak in tongues with divine results, possess my tongue, in the name of Jesus.

15. O Lord, empower me with gifts of healing to heal all sicknesses and diseases, in the name of Jesus.

16. Power to prophesy exactly as God ordained, fall upon me, in the name of Jesus.

17. O Lord, give me the ability to discern all things, in the name of Jesus.

18. Anointing to perform supernatural miracles, what are you waiting for? Possess me immediately, in the name of Jesus.

19. Power to interpret tongues, I receive you now, in the name of Jesus.

20. Lord Jesus, empower me with the gift of faith, in the name of Jesus.

21. Let all my natural talents be made supernatural, in the name of Jesus.

22. Great God, use me to do supernatural things beyond my desires, in the name of Jesus.

23. O Lord, give me the gift of administration above Solomon, in the name of Jesus.

24. Power to interpret dreams more than Joseph, possess me, in the name of Jesus.

Go back to the words of decree and pass your decree again.

DECREE 15

AGAINST SEXUAL PERVERSION

"Professing themselves to be wise, they became fools" (Romans 1:22).

"For sin shall not have dominion over you: for ye are not under the law, but under grace" (Romans 6:14).

Serpent of sexual perversion in my life, I command you to come out now and die by the decree of God. By the decree of God, I command every demon of incest that is assigned to waste my life to die by force. Holy Ghost fire, move into the foundation of my life and consume every unclean thing in my life. Blood of Jesus, confront and conquer every iron-like curse propagating sexual perversion in my life. Every dark agent that has been assigned to destroy me with sexual perversion, be exposed and be disgraced by thunder.

Whether devil likes it or not, I decree the death of sexual perverse spirits in my life by fire. Any counterfeit blessing leading me to sexual perversion, I decree your death immediately. Blood of Jesus, flow into my foundation and destroy every marine deposit in my life. O Lord, in Your anger, command perverse spirits in my life to die forever. Any sexual demon that has hijacked my feelings and sexual life, I command you to release me and die without mercy.

Any sinful partner that has been assigned from the marine kingdom to inflate my sexual desires, go back to the waters and die. I frustrate your programs in my life and I command you to leave me alone and die by fire. Let every sexual demon that has been assigned to terminate my destiny die without mercy. Any power that came from the waters with determination to defile me sexually, drink the water of judgment and die. Blood of Jesus, speak destruction to every sexual demon in my life. Let all filthy desires for sexual sin in my life die, in the name of Jesus.

Fire of God, enter into my eyes and every organ of my body to destroy every manner of inordinate desire for sexual sin in my life. You, that sexual sin that has vowed to send me to the grave, I command you to loose your hold over my life and die by force. Blood of Jesus, sanctify my inner man and purify me spiritually and physically. Arrows of sexual perversion that are fired into my life, come out immediately and die by fire. Heavenly Father, command deliverance into my life against every manner of sexual perversion. Every mark of sexual perversion in my life, be burnt to ashes by fire now, in the name of Jesus.

PRAYERS AGAINST SEXUAL PERVERSION

1. Father Lord, deliver me from sexual sins of this generation, in the name of Jesus.

2. Every sexual demon that has been assigned to destroy me, be roasted by Holy Ghost Fire, in the name of Jesus.

3. Blood of Jesus, flow into my life and destroy sexual perverse spirits in my life, in the name of Jesus.

4. Every serpent of immorality in my life, die, in the name of Jesus.

5. Every bewitchment targeted at my sexual organ, be frustrated, in the name of Jesus.

6. Let marine spirit altars that are arranging spiritual intercourses for my life catch fire, in the name of Jesus.

7. Every yoke of sexual perversion in my life, break to pieces, in the name of Jesus.

8. Any power attacking my desires from the waters, fall down and die, in the name of Jesus.

9. Every covenant with marine kingdom, promoting sexual sins in my life, break, in the name of Jesus.

10. Every marine deposits in my life, be flushed out by fire, in the name of Jesus.

11. Every strange spirit from the waters, attacking me with sexual demons, die, in the name of Jesus.

12. I withdraw my life from evil association of my time, in the name of Jesus.

13. By the power in the blood of Jesus, I separate myself from any evil sexual partner, in the name of Jesus.

14. I reject every evil advance from demonized people, in the name of Jesus.

15. Every sex outside my marital legitimate home, die, in the name of Jesus.

16. I refuse to be manipulated into any sexual relationship that is perverse, in the name of Jesus.

17. Let the strongman of sexual perversion in my life fall down and die, in the name of Jesus.

18. O Lord, deliver me from every influence of sexual perversion, in the name of Jesus.

19. Any decision that is taken in the waters to pervert my sexual life, be cancelled, in the name of Jesus.

20. Every marine power that is planning to alter my relationship with God, die, in the name of Jesus.

21. Any evil personality that has married me in the spirit, divorce me immediately and die, in the name of Jesus.

22. I speak death unto the spirit of sexual perversion in my life, in the name of Jesus.

23. power to say no successfully to sexual sins, fall upon me now, in the name of Jesus.

24. Blood of Jesus, deliver me from sexual perversion, in the name of Jesus.

Go back to the words of decree and pass your decree again.

DECREE 16

AGAINST EVIL LATENESS FOR GOOD THINGS

"For the vision is yet for an appointed time, but at the end it shall speak, and not lie: though it tarry, wait for it; because it will surely come, it will not tarry" (Habakkuk 2:3).

Any power drawing me backward from my divine appointments, I command death to overcome you now. Let your burial ceremony be conducted immediately by force. Any evil covenant causing evil lateness to good things in my life, die by force and by fire. I decree the death of satanic weapons of lateness attached to my destiny. Father Lord, break every multiple covenant of my ancestors bringing backwardness into my life. Every iron-like curse of demonic lateness in my life, be destroyed by divine thunder.

O Lord, cause me to escape from every danger of demonic lateness in any project in my life. Power to take the first position in every good thing I do in my life, possess me by force, whether the devil likes it or not. O Lord, anoint me with Your power to be a first class candidate in every good competition of life. Every contender with my divinely appointed position, I send you backward by force. Let the wind of promotion carry me by force to where I am supposed to be.

No matter the decree of devil and his agents against me, I decree that I shall move forward by fire. Blood of Jesus, take me to the mountaintop of life. Angry soldiers from the third heaven, enter into the battlefield now and destroy any power assigned to keep me behind. Arrows of lateness in marriage, blessings, anointing, etc., fired into my life, I command you to backfire immediately. Evil covenant from my father's house, taking me backward, break and break forever.

Let armies from heaven arise for my sake and scatter every progress diverter in my life. I decree the death of evil lateness that has been wasting people in my family. Let every dark agent that is pulling me backward die suddenly, and die again. O Lord, arise and deliver me completely from the grip of devil's lateness forever and ever.

Anointing for evil lateness to good thing in my life, break by force. Idols of my place of birth, drawing me backward, die, in the name of Jesus.

PRAYERS AGAINST EVIL LATENESS FOR GOOD THINGS

1. Father Lord, arise in Your power to deliver me from the spirit of evil lateness, in the name of Jesus.

2. Anointing to start good things, fall upon me, in the name of Jesus.

3. Blood of Jesus, flow into my foundation and empower me to start good works, in the name of Jesus.

4. O Lord, deliver me from every manner of demonic fear, in the name of Jesus.

5. Heavenly father, destroy every manner of witchcraft in my life, in the name of Jesus.

6. Lord Jesus, pull me out from demonic delays, in the name of Jesus.

7. Power that wastes destines, you shall not waste my life, in the name of Jesus.

8. Blood of Jesus, destroy every plan to delay my breakthroughs, in the name of Jesus.

9. I jump out from every evil prison, in the name of Jesus.

10. Any power, delaying my promotion, be frustrated by force, in the name of Jesus.

11. Every evil imagination, working against my destiny, backfire, in the name of Jesus.

12. Every arrow causing business failures that was fired into my life, backfire, in the name of Jesus.

13. Any satanic traffic in my life, clear away, in the name of Jesus.

14. Let every evil traffic on my way to success be dismantled, in the name of Jesus.

15. Every lukewarmness and perdition that are assigned to waste my time, die, in the name of Jesus.

16. Every curse of setback that is working against my life, be terminated, in the name of Jesus.

17. Every demonic clock that is keeping me behind, scatter, in the name of Jesus.

18. Every demonic pregnancy assigned to delay my miracles, be aborted, in the name of Jesus.

19. I declare by the power of God that I can do all things through Christ, in the name of Jesus.

20. Let the eagle of my destiny begin to fly high above, in the name of Jesus.

21. Every demonic padlock that is locking my success, break to pieces, in the name of Jesus.

22. Every inherited evil delay prevailing in my life, die by force, in the name of Jesus.

23. Every evil mark of satanic delays, catch fire and die, in the name of Jesus.

24. I break and loose my life from all manner of evil lateness, in the name of Jesus.

25. Every dream of evil lateness in my life, die by force, in the name of Jesus.

Go back to the words of decree and pass your decree again.

DECREE 17

AGAINST UNREPENTANT OPPOSITION

(*Study* Exodus 14)

Powers of unrelenting oppositions that have refused to let me go, I bind you, I cast you out of my life and I decree death against you by fire. Every Stubborn Pharaoh that is working against my destiny, your time is up, I decree against you, loose your hold over my life now and die by the decree of God immediately.

Lord Jesus, I drink Your blood and I swallow the fire of the Holy Spirit now. Any power that has vowed to entangle me in an evil place of destruction, I decree death and burial against you now. Let combined forces of my unrepentant enemies be scattered by divine decree. Any power that has shut my destiny in an evil forest in order to eliminate my life, by divine decree, I command you to commit suicide and die without delay.

I decree that the hearts of my unrepentant enemies shall be hardened unto their destruction. O Lord, let Your divine wrath fall upon my Pharaoh. Let him receive blindness as he approaches me for destruction. I decree that the death of unrepentant Pharaoh shall honor my God and dishonor the powers of darkness.

Let the host of unrepentant enemies opposing me scatter and die. Let unrepentant Egyptians pursing my life bow unto death now. I decree that the angels of God will arise and destroy all unrepentant enemies opposing me. Chariots of unrepentant soldiers chasing me, I command you to be confused.

I decree mass death upon Pharaoh, his chosen chariots and captains. I destroy weapons of witchcraft raised against me in the battlefield. I command them to be roasted by fire, by the decree of God. I decree that God's fear shall arrest all my unrepentant enemies now. Let the heavenly army overtake all unrepentant enemies and destroy them at once. Let graves open and bury all unrelenting oppositions that want me to be their perpetual servant. I decree against you, fall down and die now.

I decree that my eyes shall not behold unrepentant enemies possess my inheritance. Let them be disgraced unto death by fire.

> *"And the LORD said unto Moses, Stretch out thine hand over the sea, that the waters may come again upon the Egyptians, upon their chariots, and upon their horsemen. And Moses stretched forth his hand over the sea, and the sea returned to his strength when the morning appeared; and the Egyptians fled against it; and the LORD overthrew the Egyptians in the midst of the sea. And the waters returned, and covered the chariots, and the horsemen, and all the host of Pharaoh that came into the sea after them; there remained not so much as one of them"* (Exodus 14:26-28).

I stretch out my hand against all evil oppositions and command them to be overthrown in the midst of the Red Sea immediately.

PRAYERS AGAINST UNREPENTANT OPPOSITION

1. Every Stubborn enemy that has vowed to waste my life, be wasted, in the name of Jesus.

2. Let every marine witchcraft that is working against my life be disgraced, in the name of Jesus.

3. Let afflictions of the wicked that have refused to let me go backfire, in the name of Jesus.

4. Let every stubborn Pharaoh that has vowed to terminate my life die, in the name of Jesus.

5. O Lord, arise and kill any Goliath in my life, in the name of Jesus.

6. Whosoever has decided to disgrace me shall be disgraced, in the name of Jesus.

7. Any power assigned to force me to cry, you are a liar, cry forever, in the name of Jesus.

8. Any evil vow that was taken to humiliate me, backfire, in the name of Jesus.

9. Any problem in my life that is on suicide mission, die alone, in the name of Jesus.

10. Let every uncompromising enemy of my destiny be wasted unto death, in the name of Jesus.

11. Let divine whirlwind penetrate into the camp of my stubborn enemies, in the name of Jesus.

12. Lord Jesus, deliver me from the grip of devil, in the name of Jesus.

13. Every internal disorder in my body that has refused to bow, die now, in the name of Jesus.

14. Any evil altar that refuses to accept my freedom, kill your priests and scatter, in the name of Jesus.

15. Any evil pregnancy conceived to finish my life in shame, be miscarried, in the name of Jesus.

16. You, my caged stars by the wicked enemies, escape by force, in the name of Jesus.

17. Let warriors from heaven enter into every prison and deliver me now, in the name of Jesus.

18. Every evil utterance that is militating against my life, backfire, in the name of Jesus.

19. Every danger on my way, locate your owner by force, in the name of Jesus.

20. Every fear that is being released from the pit of hell against my life, kill your senders, in the name of Jesus.

21. Every uncompromising pressure assigned to pull me out from God's protection, I bury you now, in the name of Jesus.

22. Let divine destroyers, destroy all unrepentant enemies surrounding me, in the name of Jesus.

23. Fire of judgment, enter into the camp of unrepentant enemies surrounding me, in the name of Jesus.

Go back to the words of decree and pass your decree again.

DECREE 18

AGAINST EVIL GROWTHS AND INVISIBLE SICKNESSES

"Now in the morning as he returned into the city, he hungered. And when he saw a fig tree in the way, he came to it, and found nothing thereon, but leaves only, and said unto it; Let no fruit grow on thee henceforward forever. And presently the fig tree withered away. And when the disciples saw it, they marveled, saying, how soon the fig tree is withered away! Jesus answered and said unto them, Verily I say unto you, If ye have faith, and doubt not, ye shall not only do this, which is done to the fig tree, but also if ye shall say unto this mountain, Be thou removed, and be thou cast into the sea; it shall be done. And all things, whatsoever ye shall ask in prayer, believing, ye shall receive" (Matthew 21:18-22).

"The strangers shall fade away, and be afraid out of their close places" (Psalms 18:45).

Any evil utterance said against my health, I command you to backfire by force, and I decree against any form of evil growth in my life. Let all spiritual hands of Satan that have been assigned to plant evil in my life dry up and die forever. O Lord, arise for my sake and close every door of my life against evil planters.

Blood of Jesus, flow into my life and decree against all manner of evil growths in my destiny. As it is written,

"Now in the morning as he returned into the city, he hungered. And when he saw a fig tree in the way, he came to it, and found nothing thereon, but leaves only, and said unto it; Let no fruit grow on thee henceforward forever. And presently the fig tree withered away. And when the disciples saw it, they marveled, saying, how soon the fig tree is withered away! Jesus answered and said unto them, Verily I say unto you, If ye have faith, and doubt not, ye shall not only do this, which is done to the fig tree, but also if ye shall say unto this mountain, Be thou removed, and be thou cast into the sea; it shall be done. And all things, whatsoever ye shall ask in prayer, believing, ye shall receive" (Matthew 21:18-22).

I command every unprofitable tree in my life to dry up from its root now. Anything in my life that is not giving me peace, I decree your death immediately. Let evil planters and whatever they have planted in my life dry up and die henceforth. Let every evil the enemy has planted into my life in the dream be completely destroyed by fire. By faith in the Word of God, I destroy all invisible problems moving into my life. Let every satanic fig tree in my life be uprooted now by divine operation.

You, mountain of unprofitable growth in my life, be removed by force. By the power and faith in the name of Christ, I cast out all demonic deposits in my life out now. O Lord, I decree and I believe that no weapon formed against me shall prosper. As it is written,

> *"The strangers shall fade away, and be afraid out of their close places"* (Psalms 18:45).

Every stranger in my life, fade away now by force. Every stranger in my womb, fade away, in the name of Jesus. Every spirit of cancer, fibroid, and other abnormal growths in my life, be roasted by fire. I command all enemies in my life to become afraid of the voice of God and flee by force. Let evil powers giving supports to invisible sicknesses and diseases in my body die, in the name of Jesus.

I withdraw my life now from the hold and captivity of unprofitable growths.

PRAYERS AGAINST EVIL GROWTHS AND INVISIBLE SICKNESSES

1. Every manner of evil development in my life, be uprooted unto death, in the name of Jesus.

2. Any evil hand that has been assigned to plant evil in my life, wither and die, in the name of Jesus.

3. Every witchcraft deposit in my life, die, in the name of Jesus.

4. Let Holy Ghost fire burn every evil growth in my body to ashes, in the name of Jesus.

5. Every demonic arrow, fired into my destiny, I fire you back, in the name of Jesus.

6. Every powerful herb that is multiplying sicknesses and diseases in my body, die, in the name of Jesus.

7. Any power promoting invisible movements in my life, die by fire, in the name of Jesus.

8. Holy Ghost fire, dismantle every evil plantation in my life, in the name of Jesus.

9. Blood of Jesus, uproot every evil deposit in my body, in the name of Jesus.

10. Fire of God, burn every evil growth in my body to ashes, in the name of Jesus.

11. Every marine spirit operation in my life, be arrested by fire, in the name of Jesus.

12. Heavenly Father, take away every stranger in my life, in the name of Jesus.

13. O Lord, arise and destroy every work of devil in my life, in the name of Jesus.

14. Anointing for sound health in my life, fall upon me now, in the name of Jesus.

15. Blessed Jesus, destroy every evil thing that is about to grow in my life, in the name of Jesus.

16. Any power that is attacking my life with any manner of sickness, die, in the name of Jesus.

17. Let the root of every satanic work in my life dry up, in the name of Jesus.

18. Any evil plantation in my life, die, in the name of Jesus.

19. Let any evil that is living inside my body begin to come out by force, in the name of Jesus.

20. Any satanic road in my life, close now, in the name of Jesus.

21. Every satanic bungalow in my life, collapse by thunder, in the name of Jesus.

22. By the anointing of God, I destroy every handiwork of devil in my life, in the name of Jesus.

23. Any part of my body that is growing abnormally, become normalized, in the name of Jesus.

24. Let every uncompromising problem in my life die immediately, in the name of Jesus.

25. O Lord, deliver me perfectly today, in the name of Jesus.

Go back to the words of decree and pass your decree again.

DECREE 19

AGAINST SATANIC NETWORK

"Take counsel together, and it shall come to nothing; speak the word, and it shall not stand: for God is with us" (Isaiah 8:10).

I raise the banner of the Lord and I decree against satanic networks mounting against my destiny. By the power in the name of Jesus, I scatter every satanic decree against the work of God in my life. Let evil networks of powers of darkness in my life fail woefully now. It is written that I shall decree a thing and it shall be established unto me. According to the written Word of God, I command every problem in my life to perish forever.

Every evil that is gathering for my sake shall not stand.

Every evil association that is planning against my destiny shall be disgraced and be disappointed. I break the gathering of evil people for my sake. Powers of darkness, let me tell you this simple truth, the blood of Jesus covers my life, therefore all your evil plans against my life shall fail and not stand.

Blood of Jesus, arise in your power and confuse all my unrepentant enemies.

Every evil counsel that has been taken against me in the land of the dead, it shall fail woefully in the land of the living forever. Let evil counsels of the wicked against me come to nothing now. Every negative word that is spoken against me anywhere shall not stand. They shall die and die forever. Because God is with me, let every evil plan against me in the waters contribute towards my promotion. Whatever the enemy has planned against me shall not work out.

The blood of Jesus is my protector. Therefore, my enemies' powers will not affect me forever. I decree that the Word of God will be my only portion and not the words of my enemies.

Heavenly Father, arise and scatter every satanic network that is mobilizing against my life. As the enemy is planning against my life, let only the plan of God be manifesting in my life. Anointing to prevail over the entire devil's networks, fall upon my life. Spirit of the living God, take over my life and let my life prosper by fire. O Lord, deliver me and empower me to prevail over the powers of my enemies.

I drink the blood of Jesus and I receive power to frustrate every satanic network that is against my life. O Lord, by Your power, set every satanic network that is fighting to weaken my destiny ablaze. You, satanic networks in my life, be exposed immediately. Devil, wherever you are now, receive divine confusion and make mistakes that will promote me.

PRAYERS AGAINST SATANIC NETWORKS

1. Every marine witchcraft network working against my destiny, scatter and die, in the name of Jesus.

2. Blood of Jesus, deliver me from evil plans and plots, in the name of Jesus.

3. Heavenly Father, arise in Your power and make a fool of the devil, in the name of Jesus.

4. Every evil conspiracy going on against my life, be fooled by fire, in the name of Jesus.

5. O Lord, let Your wisdom in me frustrate every evil plot against me, in the name of Jesus.

6. Lord Jesus, pull me out of every satanic snare, in the name of Jesus.

7. By the anointing of the Holy Ghost, I destroy every satanic network, in the name of Jesus.

8. Holy Ghost fire, burn every meeting point of the devil against me, in the name of Jesus.

9. Every evil gathering in the waters for my sake, scatter in shame, in the name of Jesus.

10. I draw the blood of Jesus against movements of the devil for my sake, in the name of Jesus.

11. Any man, woman or power that is planning evil against me, be disgraced, in the name of Jesus.

12. Every network of marine spirits from my place of birth, fail woefully, in the name of Jesus.

13. Every demonic trap that has been assigned to catch me, catch your owners by force, in the name of Jesus.

14. Blood of Jesus, flow into my life and deliver me where I need deliverance, in the name of Jesus.

15. Every satanic network that is against me, be disgraced by thunder, in the name of Jesus.

16. Every evil padlock that is locking up my breakthroughs, break to pieces, in the name of Jesus.

17. Let my enemies fall into the pits they have dug for me, in the name of Jesus.

18. Let all evil powers on earth, planning evil against me be eliminated, in the name of Jesus.

19. I command angels of the living God to spoil the networks of devil, in the name of Jesus.

20. O Lord, give me Your wisdom to dismantle every satanic network, in the name of Jesus.

21. O Lord, let Your power defend me against evil networks, in the name of Jesus.

22. I refuse to be a victim of any satanic network, in the name of Jesus.

23. Every satanic network that is working against me, catch fire, in the name of Jesus.

Go back to the words of decree and pass your decree again.

DECREE 20

AGAINST SATANIC SPIRIT OF FEAR

> *"For the thing which I greatly feared is come upon me, and that which I was afraid of is come unto me"* (Job 3:25).

Within these 21 days, let all my fears be turned into favors, in the name of Jesus. Blood of Jesus, flow into my heart and kill every spirit of fear that has settled in my life. O Lord, give me the power to kill every demonic fear in my life by fire. Fear from the pit of hell, go back to your sender and fulfill your ministry there. Heavenly Father, turn my fears unto your own fire and use it to set me free immediately. I decree that the only fear that would remain in my life is the perfect fear of God. The fear of devil will not succeed in my life. They shall die and die permanently.

> *"For the thing which I greatly feared is come upon me, and that which I was afraid of is come unto me"* (Job 3:25).

I decree that it shall not be so with me. The thing that I greatly fear shall come upon my stubborn enemies and that which I was afraid of shall never come unto me but they shall rather come upon my enemies. O Lord, kill every evil fear in my life and establish Your own fear alone in my life.

My fears, I decree now, go and terrify my enemies. My fears, I decree now, become afraid of me and move into my enemies' camps and terrify them to death. Let the power of

God that kills fear begin to kill every satanic fear in my life. I command my life to miscarry every satanic fear in my destiny. Every fear that killed my parents and is about to kill me shall fail. Blessings in my life that fear wants to kill shall not bow down to fear. Fear, bow down to worship God in my life and die forever.

The fears that attacked Abraham, listen to me, you will not come near me, die by fire.

> *"Fear thou not; for I am with thee: be not dismayed; for I am thy God: I will strengthen thee; yea, I will help thee; yea, I will uphold thee with the right hand of my righteousness. Behold, all they that were incensed against thee shall be ashamed and confounded: they shall be as nothing; and they that strive with thee shall perish"* (Isaiah 41:10-11).

I shall not be afraid of any fear, instead fears shall be afraid of me for God is with me. I shall not be dismayed, for God will strengthen me. Satan listen to me, the Lord will help me, he will uphold me with his right hand of righteousness. As it is written, I decree that all they that were incensed against me shall be put to shame and be confounded.

I decree that they shall be as nothing. I also decree that all that strive against me or with me shall perish. Based on the above scriptures, I decree immediate death to all fears in my past, present and future. My fear are dead forever.

PRAYERS AGAINST SATANIC SPIRIT OF FEAR

1. I command every spirit of fear that is planted into my life to be dismantled by force, in the name of Jesus.

2. Blood of Jesus, break the bondage of fear in my life, in the name of Jesus.

3. Any area of my life under the torment of fear, receive deliverance, in the name of Jesus.

4. Evil powers that were assigned to destroy me in the shadow and valley of death, die, in the name of Jesus.

5. You my life, receive power to live above every manner of fear, in the name of Jesus.

6. Holy Ghost fire, burn every seed of fear planted in my life to ashes, in the name of Jesus.

7. I break, and loose myself from every yoke of satanic fear, in the name of Jesus.

8. Fear shall not waste my life, in the name of Jesus.

9. I use the power of God to overcome all the powers of fear, in the name of Jesus.

10. Let fear that is bringing failures into my life die forever, in the name of Jesus.

11. Arrows of fears, fired into my life, come out and backfire, in the name of Jesus.

12. Let fears in my life come out and terrify my enemies instead, in the name of Jesus.

13. Any spirit of death that has entered into my life because of fear, come out, in the name of Jesus.

14. Any spirit of fear moving around me, be disgraced now, in the name of Jesus.

15. I command satanic fears that want to destroy me to receive destruction, in the name of Jesus.

16. Holy Ghost Fire, burn every fear in my life to ashes, in the name of Jesus.

17. Any fear that is ripe to manufacture death in my life, die, in the name of Jesus.

18. You my life, jump out from the camp of fear by force, in the name of Jesus.

19. Let the angels of God pounce on every spirit of fear in my life, in the name of Jesus.

20. Lord Jesus, deliver me completely from every spirit of fear, in the name of Jesus.

21. Every problem that fear has caused in my life, die, in the name of Jesus.

22. I receive divine boldness against fear and death, in the name of Jesus.

23. Every pregnancy of fear in my life, be aborted immediately, in the name of Jesus.

Go back to the words of decree and pass your decree again.

DECREE 21

AGAINST WATER SPIRIT ATTACKS

> *"He sent from above, he took me, he drew me out of many waters. He delivered me from my strong enemy, and from them which hated me: for they were too strong for me"* (Psalms 18:16-17).

I decree that my life will be invisible to water spirit attacks from henceforth. Every water spirit assigned against me shall miss their way. Wherever and whenever water spirits arise against me, they shall fail, in the name of Jesus.

> *"He sent from above, he took me, he drew me out of many waters. He delivered me from my strong enemy, and from them which hated me: for they were too strong for me"* (Psalms 18:16-17).

Therefore, I decree that powers from above will lay hold on me and deliver me from evil arrests and from the powers of the waters. I command my deliverance to come from above. Let all my strong enemies from the waters be disgraced and be disappointed. Any power that hates me shall not rejoice over me, they shall cry and be disgraced, in the name of Jesus.

Blood of Jesus, arise in Your power and enter into the waters for my sake and kill all my enemies in the waters. Angels of the living God, launch Your unmerciful attack against water spirits that were assigned to disgrace me.

You, water spirits, begin to fight against yourselves until you are all perfectly dead. Every evil plantation of water spirits in my life, die immediately. Holy Ghost fire, burn in my life and destroy all deposits of marine powers in my life. Let the hand of God take away every marine spirit of sickness and disease in my life. O Lord, by Your decree, I scatter every evil gathering of the wicked and I command it to die one after the other, in the name of Jesus. As it is written,

> "As soon as they hear of me, they shall obey me: the strangers shall submit themselves unto me. The strangers shall fade away, and be afraid out of their close places" (Psalms 18:44-45).

I raise my voice aloud and I decree that all powers in the waters shall obey me. Let every water spirit and demons submit themselves to me forever, in the name of Jesus. I command every water spirit agents and their powers to fade away and suddenly become afraid in their closed places. I send the sword of the Lord into the midst of the waters to kill, without mercy, in the name of Jesus. I poison the waters and command that every marine animal that is assigned against me shall die and be destroyed by fire. Heavenly Father, arise in Your power and defend my decrees to your own glory.

Lord Jesus, let my decree be accepted by you. Every seed of impossibility in my life from the waters, I command you to die and die forever. You, evil problems from the waters, you will not make it, die immediately without negotiation. Angry soldiers from heaven, enter into the waters and fight for me now.

Let that evil personality that has been claiming to be my wife or husband die immediately. Let all evil and spiritual relationships fashioned for my sake in the waters gather together and die without delay. Blood of Jesus, flow into the waters and destroy satanic kingdom by Your divine power.

PRAYERS AGAINST WATER SPIRIT ATTACKS

1. Every hold of water spirits in my life, cease by force, in the name of Jesus.

2. I disengage my destiny from the power of marine spirit attacks, in the name of Jesus.

3. Any problem in my life emanating from marine altars, die, in the name of Jesus.

4. Heavenly Father, banish every enemy of my life and deliver me, in the name of Jesus.

5. O Lord, by Your power, break every marine spirit power in my life, in the name of Jesus.

6. Any power, assigned to pollute my life from the waters, be disgraced, in the name of Jesus.

7. Blood of Jesus, speak destruction to any marine spirit attacks in my life, in the name of Jesus.

8. O Lord, deliver me from evil attacks coming from marine kingdom, in the name of Jesus.

9. Every reproach of marine spirits in my life, catch fire, in the name of Jesus.

10. Let water spirits attacking my life from my foundation die, in the name of Jesus.

11. I receive the anointing to deal with water spirit attacks, in the name of Jesus.

12. Holy Ghost fire, burn every marine spirit attacks in my life, in the name of Jesus.

13. Every property of water spirits in my life, I spoil you by fire, in the name of Jesus.

14. I deliver every area of my life arrested by marine powers, in the name of Jesus.

15. Blood of Jesus, scatter every evil brain in the waters planning evil against me, in the name of Jesus.

16. Every agent from marine kingdom that is assigned to waste me, be wasted, in the name of Jesus.

17. I stand against every problem emanating water spirits in my life, in the name of Jesus.

18. O Lord, quench the fires of water spirits in my life, in the name of Jesus.

19. Arrows of marine powers that is coming towards me, backfire, in the name of Jesus.

20. Any power, fighting against me from the waters, be disgraced unto death, in the name of Jesus.

21. Let evil spirits attacking that are me from my village altars be wasted, in the name of Jesus.

22. I reject every evil, coming against me from the waters, in the name of Jesus.

23. Attackers of my destiny from the waters, die, in the name of Jesus.

Go back to the words of decree and pass your decree again.

40 DECREES

"Thou shalt also decree a thing, and it shall be established unto thee: and the light shall shine upon thy ways. When men are cast down, then thou shalt say, There is lifting up; and he shall

DECREE 1

TO KILL UNCOMPROMISING HAMAN

(*Study* Esther 7)

Any personality of Haman that is promoted against my destiny, fall down and die without negotiation. No matter how much this Haman personality has advanced, O Lord, arise and destroy his powers. I command you, uncompromising Haman personality, to be disgraced and removed from the throne. Let your seat in the throne be given to my Mordecai, in the name of Jesus. I decree that you shall bow down to me; that I will never bow down to you, in the name of Jesus.

Every command and decree of the king for me to bow down to Haman, I reverse you by force. Let my personified Mordecai prevail over Haman, whether devil likes it or not. Power to transgress the decree of the king and prevail over the decree of Haman, possess me by fire, in the name of Jesus. I receive power to mock unrepentant Haman and I decree that his position shall be given to me today.

Any Haman personality that has been assigned to destroy my people, destroy your own people by yourself, in the name of Jesus. Any evil meeting that is going on between Haman and any leadership for the sake of my people and I, scatter immediately and end to our favor. I reverse evil writings and decrees against my people and I to our favor.

Let evil scribes of my generation write against Haman, whether they like it or not. I force the mouth of the queen on the throne to open to my favor. Let the queen of the throne open her mouth and condemn this Haman personality to death now.

> *"Then the king Ahasuerus answered and said unto Esther the queen, who is he, and where is he, that durst presume in his heart to do so? And Esther said, the adversary and enemy is this wicked Haman. Then Haman was afraid before the king and the queen"* (Esther 7:5-6).

I decree that you, Haman personality, shall make unpardonable mistakes that will destroy you and set my people and I free. Every soldier in the throne, arise and arrest this Haman. Let Haman be confused, disgraced and be hanged on the same gallows he built himself. I command you, Haman personality, to be hanged immediately without delay.

> *"And the king arising from the banquet of wine in his wrath went into the palace garden: and Haman stood up to make request for his life to Esther the queen; for he saw that there was evil determined against him by the king. Then the king returned out of the palace garden into the place of the banquet of wine; and Haman was fallen upon the bed whereon Esther was. Then said the king, Will he force the queen also before me in the house? As the word went out of the king's mouth, they covered Haman's face. And Harbonah, one of the chamberlains, said before the king, Behold also, the gallows fifty cubits high, which Haman had made for Mordecai, who had spoken good for the king,*

standeth in the house of Haman. Then the king said, Hang him thereon. So they hanged Haman on the gallows that he had prepared for Mordecai. Then was the king's wrath pacified" (<u>Esther 7:7-10</u>).

I receive the authority to write against all Haman personalities and their supporters now. O Lord, decorate my personified Mordecai and promote me by Your own power.

"And Mordecai went out from the presence of the king in royal apparel of blue and white, and with a great crown of gold, and with a garment of fine linen and purple: and the city of Shushan rejoiced and was glad. The Jews had light, and gladness, and joy, and honor. And in every province, and in every city, whithersoever the king's commandment and his decree came; the Jews had joy and gladness, a feast and a good day. And many of the people of the land became Jews; for the fear of the Jews fell upon them" (<u>Esther 8:15-17</u>).

All uncompromising Haman personalities, die and die again, in the name of Jesus.

DECREES TO KILL UNCOMPROMISING HAMAN

1. Every Haman spirit in my life, what are you waiting for? Die now, in the name of Jesus.

2. Blood of Jesus, locate every stubborn problem in my life and destroy it, in the name of Jesus.

3. Let every uncompromising bondage in my life be destroyed, in the name of Jesus.

4. I break and loose myself from every evil arrest of the enemy, in the name of Jesus.

5. Heavenly Father, let Your strong hand take me away from strong enemies, in the name of Jesus.

6. Any witchcraft power that has refused to let me go, die immediately, in the name of Jesus.

7. Let the judgment of God fall upon every evil power assigned to waste my life, in the name of Jesus.

8. You serpent, I destroy your head that has been assigned to bite me to death, in the name of Jesus.

9. Every curse that is placed upon my life by devil and his agents, catch fire, in the name of Jesus.

10. Any problem that has vowed to kill me, die now, in the name of Jesus.

11. Blood of Jesus, flow into my brain and deliver me by fire, in the name of Jesus.

12. Holy Ghost fire, burn every enemy of my progress to ashes, in the name of Jesus.

13. Any evil power that has risen up against me, be broken, in the name of Jesus.

14. Any witchcraft altar, militating against me, scatter, in the name of Jesus.

15. Let the strong man of my father's house die by fire, in the name of Jesus.

16. Every yoke of untimely death that is placed upon my life, break, in the name of Jesus.

17. Any problem on suicide mission against my life, die alone, in the name of Jesus.

18. Let all representatives of Haman in my life die on their own gallows, in the name of Jesus.

19. Angels of the living God, arise and kill all representatives of Haman in my life, in the name of Jesus.

20. Divine aircraft, take me away from wicked and uncompromising enemies, in the name of Jesus.

21. I refuse to die; my uncompromising enemies shall die, in the name of Jesus.

Go back to the words of decree and pass your decree again.

DECREE 2

FOR SPIRITUAL CLEANSING

> *"And Jesus went into the temple of God, and cast out all them that sold and bought in the temple, and overthrew the tables of the moneychangers, and the seats of them that sold doves"* (Matthew 21:12).

I command my body, soul and spirit to receive cleansing now by the blood of Jesus. Heavenly Father, arise in Your power and purify my inner man. Let my conscience be purged by the power in the blood of Jesus. O Lord, send Your fire into my inner man to burn every impurity living inside me to ashes. Lord Jesus, as You went into the temple of God in the past, come into my life now. Let the anointing of God sanctify my life wholly.

You the temple of my life, receive total cleansing by the power in the Word of God. Blessed Jesus, the same way You walked into the temple of God, walk into my life now and cast out every unholy thing living inside me by the force of Your power. I cast out every marine spirit seed that is carrying out any manner of transaction in my life. Every hidden demon that is selling and buying with my destiny in the temple of my life, be cast out by fire.

Lord Jesus, arise and overturn tables of witchcraft powers in my life. I decree that the fire of the Holy Ghost should arise and burn every occult table containing my destiny to ashes.

I decree against every demonic moneychanger in the circle of my life. O Lord, pull down every satanic supermarket in my heart. Let the judgment fire of God burn every covetous spirit in my life.

Blood of Jesus, advertise Your divine nature in my life. I break every covenant of sin, and unclean character in my life. Every seat of witchcraft that is polluting my destiny, I decree death against you. Let the throne of witchcraft that is defiling my heart be dethroned by fire.

Any power assigned to merchandise with my destiny, I command you to die by fire. Every witchcraft dove that is sold to destroy souls, catch fire and die by force.

> *"And Jesus went into the temple of God, and cast out all them that sold and bought in the temple, and overthrew the tables of the moneychangers, and the seats of them that sold doves"* (Matthew 21:12).

I command the death of all evil merchandises that are polluting the house of God in my life. Father Lord, conduct spiritual cleansing in the body of Christ, which is the church, against every agent of marine power, defiling your church. Let the Word of God cleanse God's congregation. I fire back all enemies' arrows of pollution fired at the church of Christ. Any evil power that is trading with the souls of men, catch fire and be destroyed.

Let there be spiritual cleansing in my life now. Every spirit of pollution, living inside me, be arrested unto death.

> *"And the merchants of the earth shall weep and mourn over her; for no man buyeth their merchandise any more: The merchandise of gold, and silver, and precious stones, and of pearls, and fine linen, and purple, and silk, and scarlet, and all thyine wood, and all manner*

vessels of ivory, and all manner vessels of most precious wood, and of brass, and iron, and marble, And cinnamon, and odors, and ointments, and frankincense, and wine, and oil, and fine flour, and wheat, and beasts, and sheep, and horses, and chariots, and slaves, and souls of men. And the fruits that thy soul lusted after are departed from thee, and all things which were dainty and goodly are departed from thee, and thou shalt find them no more at all. The merchants of these things, which were made rich by her, shall stand afar off for the fear of her torment, weeping and wailing" (Revelation 18:11-15).

I command the purging fire of the Holy Ghost to penetrate into my foundation and purify me, in the name of Jesus. Father Lord, put Your divine oil into my heart and purify me, in the name of Jesus.

DECREES FOR SPIRITUAL CLEANSING

1. Father Lord, purge my inner man and cleanse me from every pollution, in the name of Jesus.

2. Blood of Jesus, cleanse me from every spiritual impurity by Your power, in the name of Jesus.

3. Heavenly Father, arise in Your power and wash me with divine waters, in the name of Jesus.

4. Ancient of days, sanctify me and make me holy by Your power, in the name of Jesus.

5. O Lord, arise in Your anger and destroy the root of sin in my life, in the name of Jesus.

6. Every impurity in my life, catch fire and burn to ashes, in the name of Jesus.

7. Lord Jesus, enter into dark rooms of my life and deliver me by fire, in the name of Jesus.

8. Every good thing in my life, be purified by the fire of God, in the name of Jesus.

9. Anointing for holy living, fall upon me now and make me holy, in the name of Jesus.

10. Blood of Jesus, flow into my life and purify my inner man, in the name of Jesus.

11. Anything in my life that is fighting against my purity, be disgraced to death, in the name of Jesus.

12. O Lord, revive my life and quicken my body by the Holy Ghost fire, in the name of Jesus.

13. Every yoke of sin in my life, break by thunder now, in the name of Jesus.

14. Let the spirit of self-righteousness in my life be cast out by fire, in the name of Jesus.

15. Every spiritual sickness in my life, die, in the name of Jesus.

16. Any witch or wizard, polluting my life, be disgraced, in the name of Jesus.

17. Any power, polluting my mind with evil thoughts, die by fire, in the name of Jesus.

18. Every corruption in my life, receive divine destruction now, in the name of Jesus.

19. Any evil power, defiling me in the dream, I cast you out, die, in the name of Jesus.

20. O Lord, with Your fire, burn every evil garment in my life, in the name of Jesus.

21. Any power from the tomb, polluting my destiny, receive destruction, in the name of Jesus.

22. Every unclean demon, assigned to defile me, be destroyed by fire, in the name of Jesus.

23. Every spiritual and physical sickness in my life, die immediately, in the name of Jesus.

24. Every demon in my tongue that has refused to let me go, come out and die, in the name of Jesus.

25. Any evil power that is defiling God's temple in me, fall down and die, in the name of Jesus.

26. Any great storm, rising up against my destiny, be calmed to the shame of devil, in the name of Jesus.

27. Blood of Jesus, empower me for holiness, in the name of Jesus.

Go back to the words of decree and pass your decree again.

DECREE 3

TO INTIMIDATE YOUR ENEMIES

> *"When thou goest out to battle against thine enemies, and Seest horses, and chariots, and a people more than thou, be not afraid of them: for the LORD thy God is with thee, which brought thee up out of the land of Egypt"* (Deuteronomy 20:1).

I stand against any demonic fear coming to attack me from my enemies. Let the perfect fear of God possess me completely by force. I receive an overwhelming power to face my enemies with boldness. No matter the size of my enemies and the power behind them, I destroy their strength. Spirit of the living God, living inside me, manifest and intimidate all my enemies. Let demonic soldiers that were mobilized against me receive divine fear, collapse and die for my sake.

No matter the powers backing up my enemies, I command then to be afraid of me. The glory of God in me shall manifest and destroy every enemy of my destiny. O Lord, show my enemies that You are with me and intimidate them with Your multitude of fear. You, my enemies, whether you like it or not, receive divine fear and be intimidated immediately.

All my spiritual enemies, be intimidated, be frustrated and be destroyed. By the power in the blood of Jesus, let my enemies bow in shame. O Lord, I decree against all enemies of Your children, let them be intimidated by force. I shall not be intimidated in the battlefield, my enemies shall be intimidated all round.

> *"When thou goest out to battle against thine enemies, and Seest horses, and chariots, and a people more than thou, be not afraid of them: for the LORD thy God is with thee, which brought thee up out of the land of Egypt"* (<u>Deuteronomy 20:1</u>).

Let spiritual armies of Philistine that have gathered for my sake with Goliath be intimidated, scattered and defeated. Any Philistine that has stood against God's children, I decree immediate fear of God against you, and die in fear now.

I command fear and destructive intimidation to fall upon Philistine champions. Every bold Goliath against me, receive fear, intimidation, confusion and destruction. I decree destruction against every weapon of my enemies in the battlefield.

Every witch or wizard that is doing any incantation against me, receive multiple fear and explosive intimidation now. I decree against my enemies who are stronger than me.

> *"Now the Philistines gathered together their armies to battle, and were gathered together at Shocho, which belongeth to Judah, and pitched between Shocho and Azekah, in Ephesdammim. And Saul and the men of Israel were gathered together, and pitched by the valley of Elah, and set the battle in array against the Philistines. And the Philistines stood on a mountain on the one side, and Israel stood on a mountain on the other side: and there was a valley between them. And there went out a champion out of the camp of the*

Philistines, named Goliath, of Gath, whose height was six cubits and a span" (1 Samuel 17:1-4).

Let my weapon of war intimidate my enemies in the battlefield unto death. Let my words enter into the hearts of my stubborn enemy and let my stone break their foreheads now.

"Then said David to the Philistine, Thou comest to me with a sword, and with a spear, and with a shield: but I come to thee in the name of the LORD of hosts, the God of the armies of Israel, whom thou hast defied. This day will the LORD deliver thee into mine hand; and I will smite thee, and take thine head from thee; and I will give the carcasses of the host of the Philistines this day unto the fowls of the air, and to the wild beasts of the earth; that all the earth may know that there is a God in Israel. And all this assembly shall know that the LORD saveth not with sword and spear: for the battle is the LORD'S and he will give you into our hands. And it came to pass, when the Philistine arose, and came and drew nigh to meet David that David hasted, and ran toward the army to meet the Philistine. And David put his hand in his bag, and took thence a stone, and slang it, and smote the Philistine in his forehead that the stone sunk into his forehead; and he fell upon his face to the earth. So David prevailed over the Philistine with a sling and with a stone, and smote the Philistine, and slew him; but there was no sword in the hand of David" (1 Samuel 17:45-50).

Every enemy of my destiny in the battlefield, you are finished, I disgrace and disorganize your brain, in the name of Jesus. Let the angel of God with divine sword confront and conquer all uncompromising enemies, in the name of Jesus.

DECREES TO INTIMIDATE YOUR ENEMIES

1. Every enemy of my destiny, wherever you are now, be intimidated, in the name of Jesus.

2. Father Lord, confront and conquer every enemy of my destiny, in the name of Jesus.

3. Heavenly Father, send Your fears into the heart of all my enemies, in the name of Jesus.

4. Any power, attacking me with fear, receive fear and die by fire, in the name of Jesus.

5. Blood of Jesus, speak fear into the camp of my enemies, in the name of Jesus.

6. Any power, assigned to manipulate my decisions, fall down and die by fire, in the name of Jesus.

7. By the power in the Word of God, I challenge every Goliath in my life, in the name of Jesus.

8. Let the anointing that destroys the power of devil fall upon me now, in the name of Jesus.

9. Every satanic barrier that is standing against my life, clear away by fire, in the name of Jesus.

10. Let all warring demons that are working against my destiny be scattered by thunder, in the name of Jesus.

11. Blood of Jesus, flow into the camp of my enemies and intimidate them, in the name of Jesus.

12. I reject every evil gift that has been assigned to intimidate me and divert my destiny, in the name of Jesus.

13. Every inherited fear that is assigned to intimidate me, die by force, in the name of Jesus.

14. Any evil diversion, working against my life from the camp of devil, die, in the name of Jesus.

15. I command the fire of God to burn every intimidating fear of devil, in the name of Jesus.

16. Any evil giant, planted on my path to breakthrough, collapse and die, in the name of Jesus.

17. Every satanic angel, assigned to intimidate me, fall down and die, in the name of Jesus.

18. Every giant in my father's house that is standing against me, fall down and die, in the name of Jesus.

19. Every agent of frustration that is working against my destiny, catch fire, in the name of Jesus.

20. Any human altar, burning incense against my life, receive stroke, in the name of Jesus.

21. Let evil altars of my father's house catch Holy Ghost fire, in the name of Jesus.

22. Blood of Jesus, flow into my family altars and scatter every demon, in the name of Jesus.

23. Every intimidating voice of the wicked, directed towards me, backfire, in the name of Jesus.

24. Let my appearance before all my enemies intimidate them by fire, in the name of Jesus.

25. 26. Every fear that was programmed into my life, move away, in the name of Jesus.

27. Every evil tongue, speaking against me, I cut you off, in the name of Jesus.

28. Glory of God, arise and overshadow my life, in the name of Jesus.

Go back to the words of decree and pass your decree again.

DECREE 4

TO MAKE WISE DECISIONS

"There are many devices in a man's heart; nevertheless the counsel of the LORD, that shall stand" (Proverbs 19:21).

I stand against every decision to counter holiness. I stand against evil decisions that dull my heart and love for God, in the name of Jesus.

Any power, causing me to postpone good decisions, I command you to close your eyes and die by force. I decree against any power that wants me to die without deciding fully to serve God, in the name of Jesus. I command the power that broke the personal will of Paul to fall upon me now. Any power that wants me to be disobedient to heavenly visions, collapse and die immediately. Paul was not disobedient to a heavenly vision, therefore no power can keep me undecided for Christ.

> *"At midday, O king, I saw in the way a light from heaven, above the brightness of the sun, shining round about me and them which journeyed with me. And when we were all fallen to the earth, I heard a voice speaking unto me, and saying in the Hebrew tongue, Saul, Saul, why persecutest thou me? it is hard for thee to kick against the pricks. And I said, who art thou, Lord? And he said, I am Jesus whom thou persecutest. But rise, and stand upon thy feet: for I have appeared unto thee for this purpose, to make thee a minister and a witness both of these things which thou hast seen, and*

> *of those things in the which I will appear unto thee; Delivering thee from the people, and from the Gentiles, unto whom now I send thee, To open their eyes, and to turn them from darkness to light, and from the power of Satan unto God, that they may receive forgiveness of sins, and inheritance among them which are sanctified by faith that is in me. Whereupon, O king Agrippa, I was not disobedient unto the heavenly vision"* (Acts 26:13-19).

Lord Jesus, speak me into conviction until I take a sound decision for Your sake. Father Lord, do it, if You must blind me, blind me, if You must knock me down, knock me down, provided I take a sound decision for Christ's sake. Any fake authority, causing me to retain a demonic decision, catch fire and burn to ashes.

Let the light of God from the third heaven above shine on my way and lead me alright to take good decision from today. Heavenly voice, speak me unto a sound decision and let me obey you by force. Any evil device in my heart against divine decision, die and die again by force. Let the counsel of the Lord for my sake arise and stand forever and ever.

> *"There are many devices in a man's heart; nevertheless the counsel of the LORD, that shall stand"* (Proverbs 19: 21).

Any evil counsel against any good decision I have taken for the Lord, what are you waiting for? I decree your death, therefore fall down and die.

I command every negative voice speaking against sound decisions I have taken to be silenced forever. Let that power that moved Enoch into a sound decision to walk with God for three hundred years possess me by force, in the name of Jesus.

I decree by the Word of God that my sound decisions to walk with God shall stand until I fulfill my destiny. Blood of Jesus, arise and help me to take great and sound decisions for God. Anointing to be obedient to sound decisions, fall upon me by force.

> *"And Enoch lived sixty and five years, and begat Methuselah: And Enoch walked with God after he begat Methuselah three hundred years, and begat sons and daughters: And all the days of Enoch were three hundred sixty and five years: And Enoch walked with God: and he was not; for God took him"* (Genesis 5:21-24).

O Lord my God, I decree against any power that is fighting against sound decisions I have made, in the name of Jesus.

DECREES TO MAKE WISE DECISIONS

1. O God, arise and move me into making a sound decision, in the name of Jesus.

2. Anointing for great and sound decisions, fall upon me, in the name of Jesus.

3. O God, arise and take a decision against all my problems, in the name of Jesus.

4. I take a solid decision against spirit of compromise of my faith in Christ, in the name of Jesus.

5. As from this moment, I decide against every evil voice speaking against me, in the name of Jesus.

6. I refuse to remain in spiritual Egypt, a land of bondage, in the name of Jesus.

7. Every idol of my father's house, receive fire and burn to ashes, in the name of Jesus.

8. In every situation I find myself, I shall pray and wait for God, in the name of Jesus.

9. I will not join the multitude to bring evil report, in the name of Jesus.

10. Any power that want me to stop at the wrong bus terminal, die, in the name of Jesus.

11. O Lord, send Your angel to instruct me so that I will not make a mistake, in the name of Jesus.

12. I refuse to die in my sin, O Lord, help me to repent, in the name of Jesus.

13. Lord Jesus, You are invited into my family to rule and reign, in the name of Jesus.

14. From now, my prayers shall bring Jesus in action in my life, in the name of Jesus.

15. As Matthew followed Jesus, O Lord, help me to follow You to the end, in the name of Jesus.

16. As the blind Bartimæus cried to Jesus for help, O Lord, I cry also for Your help, in the name of Jesus.

17. In the midst of those who hate God, I shall arise and stand for Christ, in the name of Jesus.

18. Every Stubborn witchcraft power, influencing me to take a wrong decision, die, in the name of Jesus.

19. Every witchcraft curse that is prevalent in my life, die, in the name of Jesus.

20. Let the yoke of bondage in my life break and lose me now, in the name of Jesus.

21. Blood of Jesus, flow into my brain and control my decisions, in the name of Jesus.

22. Any power that have vowed to destroy me with wrong decisions, die, in the name of Jesus.

23. Let the Holy Ghost power lead me into sound decisions forever, in the name of Jesus.

24. Let my choice be in line with the choice of the Almighty forever, in the name of Jesus.

25. Every decision I will take from today shall be sound, in the name of Jesus.

26. Heavenly Father, arise and direct me, in the name of Jesus.

Go back to the words of decree and pass your decree again.

DECREE 5

AGAINST SATANIC TRAPS

> *"And when the tempter came to him, he said, if thou be the Son of God, command that these stones be made bread"* (Matthew 4:3).

I decree against every wicked trap set for me and I command such traps to catch unrepentant enemies, who set them, in the name of Jesus. Holy Ghost Fire, arise and burn traps set by marine spirit by fire. Blood of Jesus, flow into every evil trap set for my destiny and destroy them by force. Heavenly Father, by Your permission, I release Your warring angels to destroy every demon setting traps for my life. Father Lord, by Your power of mercy, lead me by Your spirit at all times.

I decree and declare a divinely motivated fast that would give me victory over every temptation. Let the veils of evil tempters be exposed, disgraced and destroyed by thunder. Any power that will tempt me for evil shall fall for my sake from today onward. Any manipulative voice of witchcraft assigned to speak me out of God's plan shall fail woefully today and forever. Let the tempting voice of devil be recognized and rejected, in the name of Jesus. Every trap of the enemy against me, I come against you, scatter by fire, in Jesus name.

> *"But he answered and said, it is written, Man shall not live by bread alone, but by every word that proceedeth out of the mouth of God"* (Matthew 4:4).

> *"No weapon that is formed against thee shall prosper; and every tongue that shall rise against thee in judgment thou shalt condemn. This is the heritage of the servants of the LORD, and their righteousness is of me, saith the LORD"* (Isaiah 54:17).

Any weapon of the devil formed against me, you shall not prosper, fail woefully and refuse to catch me. Every tongue of the enemy speaking destruction into my life, backfire immediately. You, traps of the wicked laid against me, you shall not prosper in my life. I condemn every judgment of the enemy against me now.

Any satanic question that has been asked to catch me, catch the questioners and disgrace them for my sake. Let evil gatherings initiated to trap me and keep me in bondage scatter by fire and thunder of God now. O Lord, arise and disgrace every evil trap against my destiny. Father Lord, I decree by Your permission that every evil trap against me shall contribute to my promotion. I command the angels of the living God to destroy every demonic trap laid against me.

> *"Behold, they shall surely gather together, but not by me: whosoever shall gather together against thee shall fall for thy sake"* (Isaiah 54:15).

Every Delilah hanging around me, with a demonic vow to disgrace me, disgrace yourself. Let every Jezebel spirit that is plotting evil against me fall in her own plan. Every evil expectation, waiting to catch me for evil, backfire now. Any evil genius assigned to waste me, be wasted.

> *"Then the devil taketh him up into the holy city, and setteth him on a pinnacle of the temple, And saith unto*

him, If thou be the Son of God, cast thyself down: for it is written, He shall give his angels charge concerning thee: and in their hands they shall bear thee up, lest at any time thou dash thy foot against a stone. Jesus said unto him, it is written again, Thou shalt not tempt the Lord thy God. Again, the devil taketh him up into an exceeding high mountain, and sheweth him all the kingdoms of the world, and the glory of them; And saith unto him, All these things will I give thee, if thou wilt fall down and worship me. Then saith Jesus unto him, get thee hence, Satan: for it is written, Thou shalt worship the Lord thy God, and him only shalt thou serve" (Matthew 4:5-10).

Wherever enemies are taking me to shall be the place of my promotion. I decree victory over all demonic traps, in the name of Jesus.

"Then the devil leaveth him, and, behold, angels came and ministered unto him" (Matthew 4:11).

By the decree of the almighty God, I scatter every evil trap set against me by the enemy, in the name of Jesus.

DECREES AGAINST SATANIC TRAPS

1. Father Lord, deliver me from every satanic trap set to trap my life, in the name of Jesus.

2. I refuse to walk into the camp of my enemies, in the name of Jesus.

3. O Lord my God, deliver me from every satanic captivity forever, in the name of Jesus.

4. Blood of Jesus, magnetize me to yourself and help me, in the name of Jesus.

5. Angels of the living God, take me away from errors of my fathers, in the name of Jesus.

6. Any Jezebel spirit around me that has set a trap for me, fall into it, in the name of Jesus.

7. Any evil personality that has vowed to destroy me with food, die, in the name of Jesus.

8. Powers that feed people with forbidden fruits, fail woefully, in the name of Jesus.

9. Any power influencing me to choose by sight, die, in the name of Jesus.

10. Any trap set against me on my way from Egypt, catch fire, in the name of Jesus.

11. Any evil question, assigned to destroy me with lies, fail woefully, in the name of Jesus.

12. Any evil personality assigned to corrupt me, be disgraced, in the name of Jesus.

13. Let traps of impatience laid against me catch their owners, in the name of Jesus.

14. Let every arrows of wickedness fired at me backfire, in the name of Jesus.

15. Any temptation that has been assigned to cause me to despise my birthright, die, in the name of Jesus.

16. Every evil visitation, assigned to waste my destiny, I reject you, in the name of Jesus.

17. Let all Pharaoh's conspiracies to destroy me at the Red Sea die, in the name of Jesus.

18. Every trap of the enemy for my marriage, catch your owner, in the name of Jesus.

19. Every enchantment, working against me, be destroyed, in the name of Jesus.

20. Any problem that wants to make me speak against God, die, in the name of Jesus.

21. Any battle that has been assigned to terminate my life, scatter, in the name of Jesus.

22. Let every counsel of Ahithophel against me fail woefully, in the name of Jesus.

23. Blood of Jesus, deliver me from every evil trap, in the name of Jesus.

24. Let the voice of the Holy Ghost speak me out of problems, in the name of Jesus.

Go back to the words of decree and pass your decree again.

DECREE 6

AGAINST THE SPIRIT OF ANTICHRIST

"For we wrestle not against flesh and blood, but against principalities, against powers, against the rulers of the darkness of this world, against spiritual wickedness in high places" (Ephesians 6:12).

Any spirit of antichrist that is already working against me, be disgraced immediately unto death by fire. Any beast or leopard from the office of antichrist that is attacking me in my dreams, let your strength fail you completely. I decree that antichrist shall not have power over me. I decree against any problem in my life from the kingdom of antichrist. Let every lion-like problem from the antichrist fall down and die immediately. I cast out by force every spirit of antichrist assigned to waste my destiny.

I command every sin introduced into my life and environment by the antichrist camp to be frustrated unto death. Blood of Jesus, flow into my life and speak death unto the works of antichrist in my life. Any power that wants me to worship other gods, I command your death to appear and kill you immediately. Any power that is attacking people to worship the dragon and the beast, I decree that your destruction shall take place now.

By the decree of God, I command the warring angels of the living God to make war and defeat antichrist spirits for my sake.

> *"And they worshipped the dragon which gave power unto the beast: and they worshipped the beast, saying, who is like unto the beast? who is able to make war with him?"* (Revelation 13:4).

Any mouth of antichrist opened for my sake, close forever and ever, in the name of Jesus. Any power, influencing me to talk against God, knowingly or unknowingly, I command you to die without mercy, in the name of Jesus.

Any satanic war going on against Christians from antichrist's camp, be won to the favor of God's people. I command soldiers of antichrist warring against me to surrender in defeat now, in the name of Jesus. O Lord, scatter antichrist soldiers assigned to ruin my destiny.

> *"And there was given unto him a mouth speaking great things and blasphemies; and power was given unto him to continue forty and two months. And he opened his mouth in blasphemy against God, to blaspheme his name, and his tabernacle, and them that dwell in heaven. And it was given unto him to make war with the saints, and to overcome them: and power was given him over all kindred's, and tongues, and nations"* (Revelation 13:5-7).

The manifestations of antichrist shall not influence my lifestyle, in the name of Jesus.

I decree that evil collaboration existing between antichrist and evil people be exposed. Any agent of antichrist prospering in my area, I command you to be rejected by the saints. I decree mass rejection to lives, works, members and marks of antichrist.

"And he had power to give life unto the image of the beast, that the image of the beast should both speak, and cause that as many as would not worship the image of the beast should be killed.. And he causeth all, both small and great, rich and poor, free and bond, to receive a mark in their right hand, or in their foreheads:. And that no man might buy or sell, save he that had the mark, or the name of the beast, or the number of his name" (Revelation 13:15-17).

Every property of antichrist in my life, catch fire and burn to ashes. Blood of Jesus, empower me to disgrace the spirit of antichrist in these last days, in the name of Jesus.

DECREES AGAINST THE SPIRIT OF ANTICHRIST

1. Father Lord, arise in Your power and deliver me from the spirit of antichrist, in the name of Jesus.

2. I receive the grace of God to be raptured to escape the battle with antichrist, in the name of Jesus.

3. O Lord, deliver me from the present tribulation, in the name of Jesus.

4. Let that personality called antichrist be disgraced in my life, in the name of Jesus.

5. Every end time charity of the antichrist against me, I reject you, in the name of Jesus.

6. Any character of the antichrist in my life, catch fire and die, in the name of Jesus.

7. Let the spirit of the beast already working against my destiny be frustrated, in the name of Jesus.

8. Any beast coming out of the sea of humanity against me, die, in the name of Jesus.

9. Let that enemy called antichrist in my ministry be judged by the Lord, in the name of Jesus.

10. Any voice of the antichrist in my life, be silenced by force, in the name of Jesus.

11. O Lord, give me the power to discover the spirit of antichrist, in the name of Jesus.

12. Any antichrist rebellion going on against my life, be frustrated, in the name of Jesus.

13. Any antichrist spirit, warring against my destiny, be exposed and be disgraced, in the name of Jesus.

14. I refuse to be in this world when the antichrist will reign, in the name of Jesus.

15. Power to escape the wrath of antichrist in this end time, possess me, in the name of Jesus.

16. O Lord, deliver me from the camp of evildoers, in the name of Jesus.

17. Any war going on in my life from the antichrist, be won to my favor, in the name of Jesus.

18. I reject every sign, wonder and miracle from the antichrist, in the name of Jesus.

19. Any evil power that wants to dominate me, fail woefully, in the name of Jesus.

20. Let the fire of God judge the horns of the antichrist that has risen against me, in the name of Jesus.

21. Every crown of antichrist against me, catch fire, in the name of Jesus.

22. Let the multiple regal powers of the antichrist against the church fail, in the name of Jesus.

23. Every antichrist spirit establishing churches around the world, be exposed unto death, in the name of Jesus.

Go back to the words of decree and pass your decree again.

DECREE 7

TO STAND AGAINST SATAN

"Thou modest him to have dominion over the works of thy hands; thou hast put all things under his feet" (Psalms 8:6).

I stand against the evil of these days and I frustrate their influences over my life, in the name of Jesus. Blood of Jesus, flow into my life and destroy every evil power trying to overcome the righteousness of God in my life, in the name of Jesus. Like Phinehas, the son of Eleazar, and grandson of Aaron the priest, I rise up against the evils of my time. With the Word of God in my mouth, I bring mercy and judgment of God upon this generation.

"And when Phinehas, the son of Eleazar, the son of Aaron the priest, saw it, he rose up from among the congregation, and took a javelin in his hand; And he went after the man of Israel into the tent, and thrust both of them through, the man of Israel, and the woman through her belly. So the plague was stayed from the children of Israel" (Numbers 25:7- 8, 11).

"Phinehas, the son of Eleazar, the son of Aaron the priest, hath turned my wrath away from the children of Israel, while he was zealous for my sake among them, that I consumed not the children of Israel in my jealousy" (Numbers 25:11).

I decree and declare that the evil of this city, in which I live, shall not swallow me. In anger, I rebuke the characters of evil cities around me.

> *"Verily I say unto you, it shall be more tolerable for the land of Sodom and Gomorrha in the day of judgment, than for that city"* (Matthew 10:15).

I arise and confront this evil generation, and I decree against it like Jesus.

> *"O generation of vipers, how can ye, being evil, speak good things? for out of the abundance of the heart the mouth speaketh. A good man out of the good treasure of the heart bringeth forth good things: and an evil man out of the evil treasure bringeth forth evil things. But I say unto you, that every idle word that men shall speak, they shall give account thereof in the day of judgment. For by thy words thou shalt be justified, and by thy words thou shalt be condemned"* (Matthew 12:34-37).

> *"But he answered and said unto them, An evil and adulterous generation seeketh after a sign; and there shall no sign be given to it, but the sign of the prophet Jonas: For as Jonas was three days and three nights in the whale's belly; so shall the Son of man be three days and three nights in the heart of the earth. The men of Nineveh shall rise in judgment with this generation, and shall condemn it: because they repented at the preaching of Jonas; and, behold, a greater than Jonas is here. The queen of the south shall rise up in the judgment with this generation, and shall condemn it: for she came from the uttermost parts of the earth to hear the wisdom of Solomon; and, behold, a greater than Solomon is here. When the unclean spirit is gone out of*

> *a man, he walketh through dry places, seeking rest, and findeth none. Then he saith, I will return into my house from whence I came out; and when he is come, he findeth it empty, swept, and garnished. Then goeth he, and taketh with himself seven other spirits more wicked than himself, and they enter in and dwell there: and the last state of that man is worse than the first. Even so shall it be also unto this wicked generation"* (Matthew 12:39-45).

Let all persisting tongues that are speaking against my destiny, be rebuked and destroyed by force. You, this generation and cities that reject the gospel, you shall not stand. Every evil plan against Christ, His kingdom and children, be frustrated by force. Any power that is despising the Lord Jesus and His gospel, I stand against you now. Let all evil traditions in the cities and the churches be disgraced. Every blind leader in the cities and churches, I decree against you to be overthrown immediately.

> *"But he answered and said unto them, why do ye also transgress the commandment of God by your tradition? For God commanded, saying, Honor thy father and mother: and, He that curseth father or mother, let him die the death. But ye say, whosoever shall say to his father or his mother, It is a gift, by whatsoever thou mightest be profited by me; and honor not his father or his mother, he shall be free. Thus have ye made the commandment of God of none effect by your tradition. Ye hypocrites, well did Esaias prophesy of you, saying, This people draweth nigh unto me with their mouth, and honored me with their lips; but their heart is far from me. But in vain they do worship me, teaching for*

doctrines the commandments of men" ([Matthew 15:3-9](.)).

"Then came his disciples, and said unto him, Knowest thou that the Pharisees were offended, after they heard this saying? But he answered and said, every plant, which my heavenly Father hath not planted, shall be rooted up. Let them alone: they be blind leaders of the blind. And if the blind lead the blind, both shall fall into the ditch" ([Matthew 15:12-14](.)).

I stand against the wicked and adulterous generation in which I live in. Let the wicked that desire signs repent or perish in their situation.

"The Pharisees also with the Sadducees came, and tempting desired him that he would shew them a sign from heaven. He answered and said unto them, when it is evening, ye say, it will be fair weather: for the sky is red. And in the morning, it will be foul weather to day: for the sky is red and lowing. O ye hypocrites, ye can discern the face of the sky; but can ye not discern the signs of the times? A wicked and adulterous generation seeketh after a sign; and there shall no sign be given unto it, but the sign of the prophet Jonas. And he left them, and departed" ([Matthew 16:1-4](.)).

Any power that wants to bribe me from passing through trials meant for me so that I will miss my reward, I rebuke you like Jesus rebuked Peter, get behind me Satan.

Every moneychanger in the church of Jesus Christ, I cast you out of the temple. Woe unto evil people in this generation. Any evil of this day, preventing little children from being born again, die.

"But when Jesus saw it, he was much displeased, and said unto them, Suffer the little children to come unto me, and forbid them not: for of such is the kingdom of God. Verily I say unto you, whosoever shall not receive the kingdom of God as a little child, he shall not enter therein. And he took them up in his arms, put his hands upon them, and blessed them" (Mark 10:14-16).

By the anointing that breaks every yoke, I break the yokes of devil upon my life. I issue an order against devil and I invite divine presence to rebuke the devil for my sake in the name of Jesus.

DECREES TO STAND AGAINST SATAN

1. I receive power to stand against Satan and all his agents in the land, in the name of Jesus.

2. Every satanic power, working against my destiny, catch fire, in the name of Jesus.

3. I command every evil fear in my life to die by fire, in the name of Jesus.

4. Blood of Jesus, speak devil out of my life and ministry, in the name of Jesus.

5. Any power that wants me to worship devil, fall down and die, in the name of Jesus.

6. Let the terror of God destroy every evil terror in my life, in the name of Jesus.

7. Every demonic agent assigned to kill me, kill yourself, in the name of Jesus.

8. Every weapon of devil that is assigned to waste my life, be wasted, in the name of Jesus.

9. Any power that has risen against me from the sun, die, in the name of Jesus.

10. Every arrow of devil that is fired at me, backfire, in the name of Jesus.

11. Blood of Jesus, deliver me from the plans of devil, in the name of Jesus.

12. O Lord, set me free from bondage of Satan, in the name of Jesus.

13. Any war going on against me from the office of Satan, be terminated, in the name of Jesus.

14. Every satanic wound in my life, receive immediate healing, in the name of Jesus.

15. Let the reign of devil in my life come to an end by fire, in the name of Jesus.

16. Every dragon of darkness, working against me, fall down and die, in the name of Jesus.

17. Let any serpent dwelling in the garden of my life come out and die, in the name of Jesus.

18. Any power, blaspheming God in my life, be silenced by death, in the name of Jesus.

19. Every diabolic personality that is working against my life, collapse and die, in the name of Jesus.

20. Any satanic power pretending to come from God, I reject you, in the name of Jesus.

21. Let false prophets from devil be exposed and disgrace, in the name of Jesus.

22. Let the earth open its mouth and swallow evil powers against me, in the name of Jesus.

23. I refuse to enter into hell fire; let Satan dwell there alone, in the name of Jesus.

24. Let the angels of devil that are working against me be frustrated, in the name of Jesus.

Go back to the words of decree and pass your decree again.

DECREE 8

TO RECEIVE THE RESURRECTION POWER

> "That I may know him, and the power of his resurrection, and the fellowship of his sufferings, being made conformable unto his death" (Philippians 3:10).

> "But if the Spirit of him that raised up Jesus from the dead dwell in you, he that raised up Christ from the dead shall also quicken your mortal bodies by his Spirit that dwelleth in you" (Romans 8:11).

O Lord my God, by Your holy decree, I invoke the power of the resurrection. Because I have no confidence in the flesh, no power of the flesh can control me. The law of nature cannot control me or limit me. I decree that the power that resurrected Christ from the grave shall arise and fight for me now.

Every dead organ in my body, be touched by the resurrection power of God. O Lord, send Your angels from heaven to roll away stones of hindrances in my life.

You my spiritual sepulcher, you can no longer hold my body, I command the resurrection power to manifest in every area of my life immediately. Let there be great earthquake for my sake and let the angel of God descend from heaven for my sake and remove every evil material hindering my moving forward by force of his power. Let the divine fear of God and heavenly lightening strike down every evil agent against my deliverance. Blood of Jesus, flow into the blood of my destiny and take me away from every evil situations.

> "And, behold, there was a great earthquake: for the angel of the Lord descended from heaven, and came and rolled back the stone from the door, and sat upon it. His countenance was like lightning, and his raiment white as snow: And for fear of him the keepers did shake, and became as dead men. And the angel answered and said unto the women, Fear not ye: for I know that ye seek Jesus, which was crucified. He is not here: for he is risen, as he said. Come; see the place where the Lord lay" (Matthew 28:2-6).

Let the spirit of the living God that resurrected Jesus from the grave touch my body, soul and spirit for salvation, healing of my body, miracles, signs and wonders now.

> "But if the Spirit of him that raised up Jesus from the dead dwell in you, he that raised up Christ from the dead shall also quicken your mortal bodies by his Spirit that dwelleth in you" (Romans 8:11).

I decree that the spirit that raised Jesus from the dead shall appear for my sake now and destroy sorcerers that have buried my destiny. Let the spirit that filled the apostles in the upper room fill me now. I decree that the same spirit that energized the feet of the lame man after 40 years shall touch every part of my life now. Every lame part of my body, begin to walk by force.

That power that converted Paul on his way to Damascus, possess me and change me by force. I decree that the earthquake that delivered Paul and Silas shall appear in my situation wherever I am now. Let the foundation that is holding my destiny shake violently and set me perfectly free from every demonic captivity. Let that power that raised up Eutychus touch me now, in the name of Jesus.

> *"And upon the first day of the week, when the disciples came together to break bread, Paul preached unto them, ready to depart on the morrow; and continued his speech until midnight. And there were many lights in the upper chamber, where they were gathered together. And there sat in a window a certain young man named Eutychus, being fallen into a deep sleep: and as Paul was long preaching, he sunk down with sleep, and fell down from the third loft, and was taken up dead. And Paul went down, and fell on him, and embracing him said, Trouble not yourselves; for his life is in him. When he therefore was come up again, and had broken bread, and eaten, and talked a long while, even till break of day, so he departed. And they brought the young man alive, and were not a little comforted"* (Acts 20:7-12).

By the decree of the Almighty God, I command the earth to quake for my sake and release all my buried blessings, in the name of Jesus. Let the destroying flood of God carry enemies sitting upon my blessings, in the mighty name of Jesus

DECREES TO RECEIVE THE RESURRECTION POWER

1. Lord Jesus, empower me with the power of Your resurrection today, in the name of Jesus.

2. Let the power of God visit every evil grave and remove any part of my life, in the name of Jesus.

3. Blood of Jesus, flow into my graveyard and deliver my imprisoned destiny, in the name of Jesus.

4. I command every wicked power that is holding my life to give up by force, in the name of Jesus.

5. 6. Heavenly Father, arise and set me free from every evil captivity, in the name of Jesus.

7. Let the resurrection power visit my family altar and set every captive free, in the name of Jesus.

8. Any power that is assigned to keep me in perpetual bondage, released me and die, in the name of Jesus.

9. O Lord, perfect Your deliverance work in my life and set me free, in the name of Jesus.

10. You, eagle of my life, what are you waiting for? Fly now, in the name of Jesus.

11. Let every satanic limitation that is working against my life disappear, in the name of Jesus.

12. Let the power of resurrection arrest me and take me away from every evil, in the name of Jesus.

13. Angry soldiers from heaven, take me away from the camp of my enemies, in the name of Jesus.

14. Let warring angels from heaven take hold of me and move me forward, in the name of Jesus.

15. By the power in the Word of God, I remove my destiny from devil, in the name of Jesus.

16. Blood of Jesus, flow into my family altar and advertise Your power, in the name of Jesus.

17. O Lord, set me free from powers of my family's strongman, in the name of Jesus.

18. You, my spiritual evil partner, release me now and die by fire, in the name of Jesus.

19. Let miracles that will advertise my glory appear immediately, in the name of Jesus.

20. Any yoke in my life from water spirits, break and loose your hold, in the name of Jesus.

21. Every evil trader that has purchased me, release me and die, in the name of Jesus.

22. By the power in the name of Jesus, I walk out from every marine arrest, in the name of Jesus.

23. O Lord my God, pull me out from any evil group, in the name of Jesus.

24. Heavenly Father, catapult my destiny to the mountaintop of life, in the name of Jesus.

25. You my eagle, fly and deliver me from captivity, in the name of Jesus.

26. Every unholy soul tie in my life, be broken, in the name of Jesus.

27. Every yoke of slavery in my life, break, in the name of Jesus.

28. Whether devil likes it or not, I will make it in this life, in the name of Jesus.

Go back to the words of decree and pass your decree again.

DECREE 9

TO LAUGH AT LAST

"Plead my cause, O LORD, with them that strive with me: fight against them that fight against me. Take hold of shield and buckler, and stand up for mine help. Draw out also the spear, and stop the way against them that persecute me: say unto my soul, I am thy salvation. Let them be confounded and put to shame that seek after my soul: let them be turned back and brought to confusion that devise my hurt. Let them be as chaff before the wind: and let the angel of the LORD chase them. Let their way be dark and slippery: and let the angel of the LORD persecute them. For without cause have they hid for me their net in a pit, which without cause they have digged for my soul. Let destruction come upon him at unawares; and let his net that he hath hid catch himself: into that very destruction let him fall. And my soul

shall be joyful in the LORD: it shall rejoice in his salvation. All my bones shall say, LORD, who is like unto thee, which deliverest the poor from him that is too strong for him, yea, the poor and the needy from him that spoileth him? False witnesses did rise up; they laid to my charge things that I knew not. They rewarded me evil for good to the spoiling of my soul. But as for me, when they were sick, my clothing was sackcloth: I humbled my soul with fasting; and my prayer returned into mine own bosom. I behaved myself as though he had been my friend or brother: I bowed down heavily, as one that mourneth for his mother. But in mine adversity they rejoiced, and gathered themselves together: yea, the abjects gathered themselves together against me, and I knew it not; they did tear me, and ceased not: With hypocritical mockers in feasts, they gnashed upon me with their teeth. Lord, how long wilt thou look on? rescue my soul from their destructions, my darling from the lions. I will give thee thanks in the great congregation: I will praise thee among much people. Let not them that are mine enemies wrongfully rejoice over me: neither let them wink with the eye that hates me without a cause. For they speak not peace: but they devise deceitful matters against them that are quiet in the land. Yea, they opened their mouth wide against me, and said, aha, aha, our eye hath seen it. This thou hast seen, O LORD: keep not silence: O Lord, be not far from me. Stir up thyself, and awake to my judgment, even unto my cause, my God and my Lord. Judge me, O LORD my God, according to thy righteousness; and let them not rejoice over me. Let them not say in their hearts, Ah, so would we have it: let them not say, we have swallowed him up" (Psalms 35:1-25).

I decree that the power to start well and end well would fall upon me now, in the name of Jesus. O Lord, advertise Your glory in my life and empower me to live above all manner of reproaches. Let my prophetic Joseph cheer up for he must laugh at last to the glory of God. I decree that my sorrows shall perish from today, in the name of Jesus. I command all my lost peace to return to me double, in the name of Jesus.

O Lord, arise and cause me to laugh at last in this matter, in the name of Jesus. Abel offered to God a good offering by faith and laughed last in the presence of God. Enoch walked with God and laughed at last before the presence of God. Noah built the ark remained righteous and God saved him from the flood. As others were weeping, he was well protected inside the ark. I decree that I must laugh at last whether my enemies like it or not, in the name of Jesus. The power that helped Abraham to answer the call of God and laugh at last, fall upon me by force, in the name of Jesus. I decree that all my regrets shall be converted to joy.

The power that made Sarah and Abraham to laugh at last, carrying Isaac in their hands, fall upon me now, in the name of Jesus. I shall carry my own covenant child with my two hands. I decree that sicknesses and diseases will not prevent me from laughing at last. I decree death unto every problem of life that says I shall not end my life well. The power that attacks people at the time of the fullness of joy, I decree death unto you now, in the name of Jesus. O Lord, cause me to laugh well at last. In the end, even an armed robber who trusted God laughed last, I decree that no matter what is happening to me now, I shall arise and laugh at last.

> *"And one of the malefactors which were hanged railed on him, saying, if thou be Christ, save thyself and us. But the other answering rebuked him, saying, dost not thou fear God, seeing thou art in the same condemnation? And we indeed justly; for we receive the due reward of our deeds: but this man hath done nothing amiss. And he said unto Jesus, Lord; remember me when thou comest into thy kingdom. And Jesus said unto him, Verily I say unto thee, to day shalt thou be with me in paradise"* (Luke 23:39-43).

O Lord, show me where to cast my nets, so that I shall laugh in the end. My life's works shall not be in vain. O Lord, begin to change my situation by fire. Heavenly Father, lead me to launch out into the deep by Your power.

> *"Now when he had left speaking, he said unto Simon, Launch out into the deep, and let down your nets for a draught. And Simon answering said unto him, Master, we have toiled all the night, and have taken nothing: nevertheless at thy word I will let down the net. And when they had this done, they enclosed a great multitude of fishes: and their net brake"* (Luke 5:4-6).

I decree that from today henceforth, I shall begin to move forward. Blood of Jesus, flow into my life and begin to bring wonderful changes.

> *"And the thing was good in the eyes of Pharaoh, and in the eyes of all his servants. And Pharaoh said unto his servants, Can we find such a one as this is, a man in whom the Spirit of God is? And Pharaoh said unto Joseph, Forasmuch as God hath shewed thee all this, there is none so discreet and wise as thou art: Thou shalt be over my house, and according unto thy word*

shall all my people be ruled: only in the throne will I be greater than thou. And Pharaoh said unto Joseph, See, I have set thee over all the land of Egypt. And Pharaoh took off his ring from his hand, and put it upon Joseph's hand, and arrayed him in vestures of fine linen, and put a gold chain about his neck; And he made him to ride in the second chariot which he had; and they cried before him, Bow the knee: and he made him ruler over all the land of Egypt. And Pharaoh said unto Joseph, I am Pharaoh, and without thee shall no man lift up his hand or foot in all the land of Egypt" (Genesis 41:37-44).

Any evil power sitting upon my joy, be unseated by thunder. I command the heavens to release great miracles that will bring laughter from God into my life, in the name of Jesus.

DECREES TO LAUGH AT LAST

1. Father Lord, thank You for the power to change every evil situation, in the name of Jesus.

2. Let the power that created man in God's own image fall upon me, in the name of Jesus.

3. Lord Jesus, arise in Your power, and take me to my earthly paradise, in the name of Jesus.

4. Anointing to laugh in holiness and power, fall upon me now, in the name of Jesus.

5. O Lord, bless me mightily in this generation, in the name of Jesus.

6. Every curse of poverty in my life, break, in the name of Jesus.

7. I command any inherited yoke of suffering in my life to break, in the name of Jesus.

8. Blood of Jesus, multiply the grace of God in my life by fire, in the name of Jesus.

9. Heavenly Father, increase Your divine mercy into my life, in the name of Jesus.

10. O Lord, fill my life with Your holy laughter, in the name of Jesus.

11. Wind of Holy Ghost, take me into the ark of God, in the name of Jesus.

12. Father Lord, baptize me with Your holy laughter, in the name of Jesus.

13. Every evil gang-up against my destiny, scatter by fire, in the name of Jesus.

14. Every evil structure that is contributing to my sorrow, collapse, in the name of Jesus.

15. Let every good thing around me be used to the glory of God, in the name of Jesus.

16. Let every bitter thing in my life receive divine honey by fire, in the name of Jesus.

17. Lord Jesus, take me away from the land of sorrow, in the name of Jesus.

18. Let the joy of salvation in my life be multiplied by fire, in the name of Jesus.

19. O Lord, let Your promise begin to manifest in my life, in the name of Jesus.

20. Even at old age, I will still be rejoicing and laughing at the devil, in the name of Jesus.

21. O Lord, comfort me with an overcoming laughter, in the name of Jesus.

22. You my life, you shall laugh last to the glory of God, in the name of Jesus.

23. O Lord, help me to overcome every problem so that I can laugh at the devil, in the name of Jesus.

24. You my life, escape the judgment of devil, in the name of Jesus.

25. As I received my own portion, I shall be laughing at the devil, in the name of Jesus.

Go back to the words of decree and pass your decree again.

DECREE 10

FOR A NEW WIND OF OPPORTUNITIES

"Behold, I will do a new thing; now it shall spring forth; shall ye not know it? I will even make a way in the wilderness, and rivers in the desert" (Isaiah 43:19).

By the anointing of the Holy Ghost, I decree against every hindrance preventing from beginning again. I command wonderful and new opportunities to begin to open for me whether devil likes it or not. O Lord, protect Your great miracles, signs and wonders in my life by Your power. Heavenly Father, arise in Your power and take me to where I will make it better, in the name of Jesus.

"For I am the LORD thy God, the Holy One of Israel, thy Savior: I gave Egypt for thy ransom, Ethiopia and Seba for thee. Since thou wast precious in my sight, thou hast been honorable, and I have loved thee: therefore will I give men for thee, and people for thy life. Fear not: for I am with thee: I will bring thy seed from the east, and gather thee from the west; I will say to the north, Give up; and to the south, Keep not back: bring my sons from far, and my daughters from the ends of the earth; Even every one that is called by my name: for I have created him for my glory, I have formed him; yea, I have made him. Bring forth the blind people that have eyes, and the deaf that have ears. Let all the nations be gathered together, and let the people be assembled: who among them can declare this, and shew us former

things? Let them bring forth their witnesses, that they may be justified: or let them hear, and say, it is truth. Ye are my witnesses, saith the LORD, and my servant whom I have chosen: that ye may know and believe me, and understand that I am he: before me there was no God formed, neither shall there be after me. I, even I, am the LORD; and beside me there is no savior. I have declared, and have saved, and I have shewed, when there was no strange god among you: therefore ye are my witnesses, saith the LORD, that I am God. Yea, before the day was I am he; and there is none that can deliver out of my hand: I will work, and who shall let it? Thus saith the LORD, your redeemer, the Holy One of Israel; for your sake I have sent to Babylon, and have brought down all their nobles, and the Chaldeans, whose cry is in the ships. I am the LORD, your Holy One, the creator of Israel, your King. Thus saith the LORD, which maketh a way in the sea, and a path in the mighty waters; Which bringeth forth the chariot and horse, the army and the power; they shall lie down together, they shall not rise: they are extinct, they are quenched as tow. Remember ye not the former things, neither consider the things of old. Behold, I will do a new thing; now it shall spring forth; shall ye not know it? I will even make a way in the wilderness, and rivers in the desert" (Isaiah 43:3:19).

O Lord, do a new thing in my life by fire as You have promised. Open a new way for me in the dry places. Where people have never made it before, O Lord, make life easy for me there. I decree that I will succeed without pains from today. O Lord, with Your power, I decree open doors of greatness. I command great and miraculous ways to begin to open for me in the wilderness in the name of Jesus. Let the rivers in the wilderness begin to release the hidden miracles captured by mermaid kingdom, in the name of Jesus.

Every evil personality, sitting upon the wealth in the rivers, be unseated by force. O Lord, I decree that every desert in my life will be turned into rivers of miracles, in the name of Jesus. I decree that difficulties in my life shall become easy from now. Henceforth, my life shall be fruitful, productive and fertile for all manners of miracles, signs and wonders, in the name of Jesus.

Wherever I will set my feet upon in this month, there shall be a new and great opening for good things, in the name of Jesus. Blood of Jesus, command into my life unmerited favor from all manners of people.

> "Then the king said to Haman, Make haste, and take the apparel and the horse, as thou hast said, and do even so to Mordecai the Jew, that sitteth at the king's gate: let nothing fail of all that thou hast spoken.. Then took Haman the apparel and the horse, and arrayed Mordecai, and brought him on horseback through the street of the city, and proclaimed before him, Thus shall it be done unto the man whom the king delighteth to honor" (Esther 6:10-11).

I decree promotion above my enemies from now henceforth. I command all superior enemies to suddenly become my servants, in the name of Jesus.

As I pass through the waters this month, my enemies must bow, they shall serve me. As I enter into this month, my life shall enter into its rest and peace. I shall suffer no more, in the name of Jesus. No problem will swallow me. No fire will burn me, no mountain shall stop me in the name of Jesus.

No evil will harm me, in the name of Jesus. Powers of darkness will give way and my greatness shall appear, in the name of Jesus.

> *"Lift up your heads, O ye gates; and be ye lift up, ye everlasting doors; and the King of glory shall come in. Who is this King of glory? The LORD strong and mighty, the LORD mighty in battle. Lift up your heads, O ye gates; even lift them up, ye everlasting doors; and the King of glory shall come in. Who is this King of glory? The LORD of hosts, he is the King of glory"* (Psalms 24:7-10).

Ancient powers shall surrender all that they have captured from me, in the name of Jesus. They shall bow and die, in the name of Jesus.

DECREES FOR A NEW WIND OF OPPORTUNITIES

1. Heavenly father, arise in Your power and change my situation, in the name of Jesus.

2. Ancient of days, give me new breakthrough skills that will advertise Your glory in me, in the name of Jesus.

3. Blood of Jesus, do a new thing in my life that will move my life forward, in the name of Jesus.

4. Father Lord, show me a new way that no one has known before, in the name of Jesus.

5. Among the people that will make it this season, I am the first, in the name of Jesus.

6. Let the grace of God that would enable me to climb high mountains of success possess me, in the name of Jesus.

7. O Lord, make me a terror to my adversaries, in the name of Jesus.

8. I walk out from evil habits into holy character, in the name of Jesus.

9. Every old or phased out model of victory, give way for the new from God, in the name of Jesus.

10. Any old demonic fashion that is assigned to keep me outdated, die, in the name of Jesus.

11. O Lord, take me to a new land of victory in Christ, in the name of Jesus.

12. Lord Jesus, renew my strength for greatness, in the name of Jesus.

13. Every evil reputation in my life, perish, in the name of Jesus.

14. Any parental evil that wants to begin with me, die, in the name of Jesus.

15. Let every re-occurring evil in my life be terminated, in the name of Jesus.

16. Any evil power that woke up with me today shall not continue. Die, in the name of Jesus.

17. Blood of Jesus, lay the foundation of my greatness today by fire, in the name of Jesus.

18. Power to discover what will make me great, appear, in the name of Jesus.

19. O Lord, lay my foundation in righteousness, in the name of Jesus.

20. Any available demon on my way to a new thing, die, in the name of Jesus.

21. Any evil seed that was planted into my life the day I was born, die, in the name of Jesus.

22. Every evil utterance that has been said against me at conception, die, in the name of Jesus.

23. I claim all good things that God has prepared for me from the beginning, in the name of Jesus.

24. O Lord, enter into my root and perfect Your plans for my life, in the name of Jesus.

25. Whether devil likes it or not, I shall start well and end well, in the name of Jesus.

Go back to the words of decree and pass your decree again.

DECREE 11

AGAINST WITCHCRAFT POWERS

> *"What is man, that thou art mindful of him? and the son of man, that thou visitest him? For thou hast made him a little lower than the angels, and hast crowned him with glory and honor. Thou madest him to have dominion over the works of thy hands; thou hast put all things under his feet: All sheep and oxen, yea, and the beasts of the field; The fowl of the air, and the fish of the sea, and whatsoever passeth through the paths of the seas"* (Psalms 8:4-8).

Any witchcraft power prospering in my life, I come against you, die by the decree of the Lord. Let the strength of witchcraft powers that is attacking my life be frustrate immediately. O Lord, by Your decree, let the power of witchcraft assigned against my destiny be wasted by fire.

Any instrument of witchcraft that is targeted against me, I command you to catch Holy Ghost fire and burn to ashes now. Any witch or wizard using manipulations to disorganize my life, receive confusion and be perfectly frustrated. I decree against every witchcraft divination that is assigned to work against my destiny, in the name of Jesus. O Lord, let Your Word of decree destroy every witchcraft decree against my life forever.

Any power that is following me about to destroy me through weapons of witchcraft, I command you to go back to your senders and destroy them now, in the mighty name of Jesus. By the power in the Word of God, I destroy every evil power using soothsaying against my life, in the name of Jesus. Let the plans of occult grand masters against my destiny backfire now, in the name of Jesus. O Lord, I decree that by Your power, my deliverance from witchcraft captivity will be immediate.

I command evil personalities working against my life to bow and surrender to God's perfect plan for my life, in the name of Jesus. Every evil dominion over my life shall not stand, I command every problem in my life caused by water spirits to bow and surrender by force, in the name of Jesus. Every work of witches and wizards against my life, I bring you under my feet and I command you to remain there forever and ever, in the name of Jesus. Any witchcraft animal that is being used against my life shall surrender and die. Blood of Jesus, envelope my life with the Holy Ghost fire and intimidate witches and wizards working against my destiny, in the name of Jesus.

> *"What is man, that thou art mindful of him? and the son of man, that thou visitest him? For thou hast made him a little lower than the angels, and hast crowned him with glory and honor. Thou madest him to have dominion over the works of thy hands; thou hast put all things under his feet: All sheep and oxen, yea, and the beasts of the field; The fowl of the air, and the fish of the sea, and whatsoever passeth through the paths of the seas"* (Psalms 8:4-8).

By the decree of the Almighty, I cut off every attachment of witchcraft in my life. Any witchcraft power seeking after my soul shall be disgraced and brought to confusion. I command their devices to manifest on their heads, in the name of Jesus. I decree that the weapons of witchcraft powers against me shall not prosper. Blood of Jesus, turn witches and wizards against me to chaffs before the wind and let angels of the Lord disgrace them forever, in the name of Jesus. I decree that their ways shall be converted to thick darkness and slippery. Let the destruction they planned against me come upon their own heads, in the name of Jesus.

> *"Let them be confounded and put to shame that seek after my soul: let them be turned back and brought to confusion that devise my hurt. Let them be as chaff before the wind: and let the angel of the LORD chase them. Let their way be dark and slippery: and let the angel of the LORD persecute them"* (Psalms 35:4-6).

I release flood of confusion and destruction upon their heads and I command them to fail, in the name of Jesus.

DECREES AGAINST WITCHCRAFT POWERS

1. I command every witchcraft power working against my life to be destroyed, in the name of Jesus.

2. Father Lord, by Your power, I command the ministry of witchcraft to be frustrated, in the name of Jesus.

3. Every instrument of witchcraft against my life, catch fire, in the name of Jesus.

4. Blood of Jesus, pursue witchcraft powers in my life to death, in the name of Jesus.

5. Every yoke of witchcraft in my life, break to pieces, in the name of Jesus.

6. Any witch or wizard, ministering against God's purpose for my life, fail, in the name of Jesus.

7. Every altar of witchcraft in my father's house, scatter, in the name of Jesus.

8. Let the strongman of my father's house using witchcraft against me die, in the name of Jesus.

9. Holy Ghost Fire, burn every garden of witchcraft to ashes, in the name of Jesus.

10. Anointing to terminate witchcraft powers, fall upon me, in the name of Jesus.

11. Heavenly Father, deliver me from every witchcraft power, in the name of Jesus.

12. Any evil personality that has entered witchcraft because of me, fail, in the name of Jesus.

13. Let the chains of witchcraft that is holding me break now, in the name of Jesus.

14. I command every stronghold of witchcraft to break by fire, in the name of Jesus.

15. Every witchcraft bungalow built against me, collapse, in the name of Jesus.

16. I reject every witchcraft load that is upon my life, in the name of Jesus.

17. Every witchcraft problem assigned to waste me, be wasted, in the name of Jesus.

18. Every marine spirit altar of witchcraft, catch fire, in the name of Jesus.

19. Blood of Jesus, flow into every throne of witchcraft for my sake, in the name of Jesus.

20. Every Stubborn witchcraft sickness in my life, die, in the name of Jesus.

21. Every arrow of witchcraft fired into my life, I fire you back, in the name of Jesus.

22. Every judgment of witchcraft against my life, be reversed, in the name of Jesus.

23. O Lord, deliver me from witchcraft curses, in the name of Jesus.

Go back to the words of decree and pass your decree again.

DECREE 12

TO GET WEALTH

(Study 2 Kings 7)

I decree against the spirit of lack and famine in my life, in the name of Jesus. Let the power of prosperity begin to fall upon my life from the third heaven by fire, in the name of Jesus. Let my enemies begin to hear the noise of great hosts and let them flee for my sake, in the name of Jesus. I decree that the wealth of the gentiles shall be my portion, in the name of Jesus. I begin to inherit the wealth of the gentiles by fire. I decree that by this time tomorrow, I shall be greatly rich beyond my imagination, in the name of Jesus.

> *"Then Elisha said, Hear ye the word of the LORD; Thus saith the LORD, To morrow about this time shall a measure of fine flour be sold for a shekel, and two measures of barley for a shekel, in the gate of Samaria"* (2 Kings 7:1).

I command miracles that will make me a great millionaire to appear by force, in the name of Jesus. O Lord, multiply every good thing in my life as You did for the wife of one of the prophets, in the name of Jesus. I decree that my coast shall be expanded and enlarged, in the name of Jesus. Let all my empty vessels be filled miraculously with divine blessings, in the name of Jesus.

> *"Now there cried a certain woman of the wives of the sons of the prophets unto Elisha, saying, Thy servant*

my husband is dead; and thou knowest that thy servant did fear the LORD: and the creditor is come to take unto him my two sons to be bondmen. And Elisha said unto her, what shall I do for thee? tell me, what hast thou in the house? And she said, Thine handmaid hath not any thing in the house, save a pot of oil. Then he said, Go, borrow thee vessels abroad of all thy neighbors', even empty vessels; borrow not a few. And when thou art come in, thou shalt shut the door upon thee and upon thy sons, and shalt pour out into all those vessels, and thou shalt set aside that which is full. So she went from him, and shut the door upon her and upon her sons, who brought the vessels to her; and she poured out. And it came to pass, when the vessels were full, that she said unto her son, Bring me yet a vessel. And he said unto her, there is not a vessel more. And the oil stayed. Then she came and told the man of God. And he said, Go, sell the oil, and pay thy debt, and live thou and thy children of the rest" (2 Kings. 4:1-7).

By the power in the blood of Jesus, I can never be poor again in life. I receive the power, the anointing and the grace to get wealth that has no attachments with devil. No power from hell can return me to poverty and lack again. The enemy will never steal my prosperity again. I shall not have any business with famine again because the Lord is now involved in my business.

Ancient of days, arise and bless me with wealth from Your throne, in the name of Jesus. Every curse of poverty in my life, I command you to fall down and die, in the name of Jesus. Holy Ghost fire, burn and consume every trace of poverty in my life, in the name of Jesus. I take back every good thing I have lost as a result of disobeying the voice of the Lord. Let my lost blessings return to me doubled, without negotiation or query. O Lord, I shall not suffer any loss again, because I obey Your voice now.

> *"Then spake Elisha unto the woman, whose son he had restored to life, saying, Arise, and go thou and thine household, and sojourn wheresoever thou canst sojourn: for the LORD hath called for a famine; and it shall also come upon the land seven years. And the woman arose, and did after the saying of the man of God: and she went with her household, and sojourned in the land of the Philistines seven years. And it came to pass at the seven years' end that the woman returned out of the land of the Philistines: and she went forth to cry unto the king for her house and for her land. And the king talked with Gehazi the servant of the man of God, saying, Tell me, I pray thee, all the great things that Elisha hath done. And it came to pass, as he was telling the king how he had restored a dead body to life, that, behold, the woman, whose son he had restored to life, cried to the king for her house and for her land. And Gehazi said my lord, O king, this is the woman, and this is her son, whom Elisha restored to life. And when the king asked the woman, she told him. So the king appointed unto her a certain officer, saying, Restore all that was hers, and all the fruits of the field since the day that she left the land, even until now"* (2 Kings 8:1-6).

Let every satanic storeroom locking up my blessings open by force and let my blessings be removed immediately. I command my heavens to open for my wealth to come down without hindrance, in the name of Jesus. I break every strong room of devil by force and I carry all my confiscated blessings by fire.

Any witch or wizard that has swallowed my blessings must vomit them now by force. Wherever my blessings are taken to, I command them to re-appear immediately. O Lord, don't allow my enemies to keep back any good thing that belongs to me, in the name of Jesus. Every evil sacrifice that was made against my breakthrough, I command it to expire. Whoever says that I shall not make it spiritually, physically, financially, socially, academically, materially, martially and mentally shall fail, in the name of Jesus.

DECREES TO GET WEALTH

1. O Lord my God, give me the power to get wealth, in the name of Jesus.

2. By the power in the Word of God, I receive the anointing to make divine wealth, in the name of Jesus.

3. Heavenly Father, mark me for great wealth without pains, in the name of Jesus.

4. Every seed of poverty in my life, die now, in the name of Jesus.

5. Blood of Jesus, flow into my life and create wealth in my life, in the name of Jesus.

6. O Lord my God, prosper me for greatness, in the name of Jesus.

7. Every garment of lack in my life, catch Holy Ghost fire, in the name of Jesus.

8. Spirit of the living God, possess me to gather divine blessings, in the name of Jesus.

9. Any power working against my benefits, fall down and die, in the name of Jesus.

10. O Lord, assist me to prosper in a holy and acceptable way, in the name of Jesus.

11. Father Lord, project Your great wealth into my destiny, in the name of Jesus.

12. Any witchcraft arrow that is fired into my life for the sake of my entitlements, backfire, in the name of Jesus.

13. However difficult my circumstances are in life, I shall make great wealth, in the name of Jesus.

14. I soak my life in the pool of divine favor, in the name of Jesus.

15. O Lord my God, label me for great wealth, in the name of Jesus.

16. Every marine witchcraft broom, sweeping away my wealth, catch fire, in the name of Jesus.

17. Let the doors of my victory and success open by force, in the name of Jesus.

18. Any power that has buried my wealth alive, release it now and die, in the name of Jesus.

19. Let the womb of witchcraft powers that has swallowed my breakthrough burst, in the name of Jesus.

20. Every covenant of poverty in my life, break to pieces, in the name of Jesus.

21. Heavenly Father, arise and break curses uttered against me by fire, in the name of Jesus.

22. Let the power of God magnetize wealth into my life by fire, in the name of Jesus.

23. Blood of Jesus, speak wealth into my life by fire, in the name of Jesus.

24. Father Lord, deliver me from the reproach of poverty and bless me, in the name of Jesus.

25. I bind and cast out every spirit of lack and debts in my life, in the name of Jesus.
26. Every satanic root of poverty in my life, dry up by fire, in the name of Jesus.
27. O Lord, bless me with all manner of divine wealth, in the name of Jesus.

Go back to the words of decree and pass your decree again.

DECREE 13

AGAINST THE SPIRIT OF THE TAIL

> *"And the LORD shall make thee the head, and not the tail; and thou shalt be above only, and thou shalt not be beneath; if that thou hearken unto the commandments of the LORD thy God, which I command thee this day, to observe and to do them"* (Deuteronomy 28:13).

In the mighty name of Lord Jesus, Father, I decree against the spirit of the tail in my life. Let the spirit of the tail assigned to delay progresses in my life be cut off. Every power from my place of birth drawing me backward, I come against you, die without mercy in the name of Jesus. Let your power and control over my life be frustrated and be eliminated, in the name of Jesus. O Lord, take my life and destiny away by Your decree out of evil captivity, in the name of Jesus. I decree a total deliverance of my life from the tail region of life. Blood of Jesus, flow into my life and move my life forward by fire and by force, in the name of Jesus.

I decree, as it is written, *"I shall be the head and not the tail"* everywhere I go. Let the anointing of the tail over my life be removed forever and ever, in the name of Jesus. Blood of Jesus, empower me to be the head from henceforth. Let evil powers that are assigned against my life to tie me to tail region be arrested and destroyed.

Father Lord, in Your power, I move away from the lowest class and I jump into my original divine design from the creation of life, in the name of Jesus. Any power, assigned to influence me to break God's commandment, I decree against your plans, fall down and die immediately, in the name of Jesus.

I decree immediate death for the spirit of disobedience working against my life. O Lord, by Your decree, I arrest every evil authority working against my destiny, in the name of Jesus. Angels of the living God, arise and deliver me from powers that keep and waste destinies in the tail region of life, in the name of Jesus. I command my life to embrace the life that is above, and reject perfectly the life below. I decree immediate deliverance to take place in every aspect of my life, in the name of Jesus. I decree death to the arrows of the spirit of the tail fired at my life, in the name of Jesus.

Let the blood of Jesus flow into my destiny and move me to unmerited promotion, in the name of Jesus. Every curse and covenant of backwardness in my life, break and catch fire, burn to ashes and leave me alone. I decree against all powers of darkness assigned to monitor my life in the tail region. Every altar of darkness, attacking my progress, wherever you are now, be uprooted by thunder, in the name of Jesus. Powers that hijack prosperity, which is working against me, fall down and die, in the name of Jesus. I decree immediate freedom upon all my captured progresses in life by fire, in the name of Jesus. As it is written:

> *"No weapon that is formed against thee shall prosper; and every tongue that shall rise against thee in judgment thou shalt condemn. This is the heritage of the servants of the LORD, and their righteousness is of me, saith the LORD. No weapon that is formed against thee shall prosper; and every tongue that shall rise against thee in judgment thou shalt condemn. This is*

the heritage of the servants of the LORD, and their righteousness is of me, saith the LORD" (Isaiah 54:17).

Marine spirit weapons and all the weapons of darkness shall al be wasted immediately. I decree against every evil tongue speaking against me. O Lord, arise and confuse all my enemies, in the name of Jesus. Every evil judgment against my life, by the decree of God, I reverse you by force, in the name of Jesus. I shall be the head and not the tail forever and ever, in the name of Jesus.

DECREES AGAINST THE SPIRIT OF THE TAIL

1. Blood of Jesus, take me away from the tail region to the head region, in the name of Jesus.

2. Every spirit of the tail in my life, come out and die by fire, in the name of Jesus.

3. Any power projecting tail spirit into my life, fall down and die, in the name of Jesus.

4. Angels of the living God, arise and fight for my promotion, in the name of Jesus.

5. Any evil habit in my life, dragging me to the tail region, die, in the name of Jesus.

6. I command total deliverance to take place in my life by fire, in the name of Jesus.

7. Let the Holy Ghost fire burn every anointing of the tail in my life, in the name of Jesus.

8. Any covenant of the tail in my life, break by fire, in the name of Jesus.

9. Every yoke of the tail in my life, break to pieces, in the name of Jesus.

10. Every inherited laziness in my foundation, catch fire, in the name of Jesus.

11. Any curse placed upon my life by any one dead or alive, die, in the name of Jesus.

12. Blood of Jesus, destroy tail spirits in my life, in the name of Jesus.

13. Anointing for first class position, fall upon me now, in the name of Jesus.

14. Any evil personality that has removed my name from the front, bring it back, in the name of Jesus.

15. Let the strongman of my father's house that is dragging me backward die, in the name of Jesus.

16. I take back all that my ancestors handed over to water spirits, in the name of Jesus.

17. Any witchcraft pot that is cooking my progress, break, in the name of Jesus.

18. Let my brain carry Holy Ghost fire now, in the name of Jesus.

19. Any power that wants me to come behind others shall fail, in the name of Jesus.

20. O Lord, empower me to be brighter than the brightest, in the name of Jesus.

21. Any poison of backwardness in my life, be roasted by fire, in the name of Jesus.

22. Any power attacking my divine speed, fall down and die, in the name of Jesus.

23. I arise and move out from all evil inheritance, in the name of Jesus.

24. Any evil power that has cast spell on me, remove it and die, in the name of Jesus.

25. Any satanic chain holding me back, break by force, in the name of Jesus.

Go back to the words of decree and pass your decree again.

DECREE 14

AGAINST IRON-LIKE PROBLEMS

(*Study* Psalms 18)

I stand against every iron-like problem in my life. Heavenly Father, by Your power of decree, break every stubborn situation in my life, in the name of Jesus. I command all inherited stubborn problems to loose their hold in my life, whether they like it or not, in the name of Jesus. I decree that every marine spirit yoke in my life be broken by thunder, in the name of Jesus. You, powers of evil arrest of sicknesses and diseases in my life, be broken, in the name of Jesus. Because the Lord Himself is against you, I also come against you now, clear away by force and die, in the name of Jesus.

> *"And thou shalt teach them diligently unto thy children, and shalt talk of them when thou sittest in*

thine house, and when thou walkest by the way, and when thou liest down, and when thou risest up" (Deuteronomy 1:6-7).

You are no more welcome into my life for you have overstayed, I decree against your stay in my life, enough is enough, carry your load and go by force now, in the name of Jesus.

Any problem in my life that is standing as the wall of Jericho, fall down by force, collapse immediately from your foundation and rise no more, in the name of Jesus. By the decree of God, I command every giant in the battlefield against me to fall down and die by fire, in the name of Jesus.

"Now Jericho was straightly shut up because of the children of Israel: none went out, and none came in" (Joshua 6:1).

I blow the trumpets of God against every stubborn iron like problem in my life and I command them to shake and fall from their foundation, in the name of Jesus. I decree with a shout against every evil power that has vowed to waste my life. With my great shout of victory, I command all my problems to bow in shame and disgrace, in the name of Jesus.

"So the people shouted when the priests blew with the trumpets: and it came to pass, when the people heard the sound of the trumpet, and the people shouted with a great shout, that the wall fell down flat, so that the people went up into the city, every man straight before him, and they took the city. And they utterly destroyed all that was in the city, both man and woman, young

and old, and ox, and sheep, and ass, with the edge of the sword" (Joshua 6:20-21).

I stand upon the Word of God and decree immediate release of my peace, prosperity and perfect victory over every determined enemy of my soul, in the name of Jesus. Father Lord, give me the solution that will close the mouths of my enemies in shame, in the name of Jesus. By the power and the anointing of God, I receive my perfect freedom. Let the spirit of failure assigned to promote evil in my life be frustrated forever in my life, in the name of Jesus.

Any problem that refuses to let me go, release me quickly and die by force. You stubborn problems, attack yourselves and die without mercy, in the name of Jesus. Every sin in my life, prolonging my problems, your time is up, therefore, fall down and die immediately, in the name of Jesus. Any evil arrow that is fired into my life to waste my destiny, I fire you back, go back immediately to your senders and destroy them, in the name of Jesus.

"And afterward when David heard it, he said, I and my kingdom are guiltless before the LORD for ever from the blood of Abner the son of Ner: Let it rest on the head of Joab, and on all his father's house; and let there not fail from the house of Joab one that hath an issue, or that is a leper, or that leaneth on a staff, or that falleth on the sword, or that lacketh bread" (2 Samuel 3:28-29).

Any evil bloodshed by my ancestors or anyone living or dead that is crying against me shall fail for my sake. I refuse to inherit any problem, curse and evil covenant. I reject every evil flow from my ancestors. I take back all my blessings handed over to Satan by my ancestors or anyone living or dead. The suffering I am going through now and the iron-like problems as a result of actions of my ancestors, I decree against your power, die immediately, in the name of Jesus.

> *"Our fathers have sinned, and are not; and we have borne their iniquities. Servants have ruled over us: there is none that doth deliver us out of their hand"* (Lamentations 5:7-8).

> *"Princes are hanged up by their hand: the faces of elders were not honored"* (Lamentations 5:12).

> *"Wherefore dost thou forget us for ever, and forsake us so long time? Turn thou us unto thee, O LORD, and we shall be turned; renew our days as of old"* (Lamentations 5:20-21).

Blood of Jesus, open your mouth wide and silence every evil blood speaking against me, in the name of Jesus.

DECREES AGAINST IRON-LIKE PROBLEMS

1. Father Lord, deliver me from problems that are stronger than me, in the name of Jesus.

2. Every Stubborn infirmity in my life that is assigned to waste me, be wasted, in the name of Jesus.

3. Every yoke of hardship in my life, break into pieces, in the name of Jesus.

4. I break and loose myself from every problem that has vowed to destroy me, in the name of Jesus.

5. Every demonic attack that does not want me to rest, die, in the name of Jesus.

6. Every inherited bondage in my life, die, in the name of Jesus.

7. Blood of Jesus, flow into the roots of my problems, in the name of Jesus.

8. O Lord, confront and conquer every iron-like problem in my life, in the name of Jesus.

9. Any stubborn problem in my blood, die, in the name of Jesus.

10. I command demons working day and night to destroy me to die, in the name of Jesus.

11. Any evil altar attacking me without space, catch fire, in the name of Jesus.

12. Any poison that is working hard to kill me, die, in the name of Jesus.

13. Any witchcraft reproach in my destiny, be eliminated, in the name of Jesus.

14. Every evil plantation in my life, die, in the name of Jesus.

15. Any evil pronouncement from the waters against my life, be reversed, in the name of Jesus.

16. O Lord my God, incubate my life with the Holy Ghost fire, in the name of Jesus.

17. Every arrow of death that has been fired into my life, I fire you back, in the name of Jesus.

18. My body, reject every manner of problems, in the name of Jesus.

19. Any satanic carryover of my father's battles, die, in the name of Jesus.

20. Every disgraceful evil occurrence in my life, die completely, in the name of Jesus.

21. Let the Lord that heals me remove every deadly sickness in my life, in the name of Jesus.

22. That voice that called Lazarus out of the grave, speak to my destiny now, in the name of Jesus.

23. Any evil germ in my life, what are you waiting for? Die, in the name of Jesus.

24. Let that power that is wasting my family without a challenge die, in the name of Jesus.

25. O Lord, help me to celebrate my victory over every manner of problem, in the name of Jesus.

26. Every enemy of my joy, die by fire, in the name of Jesus.

27. O Lord, take away problems from my root, in the name of Jesus.

Go back to the words of decree and pass your decree again.

DECREE 15

AGAINST SPIRIT OF STAGNATION

"The righteous cry and the LORD heareth, and delivereth them out of all their troubles" (Psalms 34:17).

My God is a God of decree and His children are also people of decrees. My God is a progressive God and those who serve Him must be progressive. Based on these, I decree against every power of stagnancy in my life. I command stagnation of life to die forever in my life immediately. Let the warring angels of God arise and remove the stone of stagnation out of my way forever, in the name of Jesus.

In the prosperous name of our Lord Jesus Christ of Nazareth, I decree against poverty in my life and I command every manner of lack to die and leave me alone, in the name of Jesus. I terminate every ministry and work of stagnancy in my life. Every satanic setback on my way to progress, be frustrated by force, in the name of Jesus. Let the powers of stagnation in my life be put to shame today.

Father Lord, by the power in Your word, I cry for your immediate deliverance from all manners of stagnancy. I decree against every trouble that stagnancy has brought into my life by fire by force. Let the evil leg of stagnancy walk out by fire now, in the name of Jesus. Any power from the marine kingdom and other demonic powers keeping my life on evil line, die, in the name of Jesus. The powers that arrested the progress of others in my family, that is now trying to arrest me or has already arrested me, you are a liar, fall down and die, in the name of Jesus.

> *"And Jabez was more honorable than his brethren: and his mother called his name Jabez, saying, because I bare him with sorrow. And Jabez called on the God of Israel, saying, O that thou wouldest bless me indeed, and enlarge my coast, and that thine hand might be with me, and that thou wouldest keep me from evil, that it may not grieve me! And God granted him that which he requested"* (1 Chronicles 4:9-10).

Father Lord, by Your power of decree, I destroy all traces of sorrow in my life by the decree of God. I reject poverty, failure, defeat and every evil setback, in the name of Jesus. O Lord my God, I cry for a change, arise and change me by Your power. Let the power and the anointing that enlarged the coast of Jabez fall upon me now, in the name of Jesus.

I decree for my life to open every door to accommodate great blessings of God. Every iniquity that promotes stagnancy, I am not your candidate, fall down and die without negotiation. As Caleb remembered himself and made a wonderful request, O Lord, I make my own request directly to you, arise and bless me more than Caleb, and let my destiny move forward.

> *"Then the children of Judah came unto Joshua in Gilgal: and Caleb the son of Jephunneh the Kenezite said unto him, Thou knowest the thing that the LORD said unto Moses the man of God concerning me and thee in Kadesh-barnea. Forty years old was I when Moses the servant of the LORD sent me from Kadesh-barnea to espy out the land; and I brought him word again as it was in mine heart. Nevertheless my brethren*

that went up with me made the heart of the people melt: but I wholly followed the LORD my God. And Moses sware on that day, saying, Surely the land whereon thy feet have trodden shall be thine inheritance, and thy children's for ever, because thou hast wholly followed the LORD my God. And now, behold, the LORD hath kept me alive, as he said, these forty and five years, even since the LORD spake this word unto Moses, while the children of Israel wandered in the wilderness: and now, lo, I am this day fourscore and five years old. As yet I am as strong this day as I was in the day that Moses sent me: as my strength was then, even so is my strength now, for war, both to go out, and to come in. Now therefore give me this mountain, whereof the LORD spake in that day; for thou heardest in that day how the Anakims were there, and that the cities were great and fenced: if so be the LORD will be with me, then I shall be able to drive them out, as the LORD said. And Joshua blessed him, and gave unto Caleb the son of Jephunneh Hebron for an inheritance. Hebron therefore became the inheritance of Caleb the son of Jephunneh the Kenezite unto this day, because that he wholly followed the LORD God of Israel" (Joshua 14:6-14).

I decree that every promise of God shall no more elude me from henceforth, in the name of Jesus.

DECREES AGAINST SPIRIT OF STAGNATION

1. Every anointing of stagnancy upon my life, break by fire, in the name of Jesus.

2. I stand against the strongman of stagnancy working against my progress, in the name of Jesus.

3. Blood of Jesus, flow into my destiny and move my life forward, in the name of Jesus.

4. I reject every bondage of stagnancy in my life, in the name of Jesus.

5. Let the eagle of my destiny fly out from the cage of the enemy, in the name of Jesus.

6. Angels of the living God, arise and give me victory over stagnancy, in the name of Jesus.

7. Heavenly Father, anoint my life to move forward by fire, in the name of Jesus.

8. Father Lord, let Your fire devour every strange fire that is burning against my progress, in the name of Jesus.

9. Every chain of oppressors against my life, break by force, in the name of Jesus.

10. Ancient of days, take me to where You want me to be, in the name of Jesus.

11. Any power that wants to keep me at one level of life, die, in the name of Jesus.

12. Every evil prison, assigned to lock me up forever, open and release me, in the name of Jesus.

13. Every covenant of stagnancy in my life, break by fire, in the name of Jesus.

14. Every evil eye, marking me for destruction, be blinded, in the name of Jesus.

15. Any evil limitation against my life, clear away, in the name of Jesus.

16. Every habitation of stagnancy in my life, receive the Holy Ghost fire, in the name of Jesus.

17. Every demon of stagnancy that is assigned to detain me for life, die, in the name of Jesus.

18. Every evil force that has magnetized my life, scatter, in the name of Jesus.

19. I command altars of my father's house holding me in bondage to scatter, in the name of Jesus.

20. Every evil imagination against my progress, be rendered impotent, in the name of Jesus.

21. Divine aircraft, take me to where I am supposed to be, in the name of Jesus.

22. I receive the Holy Ghost power to overcome every evil stagnancy, in the name of Jesus.

23. Let oppressors of my life be oppressed, in the name of Jesus.

24. I reject every evil spirit of the tail against me, in the name of Jesus.

25. Every spirit of discouragement against my life, die by fire, in the name of Jesus.

26. 27. Any evil cloud gathering against me, scatter, in the name of Jesus.

28. O Lord, move my life forward by fire, in the name of Jesus.

Go back to the words of decree and pass your decree again.

DECREE 16

FOR GOD'S SPIRIT AND SUPPORT

"God is our refuge and strength, a very present help in trouble. Therefore will not we fear, though the earth be removed, and though the mountains be carried into the midst of the sea; Though the waters thereof roar and be troubled, though the mountains shake with the swelling thereof" (Psalms 46:1-3).

By the power in the name of Jesus, I receive divine support in every area of my life from today. I shall be supported by God this year and throughout my life, in the name of Jesus. I decree that the God that saved Noah and his family shall give me all the support I needed, in the name of Jesus.

In the midst of hatred from all the people around me, I receive divine support to prosper everywhere I go from today, in the name of Jesus. As God supported Joseph and blessed him in the land of Egypt, so shall I be supported before all my enemies, in the name of Jesus. As God prospered Joseph and gave him support from heaven, I decree that my support and prosperity shall come from heaven. Every impossibility in my life, disappear and die without delay, in the name of Jesus.

O Lord of true righteousness, impart Your righteousness into my life by fire, in the name of Jesus. Blood of Jesus, flow into my life and deliver me from enemies of my destiny. The Lord I serve is my refuge and my strength therefore, I shall not fear any evil, in the name of Jesus.

> *"To the chief Musician for the sons of Korah, a Song upon Alamoth. God is our refuge and strength, a very present help in trouble. Therefore will not we fear, though the earth be removed, and though the mountains be carried into the midst of the sea; Though the waters thereof roar and be troubled, though the mountains shake with the swelling thereof. Selah"* (Psalms 46:1-3).

I decree that in the time of trouble, when all my enemies have concluded that I will not make it, the Lord will arise and support me. I decree that in the time of weakness, when all my enemies have done all they could and nothing is left to be done, the Lord will send His divine angels to support me. I command my life to move forward and receive divine support by fire, in the name of Jesus. Any power that is bringing the fear of devil into my life, I decree against you, die forever and ever.

I decree that when the whole world is in trouble, the Lord will send His support to my life. Every attack coming into my life from water spirits, I command you to scatter and be disgraced. From now, I decree that no power from the waters will prevail over my life, in the name of Jesus. When all hopes are lost, my God shall support me and bless me before my enemies. As you blessed Joseph and prospered him before his enemies, O Lord, promote me beyond my imagination. As you supported the children of Israel and disgraced their Pharaoh, I decree that my Pharaoh will be disgraced now, in the name of Jesus. You are the God of the strangers, widows and the fatherless, I decree for your support and deliverance from my oppressors, in the name of Jesus.

> *"Thou shalt neither vex a stranger, nor oppress him: for ye were strangers in the land of Egypt. Ye shall not afflict any widow, or fatherless child. If thou afflict them in any wise, and they cry at all unto me, I will surely hear their cry; And my wrath shall wax hot, and I will kill you with the sword; and your wives shall be widows, and your children fatherless"* (Exodus 22:21-24).

I command all my oppressors to receive confusion, frustration and destruction immediately. Let the wrath of God fall upon my oppressors by force, whether they like it or not, in the name of Jesus.

DECREES FOR GOD'S SPIRIT AND SUPPORT

1. O Lord my God, support me in every situation, in the name of Jesus.

2. Let the host of heaven from God arise and fight for me to the end, in the name of Jesus.

3. I confront every problem in my life with the name of Jesus, in the name of Jesus.

4. Any power that wants to disgrace me, be disgraced by force, in the name of Jesus.

5. I shall arise and shine, whether devil likes it or not, in the name of Jesus.

6. I apply the blood of Jesus in every area of my life, in the name of Jesus.

7. O Lord, let Your power set me free from every evil arrest, in the name of Jesus.

8. Any power that wants me to suffer without help, die, in the name of Jesus.

9. O Lord, give me financial help that will kill poverty in my life forever, in the name of Jesus.

10. Every dream of helpless situation in my life, die, in the name of Jesus.

11. By the anointing that breaks every evil yoke, I break the yoke of suffering in my life, in the name of Jesus.

12. Every agent of sin, chasing away God from my life, die, in the name of Jesus.

13. O Lord, let my life attract divine favors, in the name of Jesus.

14. Angels of the living God, bring divine help into my destiny, in the name of Jesus.

15. Let tormentors of my life be tormented, in the name of Jesus.

16. Every demonic fear that is attacking my peace, be disgraced by God, in the name of Jesus.

17. O Lord, give me boldness to face every challenge, in the name of Jesus.

18. Anointing to withstand devil, possess me now, in the name of Jesus.

19. Let demonic nightmares that are tormenting my life disappear forever, in the name of Jesus.

20. Divine presence, locate me and abide with me forever, in the name of Jesus.

21. From today, I shall not lack divine support, in the name of Jesus.

22. Every enemy of my helpers, die, in the name of Jesus.

23. Every arrow of wickedness fired into my life, backfire, in the name of Jesus.

24. Every marine spirit deposit in my life, catch fire, in the name of Jesus.

25. Every evil decision against my breakthrough, be reversed, in the name of Jesus.

Go back to the words of decree and pass your decree again.

DECREE 17

AGAINST EVIL INHERITANCE

> "Christ hath redeemed us from the curse of the law, being made a curse for us: for it is written, Cursed is every one that hangeth on a tree: That the blessing of Abraham might come on the Gentiles through Jesus Christ; that we might receive the promise of the Spirit through faith" (Galatians 3:13-14).

The first sons of the Egyptians died because of evil inheritance, especially for the sins of their parents. The family of Achan was stoned because of the sin of their father, who stole an accursed thing. David's foundation was corrupted because of immoral spirit of his ancestors. David built an evil foundation of adultery that affected his children and destroyed Absalom, Tamar, Ammnon and Adonijah. Gehazi raised an evil foundation of leprosy in his generation.

> "But he went in, and stood before his master. And Elisha said unto him, whence comest thou, Gehazi? And he said, Thy servant went no whither. And he said unto him, Went not mine heart with thee, when the man turned again from his chariot to meet thee? Is it a time to receive money, and to receive garments, and

> *oliveyards, and vineyards, and sheep, and oxen, and menservants, and maidservants? The leprosy therefore of Naaman shall cleave unto thee and unto thy seed forever. And he went out from his presence a leper as white as snow"* (2 Kings 5:25-27).

Levi pioneered anger that prevented Moses from entering the Promised Land. Saul initiated evil in Israel and cries of blood caused a devastated famine in Israel and killed many innocent souls.

> *"Then there was a famine in the days of David three years, year after year; and David enquired of the LORD. And the LORD answered, It is for Saul, and for his bloody house, because he slew the Gibeonites"* (2 Samuel 21:1).

David decreed against the evil in Joab, the captain of the army in Israel. I decree against evils that prevailed in the time of my ancestors, predecessors, in the name of Jesus. Let any blood crying against my family line be silenced by the blood of Jesus. I stand against every evil inheritance and I decree that my family and I are guiltless before the Lord forever from the innocent bloodshed of the past that is crying against us, in the name of Jesus.

> *"And afterward when David heard it, he said, I and my kingdom are guiltless before the LORD for ever from the blood of Abner the son of Ner: Let it rest on the head of Joab, and on all his father's house; and let there not fail from the house of Joab one that hath an issue, or that is a leper, or that leaneth on a staff, or that falleth on the sword, or that lacketh bread"* (2 Samuel 3:28-29).

No power from the kingdom of darkness can attack me because of any blood that is crying in my foundation. I shall not suffer for the sins of anyone living or dead.

> *"Now there cried a certain woman of the wives of the sons of the prophets unto Elisha, saying, Thy servant my husband is dead; and thou knowest that thy servant did fear the LORD: and the creditor is come to take unto him my two sons to be bondmen"* (2 Kings 4:1).

You, wicked creditors, that is pursing me up and down to enslave me, die now, in the name of Jesus. Any visible and invisible creditor that has been assigned to destroy me, be destroyed without mercy. O Lord, arise and scatter every evil debt collector. I recover every good thing I have lost to evil creditors from my foundation double. I command fire to burn every yoke in my life, in Jesus name.

> *"Christ hath redeemed us from the curse of the law, being made a curse for us: for it is written, Cursed is every one that hangeth on a tree: That the blessing of Abraham might come on the Gentiles through Jesus Christ; that we might receive the promise of the Spirit through faith"* (Galatians 3:13-14).

Because of the redemption I have in Christ, no curse will work against me. I am no more under the law but under the grace. I decree for the manifestation of the blessings of Abraham upon my life now, in the name of Jesus.

> *"There is therefore now no condemnation to them which are in Christ Jesus, who walk not after the flesh, but after the Spirit"* (Romans 8:1).

I command every evil inherited problem from my father's house to depart from my life forever, in the name of Jesus.

DECREES AGAINST EVIL INHERITANCE

1. Any evil investment that is waiting to destroy my efforts, catch fire and burn to ashes, in the name of Jesus.

2. By the power in the blood of Jesus, I refuse to remain under the yoke of any evil, in the name of Jesus.

3. Father Lord, arise in Your power and deliver me from any evil investment, in the name of Jesus.

4. Let my life be available for all manners of miracles, in the name of Jesus.

5. Anointing that destroys the work of devil, fall upon me, in the name of Jesus.

6. Every serpent in my foundation, die, in the name of Jesus.

7. Every strange voice, speaking from my root, be silenced, in the name of Jesus.

8. I set all my ancestral garments ablaze, in the name of Jesus.

9. Any evil sacrifice that is offered against my destiny, expire, in the name of Jesus.

10. Every manifestation of my father's problem in my life, be frustrated, in the name of Jesus.

11. I command the fire of God to burn every evil bird against me, in the name of Jesus.

12. Let my ancestral strongman fall down and die, in the name of Jesus.

13. Every evil occurrence in my father's house, disappear from my life, in the name of Jesus.

14. Every evil covenant that is working against me, break by fire, in the name of Jesus.

15. Every problem that has been designed by household witchcraft, die, in the name of Jesus.

16. Father Lord, deliver me from sins of my ancestors, in the name of Jesus.

17. Let any evil thing planted into my life by evil powers of my father's house die, in the name of Jesus.

18. Let the Holy Ghost fire consume idols of my father's house, in the name of Jesus.

19. Any power, delegated by my father's idol to destroy me, die by fire, in the name of Jesus.

20. O Lord, recover every good thing that my ancestors have handed over to devil, in the name of Jesus.

21. Any spirit of failure that has been planted into my life, come out and die, in the name of Jesus.

22. Let the mighty power of God take me away from household bondage, in the name of Jesus.

23. Any ancestral power that is covering my glory, die by fire, in the name of Jesus.

24. Any evil priest that wants to disgrace me, be disgraced, in the name of Jesus.

25. Every Goliath of my destiny, assigned to waste me, be wasted, in the name of Jesus.

26. By the power in the blood of Jesus, I shall arise and shine, in the name of Jesus.

Go back to the words of decree and pass your decree again.

DECREE 18

FOR DIVINE INCREASE

"And Elisha came again to Gilgal: and there was a dearth in the land; and the sons of the prophets were sitting before him: and he said unto his servant, Set on the great pot, and seethe pottage for the sons of the prophets. And one went out into the field to gather herbs, and found a wild vine, and gathered thereof wild gourds his lap full, and came and shred them into the pot of pottage: for they knew them not. So they poured out for the men to eat. And it came to pass, as they were eating of the pottage, that they cried out, and said, O thou man of God, there is death in the pot. And they could not eat thereof. But he said, and then bring meal. And he cast it into the pot; and he said, Pour out for the people, that they may eat. And there was no harm in the pot. And there came a man from Baalshalisha, and brought the man of God bread of the first fruits, twenty loaves of barley, and full ears of corn in the husk thereof. And he said, Give unto the people that they may eat. And his servitor said, what, should I set this before an hundred men? He said again, Give the people that they may eat: for thus saith the LORD, They shall eat, and shall leave thereof. So he set it before them, and they did eat, and left thereof, according to the word of the LORD" (2 Kings 4:38-44).

I command every foul increase in my life to fall down and die, in the name of Jesus. Let divine increases manifest in my life by fire and by force. Every spirit of lack and poverty in my life, I command you to disappear and perish from my life forever and ever, in the name of Jesus. Blood of Jesus, appear and bring divine explosive increases to my life by fire. O Lord, let my life attract every manner of divine increase henceforth. Heavenly Father, arise and move my life forward for immediate promotion, in the name of Jesus. Father Lord, anoint me greatly for divine multiplication of Your blessings.

As you multiplied the oil of one of the wives of the sons of the prophet, I decree that every good thing in my life will be greatly multiplied by force, in the name of Jesus. Any demonic idol from my place of birth, which has vowed to waste my increase, shall be uprooted by thunder, in the name of Jesus.

Every agent of death that kills divine increases, die by force immediately. I command divine increase to begin to manifest in my life whether devil likes it or not, in the name of Jesus. Every door of increase closed against me, begin to open by force immediately. O Lord of divine increase, open the womb of my increase, in the name of Jesus. Blood of Jesus, arise and speak over flowing increase into my destiny by force. Father Lord, put Your divine fertilizer into the garden of my destiny for multiple divine increases. Anointing for plenty, what are you waiting for, manifest and rust into my life by force now.

> "And the LORD shall make thee plenteous in goods, in the fruit of thy body, and in the fruit of thy cattle, and in the fruit of thy ground, in the land which the LORD sware unto thy fathers to give thee. The LORD shall open unto thee his good treasure, the heaven to give the rain unto thy land in his season, and to bless all the

> work of thine hand: and thou shalt lend unto many nations, and thou shalt not borrow. And the LORD shall make thee the head, and not the tail; and thou shalt be above only, and thou shalt not be beneath; if that thou hearken unto the commandments of the LORD thy God, which I command thee this day, to observe and to do them" (Deuteronomy 28:11-13).

I command every part of my life to begin to bear fruits in seasons and out of seasons. My life, I command you, don't be fearful of the weather or situation of things, begin to bear fruits by force, in the name of Jesus. Let a divinely motivated production that will increase and explode beyond imagination start in my life, in the name of Jesus. You, treasures of heaven, why are you just watching, open up for my sake now by force. Let my increase move forward from nation to nation, place to place until my increase becomes an r explosive increase. O Lord, begin to enlarge my coast with all manner of blessings.

I decree the manifestation of the overflowing flood of the Almighty to appear in my life now. I decree blessings of the Lord to manifest in my life spiritually, physically, financially, materially, academically and mentally, in Jesus name.

> "And God blessed them, and God said unto them, Be fruitful, and multiply, and replenish the earth, and subdue it: and have dominion over the fish of the sea, and over the fowl of the air, and over every living thing that moveth upon the earth" (Genesis 1:28).

I command divine whirlwind to blow across the four corners of all creation to bring all my lost blessings back to me, in the name of Jesus.

DECREES FOR DIVINE INCREASE

1. I command the miracles of divine increase to manifest in my life now, in the name of Jesus.

2. Let my heavens open and let my testimonies increase by fire, in the name of Jesus.

3. Blood of Jesus, empower me to qualify for business breakthroughs, in the name of Jesus.

4. Let my life be available for all manner of miracles, in the name of Jesus.

5. Let the God that answers by fire be God in my life, in the name of Jesus.

6. O Lord, give me uncommon successes, in the name of Jesus.

7. Every yoke of poverty in my life, break by fire, in the name of Jesus.

8. Every blessing that will make me great, manifest in my life, in the name of Jesus.

9. The miracle that nobody has received before in my generation, O Lord give it to me, in the name of Jesus.

10. Every good thing in my life, increase, in the name of Jesus.

11. Father Lord, let Your power multiple Your divine favor in my life, in the name of Jesus.

12. Every little effort I put in my life to succeed, O Lord, increase it, in the name of Jesus.

13. Father Lord, increase the fruits of my labor, in the name of Jesus.

14. By the power in the Word of God, I receive every manner of increase, in the name of Jesus.

15. Lord Jesus, promote me to the highest level, in the name of Jesus.

16. O Lord, take me to Your desired end for my life, in the name of Jesus.

17. Every dream of increase in my life, manifest by fire, in the name of Jesus.

18. I bind and cast out of my life every evil spirit that is destroying my life, in the name of Jesus.

19. Every evil spirit decreasing blessings in my life, die, in the name of Jesus.

20. Let the hand of God begin to put good things into my life, in the name of Jesus.

21. Any power waiting to fight divine increase in my life, die, in the name of Jesus.

22. O God, arise and increase Your signs and wonders in my life, in the name of Jesus.

23. Anointing for financial increase in my life, fall upon me now, in the name of Jesus.

24. Any evil mouth that is swallowing good things in my life, close, in the name of Jesus.

25. Any power delegated to frustrate my efforts, die, in the name of Jesus.

26. I begin to receive the miracles of increase to the highest level, in the name of Jesus.

Go back to the words of decree and pass your decree again.

DECREE 19

AGAINST THE SPIRIT OF JEZEBEL

"And it came to pass, when King Hezekiah heard it, that he rent his clothes, and covered himself with sackcloth, and went into the house of the LORD. And he sent Eliakim, which was over the household, and Shebna the scribe, and the elders of the priests, covered with sackcloth, to Isaiah the prophet the son of Amoz. And they said unto him, thus saith Hezekiah, This day is a day of trouble, and of rebuke, and blasphemy: for the children are come to the birth, and there is not strength to bring forth. It may be the LORD thy God will hear all the words of Rabshakeh, whom the king of Assyria his master hath sent to reproach the living God; and will reprove the words which the LORD thy God hath heard: wherefore lift up thy prayer for the remnant that are left. So the servants of King Hezekiah came to Isaiah. And Isaiah said unto them, thus shall ye say to your master, thus saith the LORD, Be not afraid of the words which thou hast heard, with which the servants of the king of Assyria have blasphemed me. Behold, I will send a blast upon him, and he shall hear a rumor, and shall return to his own land; and I will cause him to fall by the sword in his own land. So Rabshakeh returned, and found the king of Assyria warring against Libnah: for he had heard that he was departed from Lachish. And when he heard say of Tirhakah king of Ethiopia, Behold, he is come out to fight against thee: he sent messengers again unto Hezekiah, saying, Thus shall ye speak to Hezekiah king of Judah, saying, Let

not thy God in whom thou trustest deceive thee, saying, Jerusalem shall not be delivered into the hand of the king of Assyria. Behold, thou hast heard what the kings of Assyria have done to all lands, by destroying them utterly: and shalt thou be delivered? Have the gods of the nations delivered them which my fathers have destroyed; as Gozan, and Haran, and Rezeph, and the children of Eden which were in Thelasar? Where is the king of Hamath, and the king of Arpad, and the king of the city of Sepharvaim, of Hena, and Ivah? And Hezekiah received the letter of the hand of the messengers, and read it: and Hezekiah went up into the house of the LORD, and spread it before the LORD. And Hezekiah prayed before the LORD, and said, O LORD God of Israel, which dwellest between the cherubims, thou art the God, even thou alone, of all the kingdoms of the earth; thou hast made heaven and earth" (2 Kings 19:1-15).

I issue an order against the spirit of Jezebel, assigned to overthrow my faith. In the anointed name of our Lord Jesus Christ of Nazareth, Father, I decree against every plan of Jezebel against my destiny. Every evil messenger from the office of Jezebel against my life, carry your message to your sender immediately. Every word of Jezebel, which is coated with fear and intimidation against my life, bounce back immediately.

You the god of Jezebel that has been invoked against my life, I command you to be incapacitated by fire. Let the speeches of Jezebel directed towards me be frustrated. O Lord my God, arise and manifest Your power in my life. Let evil gods of my Jezebel turn against her and render her actions against me useless. I command all weapons of Jezebel fashioned against me to be re-directed to her kingdom. Blood of Jesus, flow into my life and give me boldness against every conspiracy of Jezebel, in the name of Jesus.

> *"And Ahab told Jezebel all that Elijah had done, and withal how he had slain all the prophets with the sword. Then Jezebel sent a messenger unto Elijah, saying, so let the gods do to me, and more also, if I make not thy life as the life of one of them by to morrow about this time. And when he saw that, he arose, and went for his life, and came to Beersheba, which belongeth to Judah, and left his servant there"* (1 Kings 19:1-3).

Every evil arrow fired against me by Jezebel and her daughters, I fire you back immediately. I command all Jezebels to be afraid of me and run away from me unto their own destruction. Every property of Jezebel in my life, catch fire. Every messenger of Jezebel anointing with a vow unto death to pull me down, run mad and enter into the wilderness. Arrows of madness from the waters that wants me to commit suicide or get tired of life, be disgraced by fire. O Lord, empower me to rise and confront any spirit of Jezebel with boldness, in the name of Jesus.

> *"But he himself went a day's journey into the wilderness, and came and sat down under a juniper tree: and he requested for himself that he might die; and said, It is enough; now, O LORD, take away my life; for I am not better than my fathers. And as he lay and slept under a juniper tree, behold, then an angel touched him, and said unto him, arise and eat. And he looked, and, behold, there was a cake baken on the coals, and a cruse of water at his head. And he did eat and drink, and laid him down again. And the angel of the*

LORD came again the second time, and touched him, and said, Arise and eat; because the journey is too great for thee. And he arose, and did eat and drink, and went in the strength of that meat forty days and forty nights unto Horeb the mount of God" (1 Kings 19:4-8).

Let combined forces of Jezebel and Ahab, planning to eliminate my life, be disappointed. Every prophet of Baal that is being sponsored against my ministry, receive the judgment of death and die without mercy, in the name of Jesus.

"And they took the bullock which was given them, and they dressed it, and called on the name of Baal from morning even until noon, saying, O Baal, hear us. But there was no voice, nor any that answered. And they leaped upon the altar which was made. And it came to pass at noon, that Elijah mocked them, and said, Cry aloud: for he is a god; either he is talking, or he is pursuing, or he is in a journey, or peradventure he sleepeth, and must be awaked. And they cried aloud, and cut themselves after their manner with knives and lancets, till the blood gushed out upon them. And it came to pass, when midday was past, and they prophesied until the time of the offering of the evening sacrifice, that there was neither voice, nor any to answer, nor any that regarded" (1 Kings 18:26-29).

Any evil plan between Jezebel and others, assigned to waste any *Naboth* figure in my life, be exposed and be disgraced. Every evil stone that Jezebel and her agents are throwing at me shall backfire and kill them. Let all the sons of Belial and evil elders planning against me be aborted unto death. O Lord, arise and disgrace the nobles working with Jezebel against me. Any cosmetic Jezebel, painting her face to seduce me, you are finished, die immediately. Every Jezebel tying her head and looking at me from the window to seduce me, there is no peace for the wicked, I throw you down from the window; die in shame, in the name of Jesus.

> "And when Jehu was come to Jezreel, Jezebel heard of it; and she painted her face, and tired her head, and looked out at a window And as Jehu entered in at the gate, she said, Had Zimri peace, who slew his master? And he lifted up his face to the window, and said, who is on my side? who? And there looked out to him two or three eunuchs. And he said, Throw her down. So they threw her down: and some of her blood was sprinkled on the wall, and on the horses: and he trode her under foot. And when he was come in, he did eat and drink, and said, Go, see now this cursed woman, and bury her: for she is a king's daughter. And they went to bury her: but they found no more of her than the skull, and the feet, and the palms of her hands. Wherefore they came again, and told him. And he said, This is the word of the LORD, which he spake by his servant Elijah the Tishbite, saying, In the portion of Jezreel shall dogs eat the flesh of Jezebel: And the carcass of Jezebel shall be as dung upon the face of the field in the portion of Jezreel; so that they shall not say, This is Jezebel" (2 Kings 9:30-37).

Every uncompromising Jezebel that has been assigned to waste my destiny, you are finished, die, in the name of Jesus.

DECREES AGAINST THE SPIRIT OF JEZEBEL

1. Let the spirit of Jezebel in my life be cast out, in the name of Jesus.

2. Every influence of the spirit of Jezebel in my life, die by fire, in the name of Jesus.

3. Every covenant with the spirit of Jezebel in my life, break by fire, in the name of Jesus.

4. O Lord, deliver me from the control of the spirit of Jezebel, in the name of Jesus.

5. Every Jezebel spirit that is tormenting my life, come out and die, in the name of Jesus.

6. Let inherited evil foundation of the spirit of Jezebel be destroyed in my life, in the name of Jesus.

7. Any inherited evil partner that is assigned to waste my life, be wasted, in the name of Jesus.

8. I command all evil partners introduced in to my life by Jezebel to be destroyed, in the name of Jesus.

9. O Lord my God, arise and frustrate every work of Jezebel in my life, in the name of Jesus.

10. By the power in the blood of Jesus, I frustrate every work of Jezebel, in the name of Jesus.

11. Every serpentine poison in my life, dry up by fire, in the name of Jesus.

12. Let the yoke of Jezebel in my life break by fire, in the name of Jesus.

13. Any Jezebel that has married me in the spirit, I break your marriage; die, in the name of Jesus.

14. Every stubborn yoke of Jezebel in my life, break by fire, in the name of Jesus.

15. Let the messengers of Jezebel against me be disgraced, in the name of Jesus.

16. Every Jezebel assigned to disgrace me, fail woefully and be disgraced, in the name of Jesus.

17. Every curse placed upon my life by the sprit of Jezebel, die, in the name of Jesus.

18. Any strongman from my father's altar, die, in the name of Jesus.

19. Any power that wants me to die in the hand of Jezebel, die, in the name of Jesus.

20. I declare and decree against the Jezebel of my destiny, in the name of Jesus.

21. Let the grave dug against me by the spirit of Jezebel bury her, in the name of Jesus.

22. O Lord, give me power to prevail over the spirit of Jezebel, in the name of Jesus.

23. I break and loose myself from the spirit of Jezebel, in the name of Jesus.

24. Every messenger of death from Jezebel, carry your message to your sender, in the name of Jesus.

25. Blood of Jesus, speak death to Jezebel's daughters, in the name of Jesus.

Go back to the words of decree and pass your decree again.

DECREE 20

FOR UNCOMMON FAVOR AND PROMOTION

"The LORD shall open unto thee his good treasure, the heaven to give the rain unto thy land in his season, and to bless all the work of thine hand: and thou shalt lend unto many nations, and thou shalt not borrow" (Deuteronomy 28:12).

Every evil spirit against uncommon promotion of my destiny and delaying my promotion, fall down and die, in the name of Jesus. Let my God who never fails arise and fight for my divine promotion and uncommon success. I receive every manner of uncommon successes, in the name of Jesus.

> "A Psalm of David. The earth is the LORD'S, and the fulness thereof; the world, and they that dwell therein" (Psalms 24:1).

I decree with the power that formed the whole world that I must be promoted beyond human imagination as never before, in the name of Jesus. I stand against any power from the waters assigned to frustrate my promotion. Father Lord, give me divine and multiple blessings from Your throne in heaven, in the name of Jesus.

> "Beloved, I wish above all things that thou mayest prosper and be in health, even as thy soul prospereth" (3 John 1:2).

I decree that my prosperity shall be boundless -north, south, east and west. Every demonic power standing against my immediate promotion, I send shock and death to visit you immediate. Powers assigned to delay my uncommon and supernatural breakthroughs, fall down and die by force, in the name of Jesus.

Father Lord, with holy determination, open unto me Your good treasure in heaven and on earth to release unto me great blessings in seasons and out of seasons. I decree that the work of my hand shall be mightily and miraculously blessed. Let my coast be enlarged and extended unto all nations of the world. My promotion will disgrace poverty and lack, but it shall enable me to lend to many nations without borrowing at all. Blood of Jesus, take me up to the topmost ladder of life and keep me blessed, in the name of Jesus.

> "The LORD shall open unto thee his good treasure, the heaven to give the rain unto thy land in his season, and

to bless all the work of thine hand: and thou shalt lend unto many nations, and thou shalt not borrow" (Deuteronomy 28:12).

I command immediate frustration against the spirit of poverty in my life. All the witchcraft powers assigned to delay my promotion shall be frustrated by force, in the name of Jesus. O Lord, by Your power of creation, create an uncommon and unmerited opportunities for me, in the name of Jesus. My promotion shall embrace internal and external promotion from now. Any witchcraft agent assigned to demote me, be demoted and be eliminated by force in the name of Jesus. With the destroying weapons of God, I destroy every power that is against my uncommon elevation by force, in the name of Jesus.

Every marine spirit altar that has received any sacrifice to work against any area of my life, be scattered by thunder fire of God, in the name of Jesus. I break every protocol standing against my uncommon promotion, in the name of Jesus.

I command all the true angels of God to arise and fight for my uncommon miracles, signs and wonders. I decree against the spirit of the tail in agreement to bring me backward for the enemy to rejoice over me. O Lord, let Your promotion in life elevate me to the top and keep me above all my equals. I command the morning to shake off every wickedness in it and usher in my uncommon and unmerited advancement. Every curse assigned to rob me of my uncommon success, fall down and die, in the name of Jesus.

Every covenant against uncommon breakthrough in my life, break and release me by force. I decree death over spirits that are in the waters with a vow to render me poor and wretched, in the name of Jesus.

DECREES FOR UNCOMMON PROMOTION

1. Heavenly Father, arise in Your power and assist me for uncommon breakthroughs, in the name of Jesus.

2. Every demonic gathering against my elevation, scatter by fire, in the name of Jesus.

3. I command the strongman blocking my uncommon elevation to be cleared, in the name of Jesus.

4. Let the power of the Holy Spirit take me to the mountain of my success, in the name of Jesus.

5. Every spiritual and physical hindrance to my breakthrough, scatter by fire, in the name of Jesus.

6. O Lord, arise and promote me above all my equals in the office, in the name of Jesus.

7. Spirit of the living God, take me to a place of unmerited favor of God, in the name of Jesus.

8. Angels of God, be loosed for my mighty victory, in the name of Jesus.

9. Every hindrance to my greatness, be violently removed by the wind of God, in the name of Jesus.

10. Any power assigned to destroy my efforts, be rendered impotent by force, in the name of Jesus.

11. Every evil power fighting against my breakthrough, die immediately, in the name of Jesus.

12. Any satanic angel that is assigned to destroy my promotion, be disgraced, in the name of Jesus.

13. O Lord my God, prepare me for special breakthrough, in the name of Jesus.

14. Let the peace of my enemies be destroyed by the news of my uncommon success, in the name of Jesus.

15. O Lord, teach me how to make wealth and remain strong in You, in the name of Jesus.

16. Every secret of uncommon elevation, be revealed to me, in the name of Jesus.

17. Father Lord, let my life magnetize every manner of success, in the name of Jesus.

18. I disband every association that is fighting against my promotion, in the name of Jesus.

19. I receive promotion and victory over all the forces of darkness, in the name of Jesus.

20. Every enemy of my progress and elevation, scatter in shame, in the name of Jesus.

21. Every demonic delay to my promotion, be cancelled by fire, in the name of Jesus.

22. Blood of Jesus, destroy every evil force gathered against my greatness in life, in the name of Jesus.

23. O God that answers by fire, answer me with great promotion, in the name of Jesus.

24. I receive divine mandate for uncommon promotion by fire, in the name of Jesus.

25. Let the power of God destroy every evil record against my advancement, in the name of Jesus.

26. Heavenly Father, by Your anointing, catapult me into Your great blessings, in the name of Jesus.

27. Every strong man that is delegated to torment my life with poverty, fall down and die, in the name of Jesus.

28. O Lord, by Your strong hand, change my situation to the best, in the name of Jesus.

29. Any ready-made devourer that is assigned to devour my promotion and greatness, die, in the name of Jesus.

Go back to the words of decree and pass your decree again.

DECREE 21

TO ENTER THE THIRD HEAVEN

> *"And it came to pass, that in the fifth year of king Rehoboam Shishak king of Egypt came up against Jerusalem, because they had transgressed against the LORD, With twelve hundred chariots, and threescore thousand horsemen: and the people were without number that came with him out of Egypt; the Lubims, the Sukkiims, and the Ethiopians. And he took the fenced cities which pertained to Judah, and came to Jerusalem"* (2 Corinthians 12:2-4).

I command every evil spirit fighting against heaven in my life to come out and die, in the name of Jesus. I decree death to powers assigned to block my vision of heaven. O Lord, arise and take me to heaven and show me great and mighty things. Let the power of the Almighty possess me and cause me to be heavenly minded by fire.

Let the power to be caught up to heaven possess me and carry me to the third heaven. I command the heavenly messengers that can enter into the third heaven without negotiation, to conduct me round in the paradise. I decree that while I am still on this earth by the power of God, I would be visiting the third heaven. Any power on earth, waters, first and second heaven that is blocking my vision into heaven, I command you to fall down and die. Every satanic roadblock that has been mounted against me in the heavenlies, be violently scattered by thunder fire of God.

Let the angels of God make way for my prayers to reach the third heaven by force. Any stain in my life that is preventing me from visiting the third heaven at will, be washed by the blood of Jesus. Any power that banishes people out of heaven, I am not your candidate, release me by force. Any sin in my past, present and future that is under a vow to block my vision into the third heaven, catch fire and burn to ashes. I refuse to be banished out of heaven by any power of devil. I decree immediately that my prayers will begin to enter into heaven to visit places in paradise. Let my prayers take me to the rivers of the water of life. I command my prayers and vision of God to take me to the tree of life yielding different types of fruits each month, in the name of Jesus.

> *"And he shewed me a pure river of water of life, clear as crystal, proceeding out of the throne of God and of the Lamb. In the midst of the street of it, and on either side of the river, was there the tree of life, which bare twelve manner of fruits, and yielded her fruit every month: and the leaves of the tree were for the healing of the nations. And there shall be no more curse: but the throne of God and of the Lamb shall be in it; and his servants shall serve him: And they shall see his face; and his name shall be in their foreheads. And there shall be no night there; and they need no candle, neither light of the sun; for the Lord God giveth them light: and they shall reign for ever and ever"* (Revelation 22:1-5).

In my dreams, I enter into the third heaven. In my prayers, I enter into the third heaven. In my praising God, I enter into the third heaven and I begin to eat the leaves and drink the water of life. As I enter heaven with my prayers, let my life be sanctified, empowered, delivered and my joy, health and peace be promoted as if am already eternally in heaven.

> *"They shall hunger no more, neither thirst any more; neither shall the sun light on them, nor any heat. For the Lamb which is in the midst of the throne shall feed them, and shall lead them unto living fountains of waters: and God shall wipe away all tears from their eyes"* (Revelation 7:16-17).

I decree by the mercy of God that I shall be extremely holy at the point of death or rapture, in the name of Jesus.

DECREES TO ENTER THE THIRD HEAVEN

1. You my heavens, be opened now by heavenly blast, in the name of Jesus.

2. I command destruction and paralysis on every satanic angel contending with my angels of blessing, in the name of Jesus.

3. You my third heaven, open for me by fire, in the name of Jesus.

4. Blood of Jesus, accompany me to the third heaven without any hindrance, in the name of Jesus.

5. O Lord my God, rend my heavens open, in the name of Jesus.

6. Divine whirlwind from above, arise and make a way for me into the third heaven, in the name of Jesus.

7. Every marine spirit hindrance against my visit to heaven, be removed, in the name of Jesus.

8. I command my heavens to open for multiple breakthroughs, in the name of Jesus.

9. Let there be a release of divine favor into my life from the heavens, in the name of Jesus.

10. I receive power from heaven to do exploitation for my God, in the name of Jesus.

11. No power will hinder my prayers from today in the heavenlies, in the name of Jesus.

12. By the mercy of God, I receive direct promotion from the third heavens, in the name of Jesus.

13. Every breakthrough meant for me that has been confiscated in the heavenlies, I receive you, in the name of Jesus.

14. Let my financial breakthroughs come down from the heavenly bank, in the name of Jesus.

15. Every enemy of my good health, stationed in the heavens, die, in the name of Jesus.

16. Blood of Jesus, arise and flow into my mind and heal me, in the name of Jesus.

17. Great God of heaven, send Your peace into my life from the third heaven, in the name of Jesus.

18. Every spirit from the dark world blocking my heaven, clear away, in the name of Jesus.

19. Let the curses in my life be frustrated by the power of God, in the name of Jesus.

20. O Lord, empower me to enter into the third heaven with my prayers at will, in the name of Jesus.

21. Blood of Jesus, in my dreams, take me to the third heavens, in the name of Jesus.

22. Father Lord, show me the vision of the third heaven, in the name of Jesus.

23. Any power that does not allow me to enter into the third heaven in the spirit shall die, in the name of Jesus.

24. Lord Jesus, prepare me every moment for the rapture, in the name of Jesus.

25. Any sin that is attacking my progress in life, die by fire, in the name of Jesus.

26. Let the mercy of God accompany my progress to heaven by fire, in the name of Jesus.

27. Any altar of my father's house that is crying against me, be silenced by fire, in the name of Jesus.

28. Angels of the living God, arise and make a way for me into the third heaven, in the name of Jesus.

Go back to the words of decree and pass your decree again.

DECREE 22

FOR DIVINE OPPORTUNITIES

> *"Therefore thy gates shall be open continually; they shall not be shut day nor night; that men may bring unto thee the forces of the Gentiles, and that their kings may be brought"* (Isaiah 60:11)

> *"For brass I will bring gold, and for iron I will bring silver, and for wood brass, and for stones iron: I will also make thy officers peace, and thine exactor's righteousness"* (Isaiah 60:17).

As Noah was promoted and delivered by divine opportunities, I decree that divine opportunities will never elude me, in the name of Jesus. I decree that as Joseph was given the grace to prosper in all that he laid his hands upon to do, I will be opportune to prosper in the way of God also. Let the power of God that helped Jacob to pray all night and he was blessed and his name was changed possess me now. Any opportunity to say no to sin like Joseph did in the bible, O Lord, give me the grace. I decree to use every divine opportunity to the glory of God. In every divine opportunity, I shall be faithful even in hard times, faithful in times of temptation, faithful to my God in times of godliness and sudden prosperity and promotion.

I decree that I shall please God in any given opportunity no matter the situation or the circumstances around me. I command my body, soul and spirit to completely and perfectly surrender to God in any given opportunity favorably or unfavorably.

"And it came to pass after these things, that his master's wife cast her eyes upon Joseph; and she said, lie with me. But he refused, and said unto his master's wife, Behold, my master wotteth not what is with me in the house, and he hath committed all that he hath to my hand; There is none greater in this house than I; neither hath he kept back any thing from me but thee, because thou art his wife: how then can I do this great wickedness, and sin against God? And it came to pass, as she spake to Joseph day by day that he hearkened not unto her, to lie by her, or to be with her. And it came to pass about this time that Joseph went into the house to do his business; and there was none of the men of the house there within. And she caught him by his garment, saying, lie with me: and he left his garment in her hand, and fled, and got him out. And it came to pass, when she saw that he had left his garment in her hand, and was fled forth" (Genesis 39:7-13, 29).

O Lord, give me the power to be faithful in every opportunity I find myself from today. Blood of Jesus, empower me to come out a better person in every situation I find myself. I decree that the opportunity to be great will be opened unto me. Let the anointing to utilize divine opportunities well fall upon me by force. I receive divine support to be promoted after any trials and tests in life. Heavenly Father, advertise Your divine opportunities in my life.

"Therefore thy gates shall be open continually; they shall not be shut day nor night; that men may bring unto thee the forces of the Gentiles, and that their kings may be brought" (Isaiah 60:11)

> *"For brass I will bring gold, and for iron I will bring silver, and for wood brass, and for stones iron: I will also make thy officers peace, and thine exactors' righteousness"* (Isaiah 60:17).

Any gate that is opened for my sake, negatively or positively as an opportunity, O Lord, use it to make me better and great. I command that every plan of the enemy in my life shall be turned to my goodness. No matter what the enemy has in mind against me, I decree that his plans shall be opportunities for me to be greatly promoted, in the name of Jesus. I decree that every negative plan of devil and other dark powers shall end to my great favor.

Blood of Jesus, create an opportunity that will advertise me and make me a better Christian. I decree that my God will be impressed in my affairs and greatly promote me and keep me holy in everything I do henceforth. I command by the decrees of God that divine opportunities will begin to manifest for my sake, in the name of Jesus.

DECREES FOR DIVINE OPPORTUNITIES

1. By divine revelations, I receive divine opportunities by fire, in the name of Jesus.

2. Heavenly Father, take me to my promised land, and establish me in Your power, in the name of Jesus.

3. Holy Spirit, open my eyes to see Your blessings around me, in the name of Jesus.

4. Any power that has vowed to waste me before my enemies, die by fire, in the name of Jesus.

5. Heavenly Father, take me to where I can survive easily, in the name of Jesus.

6. Lord Jesus, create great opportunities to make me rich, in the name of Jesus.

7. O God my Father, take me to where You want me to be, in the name of Jesus.

8. Every strongman in my family that has been assigned to block my progresses, die, in the name of Jesus.

9. Any foundational mistake that is destroying my family members, be wasted, in the name of Jesus.

10. Lord Jesus, guide me into Your rest and prosperity, in the name of Jesus.

11. Anointing for great miracles, signs and wonders, fall upon me, in the name of Jesus.

12. I stand against every evil host assigned to frustrate my destiny, in the name of Jesus.

13. O Lord my God, give me divine wisdom for new breakthrough, in the name of Jesus.

14. Father Lord, prevent me from walking away from my helpers, in the name of Jesus.

15. Lord Jesus, give me the power to create opportunities for myself, in the name of Jesus.

16. Any spiritual cataract in my eyes, catch the Holy Ghost fire, in the name of Jesus.

17. O Lord, deliver me from yokes of evil limitations, in the name of Jesus.

18. Angels of the living God, walk me into the city of divine opportunities, in the name of Jesus.

19. Let my life be revived against every evil weapon of darkness, in the name of Jesus.

20. Let the wind of the Holy Ghost take me away from here to my divine opportunities, in the name of Jesus.

21. Every evil gang-up standing against my destiny, scatter by fire, in the name of Jesus.

22. O Lord, give me sharp spiritual eyes to see great opportunities, in the name of Jesus.

23. Let the glory of God begin to manifest in my life by fire, in the name of Jesus.

24. Every enemy of divine opportunities, die, in the name of Jesus.

25. I destabilize every organized power against my destiny, in the name of Jesus.

26. Every satanic agent, hired against my moving forward, die and be disgraced, in the name of Jesus.

27. O Lord, empower me for divine opportunities, in the name of Jesus.

Go back to the words of decree and pass your decree again.

DECREE 23

AGAINST LITTLE FOXES

"Wherefore, my beloved, as ye have always obeyed, not as in my presence only, but now much more in my absence, work out your own salvation with fear and trembling" (Philippians 2:12).

Let little foxes that rob people of their blessings in life die, in the name of year. I decree against little foxes that drove Adam and Eve out of paradise, and is now working against me to catch fire and burn to ashes.

I decree against little lies and fear that took Abraham to Egypt, and that is now working in my life to come out and die, in the name of Jesus. Let the powers of strife, walking by sight, impatience and disobedience that have entered into my life as little foxes in order to destroy me be cast out and consumed by fire. I command the powers that entered into Esau as a little fox and caused him to despise his birthright, which is also working in my life now to come out, fall down and die.

You, evil spirits of envy, hatred, lies, conspiracy, subtlety, cheating and idolatry that enter into peoples' lives as little foxes and destroy them unawares, shall not destroy me. Let all that is not godly and are pretending to be harmless in my life come out and die immediately.

Let any offence in the house of God that is pretending to be harmless be exposed and disgraced forever in my life.

> *"Moreover if thy brother shall trespass against thee, go and tell him his fault between thee and him alone: if he shall hear thee, thou hast gained thy brother. But if he will not hear thee, then take with thee one or two more, that in the mouth of two or three witnesses every word may be established. And if he shall neglect to hear them, tell it unto the church: but if he neglect to hear the church, let him be unto thee as an heathen man and a publican"* (Matthew 18:15-17).

Any acts of worldliness in conversation, adornment, dressing, worldly cares, imitations, ambition, pleasures, enjoyment, dancing, etc., that have entered into my life as little foxes to waste my life, be wasted by fire.

I stand and decree against unfriendly friends in my life to be exposed and disgraced. All you little things that look harmless but they are very destructive to my soul, receive death by force. Every unrepentant character that people call greatness and discipline in my life, catch fire and burn to ashes now. Any little thing in my life that wants to banish me from entering heaven, be roasted by fire. Blood of Jesus, flow into my life and destroy sinful nicknames and demonic thoughts in my heart. Any little fox that appears as a friend but is worldly, satanic and false, be exposed as an enemy and die.

> *"But the fearful, and unbelieving, and the abominable and murderers and whoremongers and sorcerers, and idolaters, and all liars, shall have their part in the lake which burneth with fire and brimstone: which is the second death"* (Revelation 21:8).

I command fear, unbelief, immorality, sorcery spirits, witchcrafts, and other sins nicknamed in my life in order to appear harmless to die now.

> *"Now the works of the flesh are manifest, which are these; Adultery, fornication, uncleanness, lasciviousness, Idolatry, witchcraft, hatred, variance, emulations, wrath, strife, seditions, heresies, Envying, murders, drunkenness, reveling, and such like: of the which I tell you before, as I have also told you in time past, that they which do such things shall not inherit the kingdom of God"* (Galatians 5:19-21).

I release the fire of God and destruction against all little foxes in my life, in the name of Jesus.

DECREES AGAINST LITTLE FOXES

1. Any spiritual bad leg that has walked into my life, walk out by fire, in the name of Jesus.

2. Let the burning fire of the living God consume every evil fire in my life, in the name of Jesus.

3. Any spirit of pretence, assigned to waste me, be wasted, in the name of Jesus.

4. Let the spirit of disobedience that the enemy is using to torment my life die, in the name of Jesus.

5. The lying spirit that looks smart in my life, that is about to waste my life, die, in the name of Jesus.

6. Every spirit of hatred in my life, come out and die, in the name of Jesus.

7. Foundational angry spirits, assigned to keep me out of blessings, die, in the name of Jesus.

8. Let demons of corruption in my life be roasted by fire, in the name of Jesus.

9. Every enemy of peace in my life, come out and die, in the name of Jesus.

10. Any power that keeps me out of God's plan, die by fire, in the name of Jesus.

11. Let evil spirit of conspiracies that look friendly but are about to destroy me die, in the name of Jesus.

12. Any power that is causing me to despise my birthright, be destroyed, in the name of Jesus.

13. Any power, pushing me to covet evil things, be paralyzed, in the name of Jesus.

14. Every spirits of wickedness that are on mission to destroy me and others, come out and die, in the name of Jesus.

15. Let the power that is making me to be wasting my life be wasted, in the name of Jesus.

16. Every seed of impatience, planted to waste my life, be wasted, in the name of Jesus.

17. Any root of strife in my life, be violently uprooted, in the name of Jesus.

18. Every agent of subtilty in my life, I reject your advances, in the name of Jesus.

19. Let the powers of defilement in my life catch the Holy Ghost fire, in the name of Jesus.

20. Every power of immorality that has been assigned to disgrace me at appointed time, die, in the name of Jesus.

21. Any power in me keeping others in bondage, come out and die, in the name of Jesus.

22. Let blasphemous spirits living inside of me be consumed by fire, in the name of Jesus.

23. Any witchcraft spirit that has possessed me unawares, receive death, in the name of Jesus.

24. Let demons of discouragement that are assigned to separate me from God die, in the name of Jesus.

25. Any power, keeping me in an evil agreement with sinners or so-called saints, die, in the name of Jesus.

Go back to the words of decree and pass your decree again.

DECREE 24

AGAINST MAMMON

> *"For the love of money is the root of all evil: which while some coveted after, they have erred from the faith, and pierced themselves through with many sorrows"* (1 Timothy 6:10).

I decree against the spirit of mammon in my destiny and I command it to be roasted by the fire of God.

> *"Thou shalt have no other gods before me. Thou shalt not make unto thee any graven image, or any likeness of any thing that is in heaven above, or that is in the earth beneath, or that is in the water under the earth: Thou shalt not bow down thyself to them, nor serve them: for I the LORD thy God am a jealous God, visiting the iniquity of the fathers upon the children unto the third and fourth generation of them that hate me"* (Exodus 20:3-5).

Every other god in my life that refuses to let me go, catch fire and burn to ashes. Let evil gods standing between me and God be pulled down and destroyed, in the name of Jesus. Let all gods that were inherited from my ancestors be rejected completely. Let these useless gods that did not create the heaven and the earth be universally rejected and abandoned. I decree against the spirit of mammon that has taken over my life, in the name of Jesus. Every root of love of money in my life, be uprooted, destroyed and burnt by the judgment fire of God, in the name of Jesus. Every evil that is deeply rooted in my life because of love of money, dry up and be destroyed by fire and force. Blood of Jesus, open your mouth and decree against the root of the love of money in my life. I command my life to be perfectly delivered from every manner of evil, in the name of Jesus.

> *"For the love of money is the root of all evil: which while some coveted after, they have erred from the faith, and pierced themselves through with many sorrows"* (1 Timothy 6:10).

Let the love of money and glory in my life be overthrown by the power of God immediately, in the name of Jesus. I decree against any symbol that stands as god and I command it to catch fire and burn to ashes, in the name of Jesus. Every external and internal idolatry being worshipped in this area, I set you ablaze and I command men to abandon you. Any power that is influencing me to lay my treasures upon this earth without considering God first, I decree against you, die, in the name of Jesus. I command my labor to be more heavenly than earthly, in the name of Jesus. You my heart, arise out of the earth and focus on heavenly things from today.

> *"Lay not up for yourselves treasures upon earth, where moth and rust doth corrupt, and where thieves break through and steal: But lay up for yourselves treasures in heaven, where neither moth nor rust doth corrupt, and where thieves do not break through nor steal: For where your treasure is, there will your heart be also"* (Matthew 6:19-21).

I decree against the god of mammon in my life, I cast you out of my life, come out and die by fire, let that power that wants me to serve two masters be disgraced out of my destiny by force. I command my love for money to be terminated. Father Lord, increase my faith to believe and trust in You alone forever.

> "No man can serve two masters: for either he will hate the one, and love the other; or else he will hold to the one, and despise the other. Ye cannot serve God and mammon. Therefore I say unto you, Take no thought for your life, what ye shall eat, or what ye shall drink; nor yet for your body, what ye shall put on. Is not the life more than meat, and the body than raiment? Behold the fowls of the air: for they sow not, neither do they reap, nor gather into barns; yet your heavenly Father feedeth them. Are ye not much better than they? Which of you by taking thought can add one cubit unto his stature? And why take ye thought for raiment? Consider the lilies of the field, how they grow; they toil not, neither do they spin: And yet I say unto you, That even Solomon in all his glory was not arrayed like one of these. Wherefore, if God so clothe the grass of the field, which to day is, and to morrow is cast into the oven, shall he not much more clothe you, O ye of little faith? Therefore take no thought, saying, what shall we eat? or, what shall we drink? or, Wherewithal shall we be clothed? (For after all these things do the Gentiles seek:) for your heavenly Father knoweth that ye have need of all these things. But seek ye first the kingdom of God, and his righteousness; and all these things shall be added unto you" (Matthew 6:24-33).

From henceforth, I shall spend my time, resources, and energy serving God instead of acquiring evil wealth and loving money, in the name of Jesus. I command the seed of the love of money in my life to wither and die by force, in the name of Jesus.

> *"And he said unto them, Take heed, and beware of covetousness: for a man's life consisteth not in the abundance of the things which he possesseth. And he spake a parable unto them, saying, the ground of a certain rich man brought forth plentifully: And he thought within himself, saying, what shall I do, because I have no room where to bestow my fruits? And he said, this will I do: I will pull down my barns, and build greater; and there will I bestow all my fruits and my goods. And I will say to my soul, Soul, thou hast much goods laid up for many years; take thine ease, eat, drink, and be merry. But God said unto him, Thou fool, this night thy soul shall be required of thee: then whose shall those things be, which thou hast provided? So is he that layeth up treasure for himself, and is not rich toward God"* (Luke 12:15-21).

I decree against the spirit of covetousness, idolatry, banqueting and demonic pleasures to come out of my life and die by fire. Let the god of pleasure, evil entertainment and all manner of worldliness fizzle out of my life by fire, in the name of Jesus.

> *"This know also, that in the last days perilous times shall come. For men shall be lovers of their own selves, covetous, boasters, proud, blasphemers, disobedient to parents, unthankful, unholy"* (2 Timothy 3:1-2).

I decree against the spirit of mammon, possession, people, pride, plenty and pleasures in my life to come out and die.

DECREES AGAINST THE GOD OF GOLD

1. Let the spirit of mammon that was assigned to drag me to shame be disappointed by fire, in the name of Jesus.

2. O Lord, deliver me from covetousness and sensuality, in the name of Jesus.

3. Let the power that influences me to admire money above God die, in the name of Jesus.

4. Father Lord, deliver me from all manners of evil wealth, in the name of Jesus.

5. Any power that wants me to spend more time acquiring wealth than worshipping God, die, in the name of Jesus.

6. You my strength, you shall not be wasted in serving idols, in the name of Jesus.

7. Resources of this world will not keep me busy for nothing, in the name of Jesus.

8. Any power keeping me away from God to acquire possessions, die, in the name of Jesus.

9. Let the love of the things of this world more than the things of God die by fire, in the name of Jesus.

10. I refuse to dedicate my time for making money without God, in the name of Jesus.

11. The worldly wealth will not take me away from heavenly things, in the name of Jesus.

12. Let the demonic spirit of worldly abundance in me come out and die, in the name of Jesus.

13. Every spirit of ego that has dragged me away from God, die, in the name of Jesus.

14. Power that causes me to remain selfish because of money, die, in the name of Jesus.

15. Let the love of money spirit that is blocking me from loving God die by fire, in the name of Jesus.

16. Any power that is taking me from place to place to make evil money, die, in the name of Jesus.

17. Let every demon conscious of my personality be disgrace by fire, in the name of Jesus.

18. Let the spirit of worldly enjoyment in my life be cast out, in the name of Jesus.

19. Let that demon of evil entertainment in my life die, in the name of Jesus.

20. You, evil powers that influences me to seek evil pleasures at all cost, die, in the name of Jesus.

21. Let the power of the love of pleasure more than God release me and die, in the name of Jesus.

22. Let the root of the love of money in my life be uprooted, in the name of Jesus.

23. O Lord, arise in Your power and deliver me from the love of money, in the name of Jesus.

24. Every evil that the love of money has done in my life, die, in the name of Jesus.

25. Father Lord, let me love You above all things, in the name of Jesus.

Go back to the words of decree and pass your decree again.

DECREE 25

AGAINST EVIL GROUPS

"Now Korah, the son of Izhar, the son of Koath, the son of Levi, and Dathan and Abiram, the sons of Eliab, and On, the son of Peleth, sons of Reuben, took men: And they rose up before Moses, with certain of the children of Israel, two hundred and fifty princes of the assembly, famous in the congregation, men of renown: And they gathered themselves together against Moses and against Aaron, and said unto them, Ye take too much upon you, seeing all the congregation are holy, every one of them, and the LORD is among them: wherefore then lift ye up yourselves above the congregation of the LORD?" (Numbers 16:1-3).

By faith in the Word of God, I decree against evil groups that are gathering against me. Let the power in the Word of God frustrate every satanic gang-up against my destiny. Blood of Jesus, flow into the camp of every evil group that has gathered against me, in the name of Jesus.

I decree against evil gang-ups against my life and I command them all to scatter by fire now. I separate myself from among the people who are gathering against God. O Lord, before You consume any evil congregation who are gathered against You, deliver me from their midst.

> *"And Korah gathered the entire congregation against them unto the door of the tabernacle of the congregation: and the glory of the LORD appeared unto the entire congregation. And the LORD spake unto Moses and unto Aaron, saying, Separate yourselves from among this congregation, that I may consume them in a moment"* (Numbers 16:19-21).

I decree that the grace of God will appear unto all His children to depart from the midst of evil people, who are gathering against God's constituted authorities, in the name of Jesus. Let divine earthquake rend the tent of wicked people gathering against God now. I decree that the leaders of evil gatherings shall not die a common death, but they shall die in shame. Let their visitation be disastrous and destructive, in the name of Jesus. I command the earth to open her mouth and swallow them up. I open the pit and command all evil gangs to enter into it with all their properties, in the name of Jesus. You, the ground where evil gangs are standing, obey God, cleave asunder and swallow them immediately, in the name of Jesus.

> *"And it came to pass, as he had made an end of speaking all these words, that the ground clave asunder that was under them: And the earth opened her mouth,*

and swallowed them up, and their houses, and all the men that appertained unto Korah, and all their goods. They, and all that appertained to them, went down alive into the pit, and the earth closed upon them: and they perished from among the congregation" (Numbers 16:31-33).

Let the judgment fire of God appear and burn every supporter of evil gangs wherever they are. Blood of Jesus, pursue every enemy of unity in the house of God with your anger and judgment, in the name of Jesus.

"And Moses was very wroth, and said unto the LORD, Respect not thou their offering: I have not taken one ass from them, neither have I hurt one of them" (Numbers 16:15).

"Now they that died in the plague were fourteen thousand and seven hundred, beside them that died about the matter of Korah" (Numbers 16:49).

Any evil gathering, speaking against God, be silenced by the judgment of God. Heavenly Father, arise and destroy the power of gossip in the body of Christ. I stand against every evil power that has vowed to frustrate peace in this church. Any evil plan, to discourage the move of God in this fellowship, scatter by thunder, in the name of Jesus.

"And the entire congregation lifted up their voice, and cried; and the people wept that night. And all the children of Israel murmured against Moses and against Aaron: and the whole congregation said unto them, Would God that we had died in the land of Egypt! Or would God we had died in this wilderness! And wherefore hath the LORD brought us unto this land, to

fall by the sword, that our wives and our children should be a prey? were it not better for us to return into Egypt? And they said one to another, Let us make a captain, and let us return into Egypt" (Numbers 14:1-4).

Let any evil group planning against my journey into the promise land of God, be put to shame, scatter and be disgraced. Let the anger of God be kindled against those opposing God's plan for His people. Every occult gathering in any evil altar, catch fire and be destroyed. Any evil sacrifice going on now against God and His children, be put to shame immediately.

"And when the people complained, it displeased the LORD: and the LORD heard it; and his anger was kindled; and the fire of the LORD burnt among them, and consumed them that were in the uttermost parts of the camp. And the people cried unto Moses; and when Moses prayed unto the LORD, the fire was quenched. And he called the name of the place Taberah: because the fire of the LORD burnt among them. And the mixt multitude that was among them fell a lusting: and the children of Israel also wept again, and said, who shall give us flesh to eat? We remember the fish, which we did eat in Egypt freely; the cucumbers, and the melons, and the leeks, and the onions, and the garlic: But now our soul is dried away: there is nothing at all, beside this manna, before our eyes. And the manna was as coriander seed, and the color thereof as the color of bdellium. And the people went about, and gathered it, and ground it in mills, or beat it in a mortar, and baked it in pans, and made cakes of it: and the taste of it was as the taste of fresh oil. And when the dew fell upon the

camp in the night, the manna fell upon it" (Numbers 11:1-9).

I issue an order against every evil group, visible and invisible, mobilized against my destiny, in the name of Jesus.

DECREES AGAINST EVIL GROUPS

1. Every evil group, gathering against my life, scatter by thunder, in the name of Jesus.

2. Any chain of witchcraft, chaining me together with evil people, break, in the name of Jesus.

3. By the power of God, I scatter every evil gang up against my destiny, in the name of Jesus.

4. Every marine agent that is talking against my destiny in its kingdom, fail, in the name of Jesus.

5. Let the mouth of wicked agents in any evil gathering be closed, in the name of Jesus.

6. Blood of Jesus, flow into any evil group and destroy its plans against me, in the name of Jesus.

7. Any evil crowd, gathering against me, scatter, in the name of Jesus.

8. Let the host of darkness assigned to waste me be wasted, in the name of Jesus.

9. Let the hand of the Holy Ghost blow and scatter the enemies of my soul, in the name of Jesus.

10. Every stronghold of witchcraft against my life, collapse, in the name of Jesus.

11. Any evil plan against my destiny, fail woefully by fire, in the name of Jesus.

12. Any evil weapon, gathering demons against my life, catch fire, in the name of Jesus.

13. Let the ministry of evil gang-up in my life be terminated, in the name of Jesus.

14. The personality that is calling wicked people together against me shall fail, in the name of Jesus.

15. Let all my enemies be frustrated in their meeting places, in the name of Jesus.

16. By the anointing of the Holy Ghost, I destroy every satanic gathering, in the name of Jesus.

17. O Lord, send Your angels against every evil movement in the land, in the name of Jesus.

18. Ancestral powers that have gathered together against me shall be put to shame, in the name of Jesus.

19. Blood of Jesus, deliver me right now from every evil gathering, in the name of Jesus.

20. O Lord, let my life escape every marine gang-up against me, in the name of Jesus.

21. Any curse of the enemy in my life, be roasted by fire, in the name of Jesus.

22. Every evil pronouncement in any evil meeting, be cancelled, in the name of Jesus.

23. I reject every evil agreement, made against me, in the name of Jesus.

24. Lord Jesus, arise and disgrace my enemies, in the name of Jesus.

Go back to the words of decree and pass your decree again.

DECREE 26

AGAINST HOUSEHOLD WITCHCRAFTS

"But when Athaliah the mother of Ahaziah saw that her son was dead, she arose and destroyed all the seed royal of the house of Judah. But Jehoshabeath, the daughter of the king, took Joash the son of Ahaziah, and stole him from among the king's sons that were slain, and put him and his nurse in a bedchamber. So Jehoshabeath, the daughter of king Jehoram, the wife of Jehoiada the priest, (for she was the sister of Ahaziah,) hid him from Athaliah, so that she slew him not. And he was with them hid in the house of God six years: and Athaliah reigned over the land" (2 Chronicles 22:10-12).

I stand and decree against household witchcrafts that have taken counsel together against my destiny. Forcefully, I destroy every evil thing done against me by the powers of the witchcraft in my place of birth. Every harm, diversion and enslavement of household witchcraft against my life, be recovered immediately by force.

"Take counsel together and it shall come to nought; speak the word, and it shall not stand: for God is with us" (Isaiah 8:10).

I decree and overthrow household witchcrafts' continuous bombardment of problems in my life and destiny, in the name of Jesus. Let all spells, incantations, curses and deaths fashioned against me by household witchcrafts be terminated forever. I break and loose myself from the dominion, intimidation and bewitchment of household witchcraft, in the name of Jesus. I destroy all weariness and confusion brought into my life by the powers of household witchcrafts, in the name of Jesus.

I decree against every strange noise of household witchcrafts. I command all arrows of sickness, fear, madness and frustration from household witchcraft to backfire immediately.

> *"There shall not be found among you any one that maketh his son or his daughter to pass through the fire, or that useth divination, oran observer of times, or an enchanter, or a witch, Or a charmer, or a consulter with familiar spirits, or a wizard, or a necromancer"* (Deuteronomy 18:10-11).

Any witch or wizard in my family, repent or perish. I decree against every unrepentant witch and wizard in my family and I command them to release all blessings they have confiscated by force. Let the divination of the witchcraft powers and their enchantments backfire now, in the name of Jesus.

Any evil consultation in the past, or present and even the ones that will be done in the future against me shall fail woefully. Let all charms of evil charmers and consultants that have risen against me backfire, in the name of Jesus. Any family spirit, witch or wizards that is blocking my way, I decree against you, clear away by force.

> *"A man also or woman that hath a familiar spirit, or that is a wizard, shall surely be put to death: they shall*

> *stone them with stones: their blood shall be upon them"* (Leviticus 20:27).

Let all unrepentant and uncompromising enemies receive the judgment of God, fall down, and die without mercy, in the name of Jesus.

> *"Thou shalt not suffer a witch to live"* (Exodus 22:18).

Any evil brain from the witchcraft world, thinking against my life, receive madness immediately. I send divine arrows of confusion into the midst of witches and wizards that operate locally and internationally. Let the switch of my destiny be unplugged from demonic sockets by force in the name of Jesus. O Lord, arise in Your anger and destroy every witchcraft throne assigned to fight against my life, in the name of Jesus.

> *"There is no peace, saith the LORD, unto the wicked"* (Isaiah 48:22).

Every prosperity of witches and wizards in my family line, be wasted by heavenly angels from the third heaven now. Every wickedness in my family, backfire. I decree against all eaters of flesh and the drinkers of blood in my family. I command them to eat their fleshes and drink their blood now, in the name of Jesus.

> *"But when Athaliah the mother of Ahaziah saw that her son was dead, she arose and destroyed all the seed royal of the house of Judah. But Jehoshabeath, the daughter of the king, took Joash the son of Ahaziah, and stole him from among the king's sons that were slain, and put him and his nurse in a bedchamber. So Jehoshabeath, the daughter of king Jehoram, the wife of Jehoiada the*

priest, (for she was the sister of Ahaziah,) hid him from Athaliah, so that she slew him not. And he was with them hid in the house of God six years: and Athaliah reigned over the land" (2 Chronicles 22:10-12).

Let all evil personalities that are pretending to be my friend be exposed and disgraced to death, in the name of Jesus.

DECREES AGAINST HOUSEHOLD WITCHCRAFTS

1. Any witch in my family, be exposed and disgraced by fire, in the name of Jesus.

2. Let the brain of any household witchcraft scatter in confusion, in the name of Jesus.

3. Father Lord, unseat every witchcraft personality sitting upon my destiny, in the name of Jesus.

4. Any household witchcraft problem, fighting to dominate my life, die, in the name of Jesus.

5. Holy Ghost fire, burn witchcraft properties in my life to ashes, in the name of Jesus.

6. Let evil structures of witchcraft be consumed by fire, in the name of Jesus.

7. Heavenly Father, arise and deliver me from the grips of witchcraft, in the name of Jesus.

8. Every witchcraft altar, ministering against my destiny, catch fire, in the name of Jesus.

9. Blood of Jesus, speak death to every power of household witchcraft, in the name of Jesus.

10. I withdraw my name from the register of my family evil altar, in the name of Jesus.

11. Let Holy Ghost fire ignite and consume every evil fire in my life, in the name of Jesus.

12. Every bondage of my household witchcraft in my life, break by fire, in the name of Jesus.

13. Heavenly Father, use Your thunder against every witchcraft in my life, in the name of Jesus.

14. Any evil personality, using witchcraft against me, die, in the name of Jesus.

15. Every foundation of household witchcraft in my life, collapse, in the name of Jesus.

16. Let any evil agenda of household witchcraft be frustrated, in the name of Jesus.

17. O Lord, deliver me from the grip of witchcraft powers, in the name of Jesus.

18. Anointing of household witchcrafts, be disgraced, in the name of Jesus.

19. Every evil kingdom, attacking God's kingdom in my life, be overthrown, in the name of Jesus.

20. Every evil agreement of household witchcraft powers, fail woefully, in the name of Jesus.

21. I break and loose myself from every covenant of witchcraft, in the name of Jesus.

22. Any curse placed upon my life through household witchcraft, die, in the name of Jesus.

23. The works of God shall be permanent in my life, in the name of Jesus.

Go back to the words of decree and pass your decree again.

DECREE 27

FOR DIVINE PRESENCE

"And the LORD said, Because the cry of Sodom and Gomorrah is great, and because their sin is very grievous; I will go down now, and see whether they have done altogether according to the cry of it, which is come unto me; and if not, I will know. And the men turned their faces from thence, and went toward Sodom: but Abraham stood yet before the LORD. And Abraham drew near, and said, Wilt thou also destroy the righteous with the wicked? Peradventure there be fifty righteous within the city: wilt thou also destroy and not spare the place for the fifty righteous that are therein? That be far from thee to do after this manner, to slay the righteous with the wicked: and that the righteous should be as the wicked that be far from thee: Shall not the Judge of all the earth do right?" (Genesis 18:20-25).

I command the morning to bring divine presence into my day and let every evil plan of the enemy against me be converted to my promotion. I command divine light and salvation to begin to manifest in my life. Let the divine presence of God in my life appear visible to destroy every manner of fear in my life. Let every wickedness in my life disappear before my divine presence. I decree trouble to my troubles and I command my troubles to bow for the peace of God to rule over my life forever. By the decree of the Almighty, I command my life to embrace victory over all my enemies now, in the name of Jesus.

> *"And now shall mine head be lifted up above mine enemies round about me: therefore will I offer in his tabernacle sacrifices of joy; I will sing, yea, I will sing praises unto the LORD"* (Psalms 27: 6).

Blood of Jesus, take me to the presence of God and keep me there permanently. By the power of divine presence, I destroy every weapon of tribalism, occultism, nepotism, kickbacks and favoritism working against my life, in the name of Jesus. O Lord, arise in Your power and nurture Your presence in my life. Let the Spirit of righteousness, honesty and purity appear in my life to bring down divine presence over my life, in Jesus name.

Father Lord, appear in my situation and turn things around to favor me mightily, in the name of Jesus. By the divine presence of God. I receive divine promotion in every aspect of my life now, in the name of Jesus.

> *"The LORD maketh poor, and maketh rich: he bringeth low, and lifteth up"* (1 Samuel 2:7).

I command the divine presence of God to appear in my life and promote me. Let the Lord's presence make me rich above all my equals and keep me holy everyday to the end, in the name of Jesus. Shame and reproach in my life, what are you wanting for? Disappear by the force of divine presence immediately.

> *"For promotion cometh neither from the east, nor from the west, nor from the south. But God is the judge: he putteth down one, and setteth up another"* (Psalms 75:6-7).

In divine presence, I receive unmerited promotion by fire. O Lord, promote me for Your name's sake. By the power in the blood of Jesus, I walk into the company of heavenly hosts, in the name of Jesus. Father Lord, by Your decree, I seek for Your presence. I decree that Your presence shall appear and bring judgment to unrepentant and evil people. By Your decree, I overthrow every evil in our midst, let Your power manifest again to show Your power over every other power.

> "And the LORD said, Because the cry of Sodom and Gomorrah is great, and because their sin is very grievous; I will go down now, and see whether they have done altogether according to the cry of it, which is come unto me; and if not, I will know. And the men turned their faces from thence, and went toward Sodom: but Abraham stood yet before the LORD. And Abraham drew near, and said, Wilt thou also destroy the righteous with the wicked? Peradventure there be fifty righteous within the city: wilt thou also destroy and not spare the place for the fifty righteous that are therein? That be far from thee to do after this manner, to slay the righteous with the wicked: and that the righteous should be as the wicked that be far from thee: Shall not the Judge of all the earth do right?" (Genesis 18:20-25).

O Lord, let Your fire rain upon determined and unrepentant wicked people that are portraying themselves as god in the throne. I decree that brimstones from heaven will rend all evil thrones on this earth. I command soldiers of heaven to overthrow evil soldiers, cities and thrones of the wicked on earth.

"The sun was risen upon the earth when Lot entered into Zoar. Then the LORD rained upon Sodom and upon Gomorrah brimstone and fire from the LORD out of heaven; and he overthrew those cities, and all the plain, and all the inhabitants of the cities, and that which grew upon the ground. But his wife looked back from behind him, and she became a pillar of salt" (Genesis 19:23-6).

I withdraw the mercy of God from the occult, and unrepentant evil grand masters.

DECREES FOR DIVINE PRESENCE

1. Heavenly Father, arise and manifest in my life by fire, in the name of Jesus.

2. Any evil power that is living inside of me, come out by force, in the name of Jesus.

3. Every sickness in my life, receive divine presence and die, in the name of Jesus.

4. Father Lord, destroy every bewitchment in my life, in the name of Jesus.

5. By the power in the Word of God, I frustrate every evil in my life, in the name of Jesus.

6. Every seed of sickness in my life, die, in the name of Jesus.

7. O God, arise and deliver me from every manner of bondage, in the name of Jesus.

8. Let every organ of my body receive Holy Ghost fire, in the name of Jesus.

9. Any viper of darkness in my life, what are you waiting for? Die, in the name of Jesus.

10. O Lord, appear and deliver me from every danger of life, in the name of Jesus.

11. Every demonized area of my life, receive Holy Ghost fire, in the name of Jesus.

12. Any evil power that has been assigned to paralyze my destiny, die, in the name of Jesus.

13. Satan, no matter what your reasons are, you shall not prevail over me, in the name of Jesus.

14. Let every spiritual blindness in my life face the wrath of God, in the name of Jesus.

15. Every demonic leprosy attached to my life, be detached by force, in the name of Jesus.

16. Blood of Jesus, put to an end every marine power in my life, in the name of Jesus.

17. Let any satanic poison existing in my life die, in the name of Jesus.

18. Any evil power that has walked into my life, walk out by force, in the name of Jesus.

19. Power of God, destroy every infirmity in my life, in the name of Jesus.

20. Every arrow of the wicked fired into my destiny, backfire, in the name of Jesus.

21. Let demons that refused to let me go appear before God and die, in the name of Jesus.

22. O Lord, confront and conquer every problem in my life, in the name of Jesus.

23. Lord Jesus, wake me up, in the name of Jesus.

24. Let all diverse diseases in my life die, in the name of Jesus.

25. Father Lord, deliver me from every evil, in the name of Jesus.

Go back to the words of decree and pass your decree again.

DECREE 28

FOR FREEDOM AND VICTORY

"And there was a great cry of the people and of their wives against their brethren the Jews. For there were that said, we, our sons, and our daughters, are many: therefore we take up corn for them, that we may eat, and live. Some also there were that said, we have mortgaged our lands, vineyards, and houses, that we might buy corn, because of the dearth. There were also that said, we have borrowed money for the king's tribute, and that upon our lands and vineyards. Yet now our flesh is as the flesh of our brethren, our children as their children: and, lo, we bring into bondage our sons and our daughters to be servants, and some of our daughters are brought unto bondage already: neither is it in our power to redeem them; for other men have our lands and vineyards. And I was very angry when I heard their cry and these words. Then I consulted with myself, and I rebuked the nobles, and the rulers, and said unto them, ye exact usury, every one of his brother. And I set a great assembly against them. And I said unto them, we after our ability have redeemed our brethren the Jews, which were sold unto the heathen; and will ye even sell your brethren? or shall they be sold unto us? Then held they their peace, and found nothing to answer. Also I said, It is not good that ye do: ought ye not to walk in the fear of our God because of the reproach of the heathen our enemies? I likewise, and my brethren, and my servants, might exact of them money and corn: I pray you, let us

leave off this usury. Restore, I pray you, to them, even this day, their lands, their vineyards, their oliveyards, and their houses, also the hundredth part of the money, and of the corn, the wine, and the oil, that ye exact of them. Then said they, We will restore them, and will require nothing of them; so will we do as thou sayest. Then I called the priests, and took an oath of them, that they should do according to this promise. Also I shook my lap, and said, so God shake out every man from his house, and from his labor, that performeth not this promise, even thus be he shaken out, and emptied. And the entire congregation said, Amen, and praised the LORD. And the people did according to this promise" (Nehemiah 5:1-13).

I command every part of my life to receive freedom and perfect deliverance from evil powers. Any evil power that is keeping me in bondage and has vowed never to let me go, you are a liar, fall down and die now, in the name of Jesus. I receive freedom and victory from the grip of evil and marine powers. I decree against every stubborn evil power that has vowed to useless my life in satanic prison, in the name of Jesus.

I take authority over this day and I command my freedom to appear, in the name of Jesus. I decree against any evil power holding me in bondage and I command its bondage to be broken into pieces. Let all elemental forces assigned to keep me down scatter in shame. I speak destruction unto the powers from the water that are tormenting my life.

Let the power of God deliver me from every evil power that has vowed to eliminate my life. I pull down every negative structure built to block my advancement. Any evil power uttering incantations to capture my destiny and waste it, fall down and die by fire, in the name of Jesus. Let witchcraft prayers fail woefully in my life and backfire by force, in the name of Jesus. Any power holding me down in the tail region, release me and fall down and die.

> *"And the LORD shall make thee the head, and not the tail; and thou shalt be above only, and thou shalt not be beneath; if that thou hearken unto the commandments of the LORD thy God, which I command thee this day, to observe and to do them"* (Deuteronomy 28:13).

Every satanic force that has been delegated to waste my life, scatter and be put to shame forever. Blood of Jesus, flow into my foundation and set my body, soul and spirit free from every manner of captivity. Let that hand that is holding me down be cut off permanently. Any giant in the battlefield, contesting against my life, I cut off your head, die and die again, in the name of Jesus.

> *"Then said David to the Philistine, Thou comest to me with a sword, and with a spear, and with a shield: but I come to thee in the name of the LORD of hosts, the God of the armies of Israel, whom thou hast defied. This day will the LORD deliver thee into mine hand; and I will smite thee, and take thine head from thee; and I will give the carcasses of the host of the Philistines this day unto the fowls of the air, and to the wild beasts of the earth; that all the earth may know that there is a God in Israel. And all this assembly shall know that the LORD saveth not with sword and spear: for the battle is the LORD'S and he will give you into our hands. And it came to pass, when the Philistine arose, and came and drew nigh to meet David that David hasted,*

and ran toward the army to meet the Philistine. And David put his hand in his bag, and took thence a stone, and slang it, and smote the Philistine in his forehead that the stone sunk into his forehead; and he fell upon his face to the earth. So David prevailed over the Philistine with a sling and with a stone, and smote the Philistine, and slew him; but there was no sword in the hand of David. Therefore David ran, and stood upon the Philistine, and took his sword, and drew it out of the sheath thereof, and slew him, and cut off his head therewith. And when the Philistines saw their champion was dead, they fled" (1 Samuel 17:45-51).

I receive victory over the armies of the Philistines and I scatter them in the wilderness by force. I decree against the giant of Philistines and I command him to fall down and die. I cut off the head of Goliath with his own sword, in the name of Jesus.

"Therefore David ran, and stood upon the Philistine, and took his sword, and drew it out of the sheath thereof, and slew him, and cut off his head therewith. And when the Philistines saw their champion was dead, they fled. And the men of Israel and of Judah arose, and shouted, and pursued the Philistines, until thou come to the valley, and to the gates of Ekron And the wounded of the Philistines fell down by the way to Shaaraim, even unto Gath, and unto Ekron. And the children of Israel returned from chasing after the Philistines, and they spoiled their tents. And David took the head of the Philistine, and brought it to Jerusalem; but he put his armor in his tent" (1 Samuel 17:51-54).

Let the armies on the side of God arise and shout against the armies of the enemy. I decree against the evil forces of darkness, spiritually and physically. Any sickness in my life that is on a suicide mission, I cast you out, fall down and die. I decree against every power of witchcraft in my life.

Blood of Jesus, flow into my foundation and deliver me from every destructive sickness and disease, in the name of Jesus. Any evil altar, blocking my perfect victory, be roasted by the fire of the Holy Spirit. Let the anointing that breaks every yoke break the yoke of marine spirits in my life, in the name of Jesus.

> *"And they overcame him by the blood of the Lamb and by the word of their testimony; and they loved not their lives unto the death"* (Revelation 12:11).

I decree perfect victory over all powers of darkness, in the name of Jesus.

DECREES FOR FREEDOM AND VICTORY

1. I receive freedom and victory from my God, in the name of Jesus.

2. Whether devil likes it or not, I must receive my freedom and victory today, in the name of Jesus.

3. Any evil decision that has been made against my deliverance, fail woefully by fire, in the name of Jesus.

4. Every enemy of my breakthrough, fail, in the name of Jesus.

5. Blood of Jesus, speak freedom into my foundation, in the name of Jesus.

6. Any power that has tracked me to the grassroots, release me by force, in the name of Jesus.

7. Any satanic angel that is planning to re-arrest me, be disgraced, in the name of Jesus.

8. Heavenly Father, let my freedom and victory come from You alone, in the name of Jesus.

9. Let struggles in my life give way to my breakthroughs, in the name of Jesus.

10. Father Lord, I have come to You, don't let me go empty handed, in the name of Jesus.

11. Any power that is eating up my joy and peace, die, in the name of Jesus.

12. By the power in the name of Jesus, I command my deliverance to appear, in the name of Jesus.

13. O Lord, release Your divine favor into my life by fire, in the name of Jesus.

14. Every seed of evil in my life, come out and die, in the name of Jesus.

15. I cut my life off from powers of darkness assigned to waste my life, in the name of Jesus.

16. Every bondage of poverty in my life, break, in the name of Jesus.

17. Every evil foundation, laid by my ancestors, collapse, in the name of Jesus.

18. Let territorial powers that have captured my progress release it and die, in the name of Jesus.

19. I walk out by fire from every satanic yoke, in the name of Jesus.

20. I refuse to be a servant to my servants, in the name of Jesus.

21. Blood of Jesus, flow into my life and give me the deliverance I need, in the name of Jesus.

22. Every satanic garbage can in my life, be dismantled by fire, in the name of Jesus.

23. Let every good thing I have lost to devil be recovered immediately by fire, in the name of Jesus.

24. Any power that has captured me for evil, release me and die, in the name of Jesus.

25. Every enemy of my freedom and victory, you must die, die, in the name of Jesus.

26. I pull out of my life from every evil power assigned to disgrace me, in the name of Jesus.

27. O Lord, give me miracles of abundance, in the name of Jesus.

28. Let all agents of oppression in my life be oppressed, in the name of Jesus.

29. O Lord, manifest in Your power and deliver me, in the name of Jesus.

Go back to the words of decree and pass your decree again.

DECREE 29

TO BE HIGHLY PREFERRED

"Now it came to pass on the third day, that Esther put on her royal apparel, and stood in the inner court of the king's house, over against the king's house: and the king sat upon his royal throne in the royal house, over against the gate of the house. And it was so, when the king saw Esther the queen standing in the court, that she obtained favor in his sight: and the king held out to Esther the golden scepter that was in his hand. So Esther drew near, and touched the top of the scepter. Then said the king unto her, what wilt thou, queen Esther? and what is thy request? It shall be even given thee to the half of the kingdom. And Esther answered, if it seem good unto the king, let the king and Haman come this day unto the banquet that I have prepared for him. Then the king said, Cause Haman to make haste, that he may do as Esther hath said. So the king and Haman came to the banquet that Esther had prepared. And the king said unto Esther at the banquet of wine, what is thy petition? and it shall be granted thee: and what is thy request? even to the half of the kingdom it shall be performed. Then answered Esther, and said, My petition and my request is; If I have found favor in the sight of the king, and if it please the king to grant my petition, and to perform my request, let the king and Haman come to the banquet that I shall prepare for them, and I will do to morrow as the king hath said. Then went Haman forth that day joyful and with a glad heart: but when Haman saw Mordecai in the king's *gate, that he stood not up, nor moved for him, he was full of indignation against Mordecai. Nevertheless Haman refrained himself: and when he came home, he sent and called for his friends and Zeresh his wife"* (Esther 5:1-8, 2:1-20, 7:1-10, 9:12).

Let my glory appear and shine brighter and better all the times. I decree that I shall be highly preferred anywhere I go from today. I command my star to manifest from the throne of God by fire, in the name of Jesus. I shall arise and shine to the glory of God, whether my enemies like it or not, in the name of Jesus.

"And the thing was good in the eyes of Pharaoh, and in the eyes of all his servants. And Pharaoh said unto his servants, Can we find such a one as this is, a man in whom the Spirit of God is? And Pharaoh said unto Joseph, Forasmuch as God hath shewed thee all this, there is none so discreet and wise as thou art: Thou shalt be over my house, and according unto thy word shall all my people be ruled: only in the throne will I be greater than thou. And Pharaoh said unto Joseph, See, I have set thee over all the land of Egypt. And Pharaoh took off his ring from his hand, and put it upon Joseph's hand, and arrayed him in vestures of fine linen, and put a gold chain about his neck; And he made him to ride in the second chariot which he had; and they cried before him, Bow the knee: and he made him ruler over all the land of Egypt. And Pharaoh said unto Joseph, I am Pharaoh, and without thee shall no man lift up his hand or foot in all the land of Egypt" (Genesis 41:37-44)

I decree that my life and character shall be good in the eyes of the people, especially people who are successful. Father Lord, let me be locally and internationally accepted at all times, in every situation and circumstance, in the name of Jesus. I command nature to favor me and advertise me from today. Let there be no one that will qualify to replace me untimely.

O Lord, cause me to be more qualified and favored among millions of good people, in the name of Jesus. Any power that wants to separate me from the spirit of God, I decree against you, die, in the name of Jesus. Let the spirit of excellence rest upon me and bestow upon me best quality of everything in this life by fire. O Lord, equip me with divine and incomparable qualities that cannot be challenged by others. Let my appearances be better than that of angels of God. O Lord my God, show me what none other have known and advance my spiritual knowledge by Your power, in the name of Jesus.

Heavenly Father, arise in Your power and make me a celebrity in this generation. Let the spirit of administration and leadership be imported into my life from the third heaven. Father Lord, make me great in this life.

> *"Now when the turn of Esther, the daughter of Abihail the uncle of Mordecai, who had taken her for his daughter, was come to go in unto the king, she required nothing but what Hegai the king's chamberlain, the keeper of the women, appointed. And Esther obtained favor in the sight of all them that looked upon her. So Esther was taken unto king Ahasuerus into his house royal in the tenth month, which is the month Tebeth, in the seventh year of his reign. And the king loved Esther*

above all the women, and she obtained grace and favor in his sight more than all the virgins; so that he set the royal crown upon her head, and made her queen instead of Vashti. Then the king made a great feast unto all his princes and his servants, even Esther's feast; and he made a release to the provinces, and gave gifts, according to the state of the king. And when the virgins were gathered together the second time, then Mordecai sat in the king's gate. Esther had not yet shewed her kindred nor her people; as Mordecai had charged her: for Esther did the commandment of Mordecai, like as when she was brought up with him" (Esther 2:15-20).

As I appear in any competition, I shall obtain the best favor in the sight of all that will hear of me or will look upon me. I decree that influential people will love me to the glory of God. O Lord, by Your power, I decree that I will be used to replace the best candidate anywhere there is competition, in Jesus name. I decree that once I appear anywhere, I shall be generally accepted, even by the people who hate me or compete with me. My opponents will see me, accept me and chose me as the best candidate whether they like it or not, in the name of Jesus.

"Now it came to pass on the third day, that Esther put on her royal apparel, and stood in the inner court of the king's house, over against the king's house: and the king sat upon his royal throne in the royal house, over against the gate of the house. And it was so, when the king saw Esther the queen standing in the court, that she obtained favor in his sight: and the king held out to Esther the golden sceptre that was in his hand. So Esther drew near, and touched the top of the sceptre. Then said the king unto her, what wilt thou, queen

Esther? and what is thy request? it shall be even given thee to the half of the kingdom. And Esther answered, if it seem good unto the king, let the king and Haman come this day unto the banquet that I have prepared for him. Then the king said, Cause Haman to make haste, that he may do as Esther hath said. So the king and Haman came to the banquet that Esther had prepared. And the king said unto Esther at the banquet of wine, what is thy petition? and it shall be granted thee: and what is thy request? even to the half of the kingdom it shall be performed. Then answered Esther, and said, My petition and my request is; If I have found favor in the sight of the king, and if it please the king to grant my petition, and to perform my request, let the king and Haman come to the banquet that I shall prepare for them, and I will do to morrow as the king hath said" (Esther 5:1-8).

As soon as I appear at any place, other contestants shall bow by force. Let me obtain unmerited favor to receive anything I request even for the request of a kingdom. I decree that all unrepentant Haman figures shall die in my place.

"And the king arising from the banquet of wine in his wrath went into the palace garden: and Haman stood up to make request for his life to Esther the queen; for he saw that there was evil determined against him by the king. Then the king returned out of the palace garden into the place of the banquet of wine; and Haman was fallen upon the bed whereon Esther was. Then said the king, Will he force the queen also before me in the house? As the word went out of the king's mouth, they covered Haman's face. And Harbonah, one of the chamberlains, said before the king, Behold also,

the gallows fifty cubits high, which Haman had made for Mordecai, who had spoken good for the king, standeth in the house of Haman. Then the king said, Hang him thereon. So they hanged Haman on the gallows that he had prepared for Mordecai. Then was the king's wrath pacified" (Esther 7:7-10).

Blood of Jesus, speak for my perfection and complete Your good works in my life forever, in the name of Jesus.

DECREES TO BE HIGHLY PREFERRED

1. Blood of Jesus, put Your power of acceptance in my life to Your own glory, in the name of Jesus.

2. Angels of the living God, decorate me to appear as the best in the land, in the name of Jesus.

3. O Lord, anoint me to be preferred above others, in the name of Jesus.

4. Blood of Jesus, let my life attract divine favors, in the name of Jesus.

5. Anywhere I appear in this life, I shall be highly preferred, in the name of Jesus.

6. Every satanic case file against me, catch fire and burn to ashes, in the name of Jesus.

7. Every agent of oppression, that is assigned to disgrace me, be disgraced, in the name of Jesus.

8. Among all my equals, I shall be the best, in the name of Jesus.

9. As Daniel was preferred, so shall I be preferred above others, in the name of Jesus.

10. Let all that is competing with me come behind me, in the name of Jesus.

11. O Lord, make me number one in every good thing in life, in the name of Jesus.

12. Let the spirit of the tail in my life fail woefully, in the name of Jesus.

13. Every demonic rope, drawing me behind, break by fire, in the name of Jesus.

14. Every conscious or unconscious bondage in my life, break, in the name of Jesus.

15. Every poison of backwardness in my life, dry up by fire, in the name of Jesus.

16. Any satanic voice assigned to speak against me, be silenced, in the name of Jesus.

17. O Lord, open the mouth of every one of my enemies to speak to my goodness, in the name of Jesus.

18. Let God that answers by fire be my God in this competition, in the name of Jesus.

19. Father Lord, endue me with the spirit of excellence, in the name of Jesus.

20. Power to be highly preferred, fall upon me by fire, in the name of Jesus.

21. Holy Ghost fire, burn every yoke of rejection in my life to ashes, in the name of Jesus.

22. Angels of the living God, take me to the high table of promotion, in the name of Jesus.

23. Lord Jesus, announce my success and greatness by Yourself, in the name of Jesus.

Go back to the words of decree and pass your decree again.

DECREE 30

AGAINST DEBT AND DEATH

"Now there cried a certain woman of the wives of the sons of the prophets unto Elisha, saying, Thy servant my husband is dead; and thou knowest that thy servant did fear the LORD: and the creditor is come to take unto him my two sons to be bondmen. And Elisha said unto her, what shall I do for thee? tell me, what hast thou in the house? And she said, Thine handmaid hath not any thing in the house, save a pot of oil. Then he said, Go, borrow thee vessels abroad of all thy neighbors', even empty vessels; borrow not a few And when thou art come in, thou shalt shut the door upon thee and upon thy sons, and shalt pour out into all those vessels, and thou shalt set aside that which is full. So she went from him, and shut the door upon her and upon her sons, who brought the vessels to her; and she poured out. And it came to pass, when the vessels were full, that she said unto her son, Bring me yet a vessel. And he said unto her, there is not a vessel more. And the oil stayed. Then she came and told the man of God. And he said, Go, sell the oil, and pay thy debt, and live thou and thy children of the rest" (2 Kings 4:1-7).

Every arrow of poverty, debts and death in my life, come out by force, I decree against you, go back to your sender, kill them and die forever. I decree that my life shall not accommodate debts any longer. Spirit of debts, death and hell, your time is up, I cast you out of my life. Father Lord, have mercy upon me, clear my debts and deliver me from debt and shame, in the name of Jesus.

Any evil power that wanted to kill my parents with debts so as to take the entire family into slavery, you are wicked, fall and die without mercy. Any power causing me to cry and weep because of my huge debts, cry unto death yourself. I break and loose myself from the bondage of debt and death, in the name of Jesus. I decree against inherited poverty in my life and I command it to leave me alone by force.

Any bondage in my life as a result of inherited debts, break into pieces by force. I decree that the anointing of God will break every yoke of debts in my life and set me free, in the name of Jesus. I command the miracles that will terminate my poverty and make me greatly rich to appear by fire, in the name of Jesus. Any curse of debt and poverty in my life unto death, enough is enough, come out and die immediately, in the name of Jesus. Blood of Jesus, flow into my life and destroy every spirit of debts assigned to waste my life, in the name of Jesus.

Father Lord, by Your decree, arise and prosper me to be a mighty prince with all the good things around me by Your grace, in the name of Jesus. I decree that the womb of my prosperity shall open and advance my destiny. I decree against every pregnancy of poverty and debts and I command them to be aborted by force now. Father Lord, cause my prosperity to explode and reach the north, south, east and west, in the name of Jesus. Let the evil hand of poverty and debts in my life wither by fire, in the name of Jesus.

Blood of Jesus, speak heavenly manna into existence in my life. Every good thing I have lost in life, I recover you double by the decree of the Almighty. Father Lord, by Your decree, make me abundantly rich forever. This is my year of jubilee, therefore, let all my losses be recovered by divine decree, in the name of Jesus. Blood of Jesus, flow into my life and cancel my debts by Your power, in the name of Jesus.

> *"At the end of every seven years thou shalt make a release. And this is the manner of the release: Every creditor that lendeth ought unto his neighbor shall release it; he shall not exact it of his neighbor, or of his brother; because it is called the LORD'S release Of a foreigner thou mayest exact it again: but that which is thine with thy brother thine hand shall release; Save when there shall be no poor among you; for the LORD shall greatly bless thee in the land which the LORD thy God giveth thee for an inheritance to possess it: Only if thou carefully hearken unto the voice of the LORD thy God, to observe to do all these commandments which I command thee this day. For the LORD thy God blesseth thee, as he promised thee: and thou shalt lend unto many nations, but thou shalt not borrow; and thou shalt reign over many nations, but they shall not reign over thee"* (Deuteronomy 15:1-6).

I decree against any inherited debt that is assigned to take me to the grave, in the name of Jesus.

DECREES AGAINST DEBT AND DEATH

1. Any power that wants me to die in debts, die by fire, in the name of Jesus.

2. Every agent of debts in my life, receive disgrace by fire, in the name of Jesus.

3. Any power that has placed the yoke of debts in my life to kill me, die, in the name of Jesus.

4. O Lord, give me the power to be great regardless of present situation, in the name of Jesus.

5. Any evil thing that is planted into my life by enemies, be dismantled by force, in the name of Jesus.

6. Holy Ghost fire, consume every debt that is about to disgrace me, in the name of Jesus.

7. Let every demon arresting progresses in my life be put to shame, in the name of Jesus.

8. Every enemy of my prosperity, die, in the name of Jesus.

9. O Lord, arise and satisfy me with wealth, in the name of Jesus.

10. O Lord, surprise my enemies with my breakthrough, in the name of Jesus.

11. Any power that has bewitched me with poverty, fail woefully, in the name of Jesus.

12. Every demonic activity assigned to bring me into poverty, be terminated, in the name of Jesus.

13. O Lord, take me far away from shame of debts, in the name of Jesus.

14. Any satanic program, assigned to keep me in perpetual bondage, scatter, in the name of Jesus.

15. Every instrument of debts in my life, catch Holy Ghost Fire, in the name of Jesus.

16. I receive the power to be rich, to disgrace my enemies, in the name of Jesus.

17. Let my prayers secure divine appointment and visitation, in the name of Jesus.

18. O Lord, render the spirit of poverty in my life impotent, in the name of Jesus.

19. Any power assigned to kill good things in my life, receive destruction, in the name of Jesus.

20. Death must die in my life forever, in the name of Jesus.

21. I shall not surrender to devil, the devil shall surrender to me, in the name of Jesus.

22. Father Lord, arise and waste my waster, in the name of Jesus.

23. Blood of Jesus, speak into my grave, in the name of Jesus.

24. Let the spirit of death and hell in my life fail woefully, in the name of Jesus.

25. By the anointing of God in my life, let death die, in the name of Jesus.

Go back to the words of decree and pass your decree again.

DECREE 31

TO STOP WEEPING PERMANENTLY

"And it came to pass the day after, that he went into a city called Nain; and many of his disciples went with him, and much people. Now when he came nigh to the gate of the city, behold, there was a dead man carried out, the only son of his mother, and she was a widow: and much people of the city was with her. And when the Lord saw her, he had compassion on her, and said unto her, Weep not. And he came and touched the bier: and they that bare him stood still. And he said, Young man, I say unto thee, Arise And he that was dead sat up, and began to speak. And he delivered him to his mother. And there came a fear on all: and they glorified God, saying, that a great prophet is risen up among us; and, that God hath visited his people. And this rumor of him went forth throughout all Judaea, and throughout the entire region round about" (<u>Luke 7:11-17</u>).

Father Lord, by Your decree, I command miracles that will terminate my weeping to manifest by fire, in the name of Jesus. Heavenly Father, appear in my situation and wipe away my tears forever. Let the glory of God begin to follow me everywhere I go by the decree of the Almighty, in the mighty name of our Lord Jesus Christ.

Blood of Jesus, flow into my eyes and convert my tears to joy, in the name of Jesus. Holy Ghost fire, enter into my eyes and dry up my tears, in the name of Jesus.

Lord Jesus, by Your decree, restore into my life everything devil has removed from my life to torment me. I decree that the voice of Lord Jesus shall speak life into every dead organ of my life, in the name of Jesus. Let the anointing of God that breaks every yoke fall upon my life and break the yoke of untimely death in my life. Any good thing that is giving me joy, which enemies have removed from my family, be restored by force, in the name of Jesus.

O Lord my God, by Your decree, arise and work out my deliverance. Any problem in my life, causing me to weep all the time, receive immediate solution by fire. Any power that has rendered me useless, I decree against you, receive back your useless arrows and die in shame. I decree that powers of resurrection should begin to touch every aspect of my destiny, in the name of Jesus. Lord Jesus, arise and confront all my problems and conquer them unto death.

Every arrow of sorrow and weeping, fired into my destiny, I fire you back. I decree against every evil power assigned to wage war against my joy, in the name of Jesus. Angry soldiers from heaven, arise and fight for me, in the name of Jesus.

> *"And the LORD said, I have surely seen the affliction of my people which are in Egypt, and have heard their cry by reason of their taskmasters; for I know their sorrows; And I am come down to deliver them out of the hand of the Egyptians, and to bring them up out of that land unto a good land and a large, unto a land flowing with milk and honey; unto the place of the Canaanites, and the Hittites, and the Amorites, and the Perizzites, and the Hivites, and the Jebusite. Now therefore, behold, the cry of the children of Israel is come unto me: and I have also seen the oppression wherewith the Egyptians oppress them. Come now therefore, and I will send thee unto Pharaoh, that thou mayest bring forth my people the children of Israel out of Egypt"* (Exodus 3:7-10).

Father Lord, open Your eyes towards me and see my affliction and oppression in my life. Any Egyptian bondage, causing me to weep in sorrow, break and release me by force. I decree against physical and spiritual task masters assigned to torment my life daily. I come against any agent of sorrow in my life and I command them to die, in the name of Jesus.

I decree my freedom out of the hand of spiritual Egyptian tormentors and I jump into the land of freedom by faith, a land flowing with milk and honey, in the name of Jesus. Let every oppressor of my life be oppressed and be permanently disengaged out of my destiny, in the name of Jesus. I stand in the authority of the Word of God and I decree against all Pharaoh personalities in my life. I command them and all their visible and invisible soldiers to enter into the Red Sea and be drowned by force. O Lord, put Your permanent joy and laughter into my life and cause me to win every battle of my life perfectly forever and ever, in the name of Jesus.

DECREES TO STOP WEEPING PERMANENTLY

1. Every manner of suffering in my life, be terminated, in the name of Jesus.

2. O Lord, quench every voice of devil in my life forever and ever, in the name of Jesus.

3. Every evil river, flowing in my life to cause trouble, dry up by force, in the name of Jesus.

4. Holy Ghost fire, burn to ashes every evil influence in my life in the name of Jesus.

5. Let the spirit of failure in my life, die, in the name of Jesus.

6. 7. Lord Jesus, arise and fight my battles to the end, in the name of Jesus.

8. Every agent of wickedness in my life, be terminated by death, in the name of Jesus.

9. Any evil burial that has taken place in my life, receive resurrection, in the name of Jesus.

10. Angels of the living God, arise and defend me, in the name of Jesus.

11. Any area of my life that is under torment, be delivered by fire, in the name of Jesus.

12. You, evil sorrows, be replaced with joy, in the name of Jesus.

13. Every marine spirit attacks against me, catch Holy Ghost fire, in the name of Jesus.

14. Any power that is tormenting me with hardship, your time is up, die, in the name of Jesus.

15. Where the enemy says I will not get to, O Lord, take me there, in the name of Jesus.

16. Any evil presence in my life, disappear, in the name of Jesus.

17. By the power in the Word of God, I receive my deliverance today, in the name of Jesus.

18. Lord Jesus, wipe away all my tears, in the name of Jesus.

19. Anything by which the enemy is planning to disgrace me again shall fail, in the name of Jesus.

20. Every chain of bondage in my life, break by fire, in the name of Jesus.

21. Any problem in my life, forcing tears out of my eyes, die, in the name of Jesus.

22. Every evil padlock in my life, break, in the name of Jesus.

23. Any evil situation in my life, making me to weep, receive deliverance, in the name of Jesus.

24. That problem in my family that has been assigned to frustrate me, die, in the name of Jesus.

25. Every iron-like curse in my life, die, in the name of Jesus.

26. Lord Jesus, take away every marine attack in my destiny, in the name of Jesus.

27. Let the wickedness of the wicked return to their heads, in the name of Jesus.

28. Lord Jesus, give me a perfect solution I need, in the name of Jesus.

Go back to the words of decree and pass your decree again.

DECREE 32

AGAINST DESTRUCTIVE CURSES

"And the LORD said unto Cain, Where is Abel thy brother? And he said, I know not: Am I my brother's keeper? And he said, what hast thou done? the voice of thy brother's blood crieth unto me from the ground. And now art thou cursed from the earth, which hath opened her mouth to receive thy brother's blood from thy hand; When thou tillest the ground, it shall not henceforth yield unto thee her strength; a fugitive and a vagabond shalt thou be in the earth. And Cain said unto the LORD, My punishment is greater than I can bear. Behold, thou hast driven me out this day from the face of the earth; and from thy face shall I be hid; and I shall be a fugitive and a vagabond in the earth; and it shall come to pass, that every one that findeth me shall slay me. And the LORD said unto him, therefore

whosoever slayeth Cain, vengeance shall be taken on him sevenfold. And the LORD set a mark upon Cain, lest any finding him should kill him" (Genesis 4:11-15).

I stand against every destructive curse that has been assigned to waste my destiny, in the name of Jesus. Blood of Jesus, flow into my foundation and paralyze every curse planted in it by fire. Let the power in the name of Jesus remove every cursed material that is prospering in my life, in the name of Jesus. Any curse in my life that is directly opposing my blessings, I curse your strength; die now, in the name of Jesus.

"As the bird by wandering, as the swallow by flying, so the curse causeless shall not come" (Proverbs 26:2).

Any evil personality wishing me evil, receive a grand disappointment. I command every evil utterance said against me to go back to its senders, in the name of Jesus. Any satanic agent gathering evil words against my life, be disgraced immediately. I decree against any curse placed upon my life to torment my destiny. Any witch or wizard, distributing problems into my life, be frustrated and be disgraced by fire, in the name of Jesus.

Any invisible barrier created by evil curses in my life, be closed forever. Let curses in my life that are keeping me away from blessings die immediately. I command every satanic spell in my life to be terminated. I decree against any curse in my life that is causing me to struggle without success, or is frustrating my destiny. Be cancelled by fire. Every evil limitation upon my life because of ancestral curses, be removed, in the name of Jesus.

Any blood crying against me, be silenced by the blood of Jesus. I decree against the consequences of all evil atrocities done by my ancestors, which are now affecting my destiny. I command every curse of hardship in my life to be destroyed now. Every curse of fugitive and vagabond in my life break and loose your hold over my life. I recover by force any of my inheritance turned to strangers in my life. Any destructive curse that has reduced me to perpetual slavery among my people, loose your hold over my life now. I refuse to buy what belongs to me with my own money. I decree against every spirit of suffering and labor without results, in the name of Jesus.

> *"Remember, O LORD, what is come upon us: consider, and behold our reproach. Our inheritance is turned to strangers, our houses to aliens. We are orphans and fatherless, our mothers are as widows. We have drunken our water for money; our wood is sold unto us. Our necks are under persecution: we labor, and have no rest"* (Lamentations 5:1-5).

Let curses prevailing in my life, which have made my servants to rule over me, loose their hold over my destiny. I command the spirit of fear brought into my life by curses to disappear and die. I refuse to remain under curses, poverty and death, in the name of Jesus.

> *"Our fathers have sinned, and are not; and we have borne their iniquities. Servants have ruled over us: there is none that doth deliver us out of their hand. We gat our bread with the peril of our lives because of the sword of the wilderness"* (Lamentations 5:7-9).

I decree against the spirit of famine, mass death, reproach and shame. I command all manner of curses in my life to die forever.

> "Our skin was black like an oven because of the terrible famine. They ravished the women in Zion, and the maids in the cities of Judah. Princes are hanged up by their hand: the faces of elders were not honored. They took the young men to grind, and the children fell under the wood. The elders have ceased from the gate, the young men from their music. The joy of our heart is ceased; our dance is turned into mourning. The crown is fallen from our head: woe unto us that we have sinned! For this our heart is faint; for these things our eyes are dim. Because of the mountain of Zion, which is desolate, the foxes walk upon it" (Lamentations 5:10-18).

> "Then there was a famine in the days of David three years, year after year; and David enquired of the LORD. And the LORD answered, It is for Saul, and for his bloody house, because he slew the Gibeonites" (2 Samuel 21:1).

I decree that whether devil likes it or not, my life shall escape from every destructive curse, in the name of Jesus.

DECREES AGAINST DESTRUCTIVE CURSES

1. O Lord, arise and deliver me from every curse of my father's house, in the name of Jesus.

2. Blood of Jesus, take me away from every inherited curse, in the name of Jesus.

3. Every evil covenant working against my destiny, break by fire, in the name of Jesus.

4. Any aggressive altar, attacking me with aggressive curses, scatter, in the name of Jesus.

5. Heavenly Father, destroy curses that came upon me as a result of sin, in the name of Jesus.

6. Any serpentine curse that is upon my destiny, be swallowed by the Holy Ghost fire, in the name of Jesus.

7. Blood of Jesus, defy every destructive curse in my life, in the name of Jesus.

8. Any problem in my life, which is existing as a result of demonic curses, die, in the name of Jesus.

9. I render every aggressive curse in my life powerless, in the name of Jesus.

10. Every marine altar curses erected against my life, catch fire, in the name of Jesus.

11. Any evil done against my life because of inherited curses, die, in the name of Jesus.

12. Every demon delegated to my life because of an evil curse, I cast you out, in the name of Jesus.

13. Any curse that has opened satanic traffic into my life, die, in the name of Jesus.

14. Any destructive curse, diverting good things away from my life, be frustrated, in the name of Jesus.

15. O Lord, water every area of my life dried up by evil curses, in the name of Jesus.

16. Every good thing that curses have destroyed in my life, be restored by fire, in the name of Jesus.

17. Any marine power that is obstructing divine blessings in my life, die, in the name of Jesus.

18. O Lord, reestablish Your purpose in my life, in the name of Jesus.

19. Any pillar, supporting curses in my life, fall, in the name of Jesus.

20. You, sickness in my life as a result of demonic curses; you must die, die, in the name of Jesus.

21. By the power of God, I curse evil cures in my life, in the name of Jesus.

22. O Lord, purge my life and deliver me from the grip of destructive curses, in the name of Jesus.

23. Every yoke of destructive curses in my life, break, in the name of Jesus.

24. Let my God arise and break every curse in my life assigned to disgrace me, in the name of Jesus.

25. I withdraw my life from the altar of destructive curses, in the name of Jesus.

Go back to the words of decree and pass your decree again.

DECREE 33

FOR COMPLETE HOLINESS

"So Abijah slept with his fathers, and they buried him in the city of David: and Asa his son reigned in his stead. In his days the land was quiet ten years. And Asa did that which was good and right in the eyes of the LORD his God: For he took away the altars of the strange gods, and the high places, and brake down the images, and cut down the groves: And commanded Judah to seek the LORD God of their fathers, and to do the law and the commandment. Also he took away out of all the cities of Judah the high places and the images: and the kingdom was quiet before him. And he built fenced cities in Judah: for the land had rest, and he had no war in those years; because the LORD had given him rest. Therefore he said unto Judah, Let us build these cities, and make about them walls, and towers, gates, and bars, while the land is yet before us; because we have sought the LORD our God, we have sought him, and he hath given us rest on every side. So they built and prospered. And Asa had an army of men that bare targets and spears, out of Judah three hundred thousand; and out of Benjamin, that bare shields and drew bows, two hundred and fourscore thousand: all these were mighty men of valor. And there came out against them Zerah the Ethiopian with an host of a thousand, and three hundred chariots; and came unto Mareshah. Then Asa went out against him, and they set the battle in array in the valley of Zephathah at Mareshah. And Asa cried unto the LORD his God, and *said, LORD, it is nothing with thee to help, whether with many, or with them that have no power: help us, O LORD our God; for we rest on thee, and in thy name we go against this multitude. O LORD, thou art our God; let not man prevail against thee. So the LORD smote the Ethiopians before Asa, and before Judah; and the Ethiopians fled. And Asa and the people that were with him pursued them unto Gerar: and the Ethiopians were overthrown, that they could not recover themselves; for they were destroyed before the LORD, and before his host; and they carried away very much spoil. And they smote all the cities round about Gerar; for the fear of the LORD came upon them: and they spoiled all the cities; for there was exceeding much spoil in them. They smote also the tents of cattle, and carried away sheep and camels in abundance, and returned to Jerusalem"* (2 Chronicles 14:1-15).

Father Lord, by Your power of decree, I receive the anointing to live a holy life on daily basis. Lord, by Your power of decree, I command every evil in my destiny to wither and die, in the name of Jesus.

I decree for immediate power to cleanse my life from every idol. Let the altars of strange gods defiling the temple of my life be roasted by fire. Every satanic image in my memory, catch fire and die by fire. Power to seek the Lord and to influence others to seek the Lord everywhere I go, possess me. I build divine fences against sin round about my life.

I decree against territorial powers assigned to defile me in this area and I command them to become powerless before me. Every evil spirit assigned to darken my understanding and desire for holiness, fall down and die. I decree against every deceitful and desperate wicked demon attacking my heart with sin.

> *"The heart is deceitful above all things, and desperately wicked: who can know it?"* (Jeremiah 17:9).

Let powers that attack people's consciences and minds against holy living be overthrown in my life. Blood of Jesus, sanctify my life in and out and keep me holy everyday.

> *"Knowing this, that our old man is crucified with him, that the body of sin might be destroyed, that henceforth we should not serve sin"* (Romans 6:6).

I decree immediate death to the root of sin in my life. I uproot the old man and command him to bow for the Lord Jesus to take over immediately, in the name of Jesus.

Every unholy character in my life that has refused to let me go, catch fire from your root and burn to ashes. Let the body of sin in me be crucified on the cross by fire.

> *"Because the carnal mind is enmity against God: for it is not subject to the law of God, neither indeed can be. So then they that are in the flesh cannot please God. But ye are not in the flesh, but in the Spirit, if so be that the Spirit of God dwell in you. Now if any men have not the Spirit of Christ, he is none of his"* (Romans 8:7-9).

> *"Therefore, brethren, we are debtors, not to the flesh, to live after the flesh. For if ye live after the flesh, ye shall die: but if ye through the Spirit do mortify the deeds of the body, ye shall live"* (Romans 8:12-13)

I decree against my carnal mind and command it to pass through fire. Let evil powers that pollute the mind and flesh be removed from my life. Blood of Jesus, arise and rid me of unholy power. I decree that holiness and righteousness of God will dominate my inner and outer man. Any evil and sinful nature I have inherited shall die now whether devil likes it or not. I pursue every corruption in my life and command them to be perfectly purged by force, in the name of Jesus.

> "For we know that the law is spiritual: but I am carnal, sold under sin. For that which I do, I allow not: for what I would, that do I not; but what I hate, that do I. If then I do that which I would not, I consent unto the law that it is good. Now then it is no more I that do it, but sin that dwelleth in me. For I know that in me, dwelleth no good thing: for to will is present with me; but how to perform that which is good I find not. For the good that I would I do not: but the evil which I would not, that I do. Now if I do that I would not, it is no more I that do it, but sin that dwelleth in me" (Romans 7:14-20).

Let the fire of God destroy all immoral spirits in my life. O Lord my God, give me the power to live a holy life everywhere I go from today, in the name of Jesus.

> "That he would grant unto us, that we being delivered out of the hand of our enemies might serve him without fear, In holiness and righteousness before him, all the days of our life" (Luke 1:74-75).

Let the raging fire of God burn every demonic impurities in my heart, in the name of Jesus.

DECREES FOR COMPLETE HOLINESS

1. Father Lord, You are the Creator of the whole universe, keep me holy, in the name of Jesus.

2. Every agent of defilement, following me about, die, in the name of Jesus.

3. Any agent of pollution waiting for me anywhere, I bury you alive, in the name of Jesus.

4. I withdraw my entire life from any altar of pollution, in the name of Jesus.

5. O Lord, return Your divine image into my life, in the name of Jesus.

6. O Lord, release Your holy nature into my life by fire, in the name of Jesus.

7. Every spiritual impurity in my life, die, in the name of Jesus.

8. O Lord, deliver me from every inherited iniquity by Your power, in the name of Jesus.

9. Every root of evil imagination in my life, be uprooted, in the name of Jesus.

10. I receive power to be holy everywhere I go from today, in the name of Jesus.

11. Father Lord, plant holiness into my life, in the name of Jesus.

12. Let every demonic internal disorder in my life receive order by fire, in the name of Jesus.

13. Every architect of spiritual impurities in my life, catch fire, in the name of Jesus.

14. O Lord, take over the work of spiritual cleansing in my life, by Your mercy, in the name of Jesus.

15. Any sin that refuses to let me go, die, in the name of Jesus.

16. Any agent of sin, waiting for me anywhere, fall down and die, in the name of Jesus.

17. By the power in the blood of Jesus, I receive victory over sin, in the name of Jesus.

18. Let any sin that has been assigned to humiliate me fail and be humiliated, in the name of Jesus.

19. Every yoke of sin in my life, break, in the name of Jesus.

20. The power of sin that is disgracing people anywhere without being disgraced, I disgrace you, in the name of Jesus.

21. Let that evil covenant with sin in my life break, in the name of Jesus.

22. Every weapon of sin that defeated others shall not defeat me, in the name of Jesus.

23. Sin, you shall not harvest my soul, in the name of Jesus.

24. Anointing to overcome sin everywhere, possess me, in the name of Jesus.

25. O Lord, send Your help into my life from heaven to live above sin, in the name of Jesus.

Go back to the words of decree and pass your decree again.

DECREE 34

AGAINST STUBBORN ENEMIES

"In the beginning of the reign of Jehoiakim the son of Josiah king of Judah came this word from the LORD, saying, Thus saith the LORD; Stand in the court of the LORD'S house, and speak unto all the cities of Judah, which come to worship in the LORD'S house, all the words that I command thee to speak unto them; diminish not a word: If so be they will hearken, and turn every man from his evil way, that I may repent me of the evil, which I purpose to do unto them because of the evil of their doings. And thou shalt say unto them, Thus saith the LORD; If ye will not hearken to me, to walk in my law, which I have set before you, To hearken to the words of my servants the prophets, whom I sent unto you, both rising up early, and sending them, but ye have not hearkened; Then will I make this house like Shiloh, and will make this city a curse to all the nations of the earth" (Jeremiah 26:1-6).

I decree against every stubborn enemy that has taken an oath to waste my life, in the name of Jesus. Blood of Jesus, arise and flow by Your power and stand between me and every opposing enemy of my destiny. Heavenly Father, by Your decree of heaven. Let Your anger manifest in the face of all my enemies. O Lord, I decree against every stubborn evil priest that refuses to let me go, in the name of Jesus Christ.

Let my spirit, body and soul, receive power to stand and resist every attack of my stubborn enemy, in the name of Jesus. I receive the power to fight back and win every battle against my enemies by the decree of God.

> "No weapon that is formed against thee shall prosper; and every tongue that shall rise against thee in judgment thou shalt condemn. This is the heritage of the servants of the LORD, and their righteousness is of me, saith the LORD" (Isaiah 54:17).

I decree against every weapon of my enemy that is already prospering in my life and I command it to fall down and die immediately. Every evil arrow, fired into my life by the enemy of my soul, I decree by the anointing of God and I command you to backfire immediately, in the name of Jesus. Every tongue of stubborn enemy that is already speaking against me, I decree against you and I command you to receive immediate divine condemnation now by force. Let my divine heritage stolen and confiscated by enemies be released by the decree of the Almighty, in the name of Jesus.

Blood of Jesus, open your mouth wide and begin to speak destruction unto my enemies by the decree of God. Let every evil gathering against me by the enemies be scattered by the decree of God. Every gathering that is motivated by devil and my enemies, your end shall be a failure, disgrace and shame, in the name of Jesus. Let all my enemies in the battlefield begin to fall for my sake by the decree of God.

> "Behold, they shall surely gather together, but not by me: whosoever shall gather together against thee shall fall for thy sake" (Isaiah 54:15).

I command all evil doers around me to be frustrated by the destructive decree of God now. Every enemy of my destiny, be confounded, be put to shame, and be turned back and be brought to confusion forever.

I decree that all enemies that seek to hurt me shall be as chaff before the wind. Let their way be dark and slippery and let the angel of the Lord persecute them. I command destruction upon all enemies of my soul and I decree that the evil nets they have prepared against me shall catch them unawares.

> *"Let them be confounded and put to shame that seek after my soul: let them be turned back and brought to confusion that devise my hurt. Let them be as chaff before the wind: and let the angel of the LORD chase them. Let their way be dark and slippery: and let the angel of the LORD persecute them"* (Psalms 35:4-6).

> *"Let destruction come upon him at unawares; and let his net that he hath hid catch himself: into that very destruction let him fall"* (Psalms 35:8).

Every enchantment of the wicked against my life shall not work; I command and decree that by the power of God, they shall backfire. Every enemy of my divine assignment, what are you waiting for? By the decree of God, receive fire of confusion and be frustrated, in the name of Jesus.

> *"So the priests and the prophets and all the people heard Jeremiah speaking these words in the house of the LORD"* (Jeremiah 26:7).

Every gathering of evil religious people to frustrate my ministry, fail woefully and scatter. Let all enemies questioning my assignment from God be put to shame forever, in the name of Jesus. Let evil priests and leaders that have vowed to set me up, be exposed and disgraced. I command the angels of God to arise at God's anger and locate the strongholds of my enemies and destroy them all, in the name of Jesus. Blood of Jesus, speak out in your power and decree against every program of the devil against me. By the divine decree, let all my enemies begin to make mistakes that will promote me, in the name of Jesus.

DECREES AGAINST STUBBORN ENEMIES

1. Every stubborn enemy of my breakthrough, die, in the name of Jesus.

2. O Lord, deliver me from stubborn enemy that refuses to let me go, in the name of Jesus.

3. Holy Spirit, empower me to disgrace my stubborn enemies, in the name of Jesus.

4. Every marine problem in my life, die, in the name of Jesus.

5. By the power of God, I destroy every enemy in the battlefield against me, in the name of Jesus.

6. Every sickness ordained to waste me, be wasted by fire, in the name of Jesus.

7. Heavenly soldiers, box all my enemies to death, in the name of Jesus.

8. I begin to walk out from the prison of evil altars, in the name of Jesus.

9. Father Lord, use the weapons of signs and wonders to deliver me from the strong enemy, in the name of Jesus.

10. Any spiritual violence against me from the enemy, be silenced, in the name of Jesus.

11. O Lord, give me Your anointing to overcome the enemies of my soul, in the name of Jesus.

12. Every demonic door in my life, close, in the name of Jesus.

13. Let altars of darkness fighting against my soul be disgraced, in the name of Jesus.

14. Any power, announcing my name for evil, close your mouth and die, in the name of Jesus.

15. Let the wicked fire burning against me be quenched by force, in the name of Jesus.

16. Every demonic revival in my life, be terminated unto death, in the name of Jesus.

17. Any evil leg about to walk into my life, turn back, walk back to your sender, in the name of Jesus.

18. Every enemy of my promotion, be disgraced, in the name of Jesus.

19. I disband every host of the wicked gathered against me, in the name of Jesus.

20. Every uncompromising enemy of my destiny, fall down and die, in the name of Jesus.

21. I break and loose my destiny from every enemy of my soul, in the name of Jesus.

22. Any evil arrow, fired into my life, go back to my enemies, in the name of Jesus.

23. Every good thing that enemies have buried against me, be exhumed by thunder, in the name of Jesus.

24. Holy Spirit, energize me to destroy all my enemies, in the name of Jesus.

25. By the power in the blood of Jesus, I close the mouth of my enemies, in the name of Jesus.

Go back to the words of decree and pass your decree again.

DECREE 35

TO FRUSTRATE ENEMIES' PLANS

"But it came to pass, that when Sanballat heard that we builded the wall, he was wroth, and took great indignation, and mocked the Jews. And he spake before his brethren and the army of Samaria, and said, what do these feeble Jews? will they fortify themselves? Will they sacrifice? Will they make an end in a day? will they revive the stones out of the heaps of the rubbish which are burned? Now Tobiah the Ammonite was by him, and he said, even that which they build, if a fox go up, he shall even break down their stone wall. Hear, O our God; for we are despised: and turn their reproach upon their own head, and give them for a prey in the land of captivity: And cover not their iniquity, and let not their sin be blotted out from before thee: for they have provoked thee to anger before the builders. So built we the wall; and all the wall was joined together unto the half thereof: for the people had a mind to work. Ammonites, and the Ashdodites, heard that the walls of Jerusalem were made up, and that the breaches began to be stopped, then they were very wroth, And conspired all of them together to come and to fight against Jerusalem, and to hinder it. Nevertheless we made our prayer unto our God, and set a watch against them day and night, because of them" (Nehemiah 4:1-9).

By the decree of God, I frustrate every plan of my enemies and I command them to be frustrated by fire. By decision of faith, I order every evil group planning against me to scatter in shame by force, in the name of Jesus. Holy Ghost fire, begin to burn every enemy of my destiny. I take a solid decision against every evil planner against my destiny. I decree against leaders of any evil group that is planning against me. I command such evil planners to begin to fight against themselves until they destroy themselves.

I decree woes upon the heads of all evil leaders planning to put me to shame. I stand firm in the Word of God and I command all my enemies to be put to shame by force.

Every Sanballat of my destiny that is not happy because of my progress, collapse and die by force. Let the anger of my stubborn enemies be reversed against them by force. Every indignation and mockery against my life from my enemies, backfire, in the name of Jesus. Let the brethren of Sanballat personality begin to make mistakes that will frustrate their efforts against my life.

Angels of the living God, arise in Your power and put all Sanballat and Tobiah to shame and disgrace. I command all enemies that are against me to be frustrated by force, in the name of Jesus.

Father Lord, by Your decree, I command all my enemies' iniquities to be remembered and judged to their disappointments. I decree that God's anger will appear before my enemies and frustrate all their efforts and plans against me. O Lord, by Your decree, let Your programs in my life be completed to the shame of my enemies, in the name of Jesus.

Every conspiracy of my enemy that is about to manifest in my life, turn around and backfire by force. Any battle going on in my life from my enemies' camps, be won to my favor, in the name of Jesus.

> "Therefore set I in the lower places behind the wall, and on the higher places, I even set the people after their families with their swords, their spears, and their bows. And I looked, and rose up, and said unto the nobles, and to the rulers, and to the rest of the people, Be not ye afraid of them: remember the Lord, which is great and terrible, and fight for your brethren, your sons, and your daughters, your wives, and your houses. And it came to pass, when our enemies heard that it was known unto us, and God had brought their counsel to nothing, that we returned all of us to the wall, every one unto his work. And it came to pass from that time forth, that the half of my servants wrought in the work, and the other half of them held both the spears, the shields, and the bows, and the habergeons; and the rulers were behind all the house of Judah. They which builded on the wall, and they that bare burdens, with those that laded, every one with one of his hands wrought in the work, and with the other hand held a weapon. For the builders, every one had his sword girded by his side, and so builded. And he that sounded the trumpet was by me. And I said unto the nobles, and to the rulers, and to the rest of the people, the work is great and large, and we are separated upon the wall, one far from another. In what place therefore ye hear the sound of the trumpet, resort ye thither unto us: our God shall fight for us. So we labored in the work: and half of them held the spears from the rising of the morning till the stars appeared. Likewise at the same time said I unto the people, Let every one with his servant lodge within Jerusalem, that in the night they

may be a guard to us, and labor on the day. So neither I, nor my brethren, nor my servants, nor the men of the guard which followed me, none of us put off our clothes, saving that every one put them off for washing" (Nehemiah 4:13-23).

I decree immediately that my God will arise in His mercy and all my enemies would be frustrated in all their efforts against me. I command divine fear to enter into the camp of my enemies and all their weapons against me. I decree that the counsel of my enemies shall be brought to nothing, in the name of Jesus.

I decree against all demonic soldiers in the battlefield and I command them to fall down and die. I command overwhelming confusion to take hold of my enemies.

DECREES TO FRUSTRATE ENEMIES' PLANS

1. By the power of God, I disgrace every enemy of my soul, in the name of Jesus.

2. Let the plans of my enemies begin to fail them by fire, in the name of Jesus.

3. You, Goliath fighting my destiny, fall down and die, in the name of Jesus.

4. Every dangerous counsel given to my enemies against me, be fooled, in the name of Jesus.

5. The Goliath that has gathered against my life shall scatter in shame, in the name of Jesus.

6. Every Herod of my life, you are finished, die, in the name of Jesus.

7. The imagination of my enemies against my life shall not stand, in the name of Jesus.

8. Every evil plan about to manifest in my life, be frustrated by fire, in the name of Jesus.

9. Let Egyptian soldiers pursuing me to the Red Sea scatter and die, in the name of Jesus.

10. Any power laughing me to scorn, what are you waiting for? Die by force, in the name of Jesus.

11. Every enchantment released against my destiny, be cancelled by force, in the name of Jesus.

12. The enemy that is planning against me shall be disgraced, in the name of Jesus.

13. Blood of Jesus, flow into the camp of my enemies and frustrate their plans, in the name of Jesus.

14. Let the wind of the Holy Spirit blow upon the feet of my enemies, in the name of Jesus.

15. Lord Jesus, use the plans of my enemies to overthrow them, in the name of Jesus.

16. Any evil tree, planted against me by the enemies, be uprooted, in the name of Jesus.

17. Any evil tongue speaking against me, I smite you, in the name of Jesus.

18. Let heavenly soldiers arise and scatter every enemy plan against me, in the name of Jesus.

19. Any witchcraft meeting, organized against me, scatter, in the name of Jesus.

20. Heavenly Father, expose all the secret plans of the enemy, in the name of Jesus.

21. Any evil plan being made to waste my life, fail, in the name of Jesus.

22. Every territorial power, planning against me, scatter, in the name of Jesus.

23. Lord Jesus, command my enemies to favor me, in the name of Jesus.

24. Any witchcraft fire, released against me, quench, in the name of Jesus.

Go back to the words of decree and pass your decree again.

DECREE 36

AGAINST EVIL ACCUSATIONS

> *"Then was brought unto him one possessed with a devil, blind, and dumb: and he healed him, insomuch that the blind and dumb both spake and saw. And all the people were amazed, and said, Is not this the son of David? But when the Pharisees heard it, they said, This fellow doth not cast out devils, but by Beelzebub the prince of the devils. And Jesus knew their thoughts, and said unto them, Every kingdom divided against itself is brought to desolation; and every city or house divided against itself shall not stand: And if Satan cast out Satan, he is divided against himself; how shall then his kingdom stand? And if I by Beelzebub cast out devils, by whom do your children cast them out? therefore they shall be your judges. But if I cast out devils by the Spirit"* (Matthew 12:22-28).

> *"Then the whole multitude of the country of the Gadarenes round about besought him to depart from them; for they were taken with great fear: and he went up into the ship, and returned back again"* (Luke 8:37)

Any power that has vowed to waste my life with false accusation, you are a liar, collapse and die by fire immediately, in the name of Jesus. Blood of Jesus, arise, flow into my foundation and deliver me from every manner of evil accusations. I decree by the decree of God and I command every demonic power promoting evil accusation against me to perish. Heavenly Father, deliver me from the grip of evil accusers. Every evil chain that evil accusers has tied on my life, I decree against you, break to pieces, in the name of Jesus.

Father Lord, ordain terrifying noises against all my known and unknown enemies. I decree that evil accusers shall be destroyed by divine soldiers and I command that they shall be buried alive, in the name of Jesus.

Any evil group that has gathered together to accuse me for the good work I am doing in the name of the Lord, scatter, in the name of Jesus. Let all despisers that have accused me wrongly be put to shame, in the name of Jesus. Blood of Jesus, arise in your power and speak destruction to all evil accusers assigned to waste my destiny. I command all witches that have vowed to frustrate my destiny to fall down and die by fire. I decree against the Pharisees of my day that are not happy for what God is doing in my life. Let them be put to everlasting shame. Any evil personality, telling lies against me, whether you like it or not, be disgraced by fire and by force.

> *"Crying out, Men of Israel, help: This is the man, that teacheth all men every where against the people, and the law, and this place: and further brought Greeks also into the temple, and hath polluted this holy place. And the entire city was moved, and the people ran together: and they took Paul, and drew him out of the temple: and forthwith the doors were shut. And as they went about to kill him, tidings came unto the chief captain of the band, that all Jerusalem was in an uproar"* (Acts 21:28-31).

Any evil cry of false accusation against me from the pit of hell, backfire, in the name of Jesus. I decree against every satanic judgment passed against me as a result of evil accusation and I command the judgment to backfire now, in the name of Jesus. I decree against every satanic orator that has been hired to accuse me and I command confusion and madness in their brains. Every evil word of accusation that will come out of the mouth of my evil accusers, I convert you to favor me.

> *"And after five days Ananias the high priest descended with the elders, and with a certain orator named Tertullus, who informed the governor against Paul. And when he was called forth, Tertullus began to accuse him, saying, Seeing that by thee we enjoy great quietness, and that very worthy deeds are done unto this nation by thy providence, We accept it always, and in all places, most noble Felix, with all thankfulness. Notwithstanding, that I be not further tedious unto thee, I pray thee that thou wouldest hear us of thy clemency a few words. For we have found this man a pestilent fellow, and a mover of sedition among all the Jews throughout the world, and a ringleader of the sect*

of the Nazarenes: Who also hath gone about to profane the temple: whom we took, and would have judged according to our law. But the chief captain Lysias came upon us, and with great violence took him away out of our hands, Commanding his accusers to come unto thee: by examining of whom thyself mayest take knowledge of all these things, whereof we accuse him. And the Jews also assented, saying that these things were so" (Acts 24:1-9).

Father Lord, let my way of life be acceptable to You. Let my ministry arise and move people to receive Christ throughout the whole world, in the name of Jesus. I decree against every curse of witchcraft, poverty, isolation, oppression, sickness and infirmity attacking my life as a result of evil accusation. I break the head of the serpent and scorpion of evil accusation against my life. I take back by force every good thing evil accusation has stolen from my life. Every demon fighting against my destiny from the camp of my accusers, go back and attack your senders. Let every spiritual rat, bat and lizard assigned to waste my life from my accusers, die. Father Lord, by Your power, I decree against my evil accusers, in the name of Jesus.

DECREES AGAINST EVIL ACCUSATIONS

1. Any evil tongue speaking against me, I cut you off with divine matches, in the name of Jesus.

2. Every enemy of my destiny, speaking against my life, be silenced, in the name of Jesus.

3. O Lord, arise in Your power and accuse my accusers, in the name of Jesus.

4. Any evil speech spoken against me, backfire, in the name of Jesus.

5. Every pregnant mouth against me, be aborted by fire, in the name of Jesus.

6. You, strongman, that is assigned to accuse me wrongly, accuse your sender, in the name of Jesus.

7. Every giant of my evil report, fall down and die, in the name of Jesus.

8. I expel every wicked agent speaking against my life, in the name of Jesus.

9. Every anointed tongue speaking against me, receive divine cut, in the name of Jesus.

10. O Lord, overthrow the words of my enemies, in the name of Jesus.

11. Every evil word planted against me, be dismantled, in the name of Jesus.

12. Every evil spirit behind my problems, die, in the name of Jesus.

13. Any evil word that has gripped me, die, in the name of Jesus.

14. O Lord, release me from destructive words by fire, in the name of Jesus.

15. O Lord, let the words of my stubborn enemy favor me by fire, in the name of Jesus.

16. Any power accusing me from my parent's altar, be disgraced, in the name of Jesus.

17. Blood of Jesus, anoint me to overcome every evil accusation, in the name of Jesus.

18. Spirit of the living God, arise and communicate me to my helpers, in the name of Jesus.

19. Father Lord, destroy every evil word ever spoken against me, in the name of Jesus.

20. Let my life escape every evil word said against my life, in the name of Jesus.

21. Heavenly Father, speak destruction to every evil speech said against me, in the name of Jesus.

22. Blood of Jesus, speak destruction to every evil speech against me, in the name of Jesus.

23. Lord Jesus, help me to destroy every evil utterance against me, in the name of Jesus.

24. Father Lord, advertise Your peace and joy in my life, in the name of Jesus.

25. Anointing to get victory over gossipers, possess me, in the name of Jesus.

Go back to the words of decree and pass your decree again.

DECREE 37

FOR A GLORIOUS END

> *"Better is the end of a thing than the beginning thereof: and the patient in spirit is better than the proud in spirit"* (Ecclesiastes 7:8).

I stand against every evil power and I decree against their hindrances against my destiny. Blood of Jesus, by your power, I decree that my end shall be sweetened. Let every bitterness in my life be perfectly destroyed. I command divine honey to enter into my foundation and better my life by force, in the name of Jesus.

O Lord my God, arise and pronounce me victorious over every evil power. Anything in my life that does not allow me to rest, come out and die. Evil powers tormenting my life from birth, catch fire and die. Every manner of sickness, disease and infirmities, that want to follow me to the end, die today, in Jesus name.

> *"And Jesus went about all Galilee, teaching in their synagogues, and preaching the gospel of the kingdom, and healing all manner of sickness and all manner of disease among the people. And his fame went throughout all Syria: and they brought unto him all sick people that were taken with divers diseases and torments, and those which were possessed with devils, and those which were lunatick, and those that had the palsy; and he healed them. And there followed him great multitudes of people from Galilee, and from Decapolis,*

and from Jerusalem, and from Judaea, and from beyond Jordan" (Matthew 4:23-25).

Any problem in my life that is grieving me with pains, be terminated. Every demonic fear in my life, that has vowed to waste my life, I decree against you, be wasted by force. I command every manner of leprosy in my life to go back to its senders and destroy them, in the name of Jesus.

> *"When he was come down from the mountain, great multitudes followed him. And, behold, there came a leper and worshipped him, saying, Lord, if thou wilt, thou canst make me clean. And Jesus put forth his hand, and touched him, saying, I will; be thou clean. And immediately his leprosy was cleansed. And Jesus saith unto him, See thou tell no man; but go thy way, shew thyself to the priest, and offer the gift that Moses commanded, for a testimony unto them"* (Matthew 8:1-4).

Let every veil of darkness in my life that is increasing my sorrows be rent into two parts in the name of Jesus. I decree against every stubborn plague and unclean spirit in my life to die. O Lord my God, arise and calm the storms of enemies that do not allow me to rest. Let all the problems in my life receive divine judgment and be stilled forever, in the name of Jesus.

> *"And there arose a great storm of wind, and the waves beat into the ship, so that it was now full. And he was in the hinder part of the ship, asleep on a pillow: and they awake him, and say unto him, Master, carest thou not that we perish? And he arose, and rebuked the wind, and said unto the sea, Peace, be still. And the wind ceased, and there was a great calm. And he said*

unto them, why are ye so fearful? how is it that ye have no faith? And they feared exceedingly, and said one to another, what manner of man is this, that even the wind and the sea obey him?" (Mark 4:37-41).

Every wind of darkness that wants to blow in my life, receive destruction and leave me alone. I command every demonic spirit of death in my life to go back to their senders. Any power, attacking my brain, I decree against you, receive incurable madness. O Lord my God, arise and change my water into wine. Blood of Jesus, fill the water pots in my life and change them to a sweeter wine, in the name of Jesus. I decree against every problem that is eating me little by little to die.

"And a woman having an issue of blood twelve years, which had spent all her living upon physicians, neither could be healed of any, Came behind him, and touched the border of his garment: and immediately her issue of blood stanched. And Jesus said, who touched me? When all denied, Peter and they that were with him said, Master, the multitude throng thee and press thee, and sayest thou, who touched me? And Jesus said, somebody hath touched me: for I perceive that virtue is gone out of me. And when the woman saw that she was not hid, she came trembling, and falling down before him, she declared unto him before all the people for what cause she had touched him, and how she was healed immediately. And he said unto her, Daughter, be of good comfort: thy faith hath made thee whole; go in peace" (Luke 8:43-48).

I decree that as from today, every good thing I start shall end peacefully. You my beginning, embrace a perfect and good end. Every agent of bitter ends in my life, be exposed, be disgraced, fall down and die. I shall enjoy a better end in all my endeavors.

DECREES FOR A GLORIOUS END

1. Any power that wants me to end my life in hell Fire, you are a liar, die, in the name of Jesus.

2. Father Lord, help me to end my life in heaven, in the name of Jesus.

3. Any power, destroying my end, be destroyed, in the name of Jesus.

4. O Lord, assist me to perfectly continue in righteousness, in the name of Jesus.

5. Blood of Jesus, wash my life perfectly clean, in the name of Jesus.

6. I stand against any power that does not want me to succeed to the end, in the name of Jesus.

7. The spirit of almost-there syndrome working against me, die by fire, in the name of Jesus.

8. Any power fighting to stop me from reaching my goals, fall down and die, in the name of Jesus.

9. Any power standing against me at the edge of breakthrough, die, in the name of Jesus.

10. Any satanic warfare going on against my life, be terminated, in the name of Jesus.

11. Any evil power, playing games with me against my peaceful end, die, in the name of Jesus.

12. Every evil gang-up against my finishing well, scatter, in the name of Jesus.

13. Any power working against good things I started, be disgraced, in the name of Jesus.

14. Every failure waiting for me at the end, receive fire, in the name of Jesus.

15. Every evil group standing against me at the tail end, scatter in shame, in the name of Jesus.

16. Any power against my perfect progress, be frustrated, in the name of Jesus.

17. Any satanic havoc waiting for me at the end, die, in the name of Jesus.

18. Any demon at the boarder of my life, receive destruction, in the name of Jesus.

19. O Lord, don't allow the enemy to enter into the garden of my life, in the name of Jesus.

20. From the beginning to the end, O Lord, give me victory, in the name of Jesus.

21. O Lord, write my name down among those who will finish good things they started, in the name of Jesus.

22. Any power standing against my reward, fall down and die, in the name of Jesus.

23. Any evil personality assigned to take my reward, die, in the name of Jesus.

Go back to the words of decree and pass your decree again.

DECREE 38

AGAINST IMPENDING SHAME

"As they were increased, so they sinned against me: therefore will I change their glory into shame" (Hosea 4:7).

O Lord, thank You because You see everything and know everything better. By the power in the name of Jesus, I decree against every evil in store for my life. I decree against every evil plan against my destiny, in the name of Jesus. Let the power in the Word of God begin to fight for me. Let every war assigned to destroy me die in my place.

"And Cain talked with Abel his brother: and it came to pass, when they were in the field, that Cain rose up against Abel his brother, and slew him" (Genesis 4:8).

I decree that every shame the enemy wants to bring into my life through what I am going through now shall be converted to my promotion. Let my name be changed by the decree of God. Every warrior in the battlefield of my life shall bow and my glory shall appear.

"And Jacob went on his way, and the angels of God met him. And when Jacob saw them, he said, this is God's host: and he called the name of that place Mahanaim" (Genesis 32:1-2).

"And Jacob said, O God of my father Abraham, and God of my father Isaac, the LORD which saidst unto

me, Return unto thy country, and to thy kindred, and I will deal well with thee: I am not worthy of the least of all the mercies, and of all the truth, which thou hast shewed unto thy servant; for with my staff I passed over this Jordan; and now I am become two bands. Deliver me, I pray thee, from the hand of my brother, from the hand of Esau: for I fear him, lest he will come and smite me, and the mother with the children. And thou saidst, I will surely do thee good, and make thy seed as the sand of the sea, which cannot be numbered for multitude"* (Genesis 32:9-12).

"And Jacob was left alone; and there wrestled a man with him until the breaking of the day. And when he saw that he prevailed not against him, he touched the hollow of his thigh; and the hollow of Jacob's thigh was out of joint, as he wrestled with him. And he said, Let me go, for the day breaketh. And he said, I will not let thee go, except thou bless me. And he said unto him, what is thy name? And he said, Jacob. And he said, Thy name shall be called no more Jacob, but Israel: for as a prince hast thou power with God and with men, and hast prevailed And Jacob asked him, and said, Tell me, I pray thee, thy name. And he said, wherefore is it that thou dost ask after my name? And he blessed him there. And Jacob called the name of the place Peniel: for I have seen God face to face, and my life is preserved. And as he passed over Penuel the sun rose upon him, and he halted upon his thigh. Therefore the children of Israel eat not of the sinew which shrank, which is upon the hollow of the thigh, unto this day: because he touched the hollow of Jacob's thigh in the sinew that shrank" (Genesis 32:24-32).

Heavenly Father, by Your decree, arise and change my name. I command every shame in my life to be converted to my glory. Every battle in my life assigned to put me to shame, be concluded to my favor. Let soldiers of devil that have vowed to shed my blood disgracefully in the battlefield be disgraced in shame. I command every weapon of my enemy approaching me for disgrace to be diverted back to them.

> *"Then went Abimelech to Thebez, and encamped against Thebez, and took it. But there was a strong tower within the city, and thither fled all the men and women, and all they of the city, and shut it to them, and gat them up to the top of the tower. And Abimelech came unto the tower, and fought against it, and went hard unto the door of the tower to burn it with fire. And a certain woman cast a piece of a millstone upon Abimelech's head, and all to break his skull. Then he called hastily unto the young man his armor bearer, and said unto him, Draw thy sword, and slay me, that men say not of me, a woman slew him. And his young man thrust him through, and he died. And when the men of Israel saw that Abimelech was dead, they departed every man unto his place. Thus God rendered the wickedness of Abimelech, which he did unto his father, in slaying his seventy brethren: And all the evil of the men of Shechem did God render upon their heads: and upon them came the curse of Jotham the son of Jerubbaal"* (Judges 9:50-57).

Any power, living inside my life over the years to disgrace me in the day of my glory, come out and be disgraced. I command everything in me causing me to look back to the world to come out and die.

"But his wife looked back from behind him, and she became a pillar of salt" (Genesis 19:26).

The fruit that the enemy wants me to eat so that I will be disgraced like Adam and Eve, I reject you. Every seed of wrong choice that is in my life to put me to shame, catch fire and burn to ashes. Let any wickedness that wants to put me to shame before God die.

"But king Solomon loved many strange women, together with the daughter of Pharaoh, women of the Moabites, Ammonites, Edomites, Zidonians, and Hittites; Of the nations concerning which the LORD said unto the children of Israel, Ye shall not go in to them, neither shall they come in unto you: for surely they will turn away your heart after their gods: Solomon clave unto these in love. And he had seven hundred wives, princesses, and three hundred concubines: and his wives turned away his heart. For it came to pass, when Solomon was old, that his wives turned away his heart after other gods: and his heart was not perfect with the LORD his God, as was the heart of David his father. For Solomon went after Ashtoreth the goddess of the Zidonians, and after Milcom the abomination of the Ammonites. And Solomon did evil in the sight of the LORD, and went not fully after the LORD, as did David his father. Then did Solomon build an high place for Chemosh, the abomination of Moab, in the hill that is before Jerusalem, and for Molech, the abomination of the children of Ammon. And likewise did he for all his strange wives, which burnt incense and sacrificed unto their gods. And the LORD was angry with Solomon, because his heart was turned from the LORD God of

Israel, which had appeared unto him twice, And had commanded him concerning this thing, that he should not go after other gods: but he kept not that which the LORD commanded. Wherefore the LORD said unto Solomon, Forasmuch as this is done of thee, and thou hast not kept my covenant and my statutes, which I have commanded thee, I will surely rend the kingdom from thee, and will give it to thy servant" (1 Kings 11:1-11).

Let the spirit of universal and modern idolatry of my generation be aborted in my life. I decree against the sin of abortion, lust, unbelief, love of money and anger to come out of my life and die by fire.

The shame, immorality, evil gang-up and all manner of backsliding will not be my portion. I decree against every shame on my way and I command it to fall down and die, in the name of Jesus.

"And I saw a great white throne, and him that sat on it, from whose face the earth and the heaven fled away; and there was found no place for them. And I saw the dead, small and great, stand before God; and the books were opened: and another book was opened, which is the book of life: and the dead were judged out of those things which were written in the books, according to their works. And the sea gave up the dead which were in it; and death and hell delivered up the dead which were in them: and they were judged every man according to their works. And death and hell were cast into the lake of fire. This is the second death. And whosoever was not found written in the book of life was cast into the lake of fire" (Revelation 20:11-15).

I issue an order to the angels of God to arrest and destroy every satanic agenda of shame assigned to disgrace me, in the mighty name of Jesus

DECREES AGAINST IMPENDING SHAME

1. Father Lord, take me away before shame arrives, in the name of Jesus.

2. The Goliath that is destined to kill me shall die a day before me, in the name of Jesus.

3. Any curse that is placed upon my life shall be disgraced before the day of destruction, in the name of Jesus.

4. By the anointing of the Holy Ghost, let my life escape every shame, in the name of Jesus.

5. Lord Jesus, deliver me from the coming shame, in the name of Jesus.

6. O Lord, put fear into my shame and disgrace them, in the name of Jesus.

7. You my shame, receive shame and die, in the name of Jesus.

8. Any evil spirit, assigned to waste me in shame, be wasted, in the name of Jesus.

9. Any witchcraft problem about to disgrace me, be disgraced, in the name of Jesus.

10. Every evil mark, dragging me to shame, catch fire, in the name of Jesus.

11. Blood of Jesus, speak me out of shame, in the name of Jesus.

12. Every arrow of shame fired against me, backfire, in the name of Jesus.

13. Every load of shame upon my life, catch fire and burn to ashes, in the name of Jesus.

14. Anything that is producing shame against me, die in shame, in the name of Jesus.

15. Every strongman of my father's house, die in shame, in the name of Jesus.

16. Distributors of shame in my father's house, die with your shame, in the name of Jesus.

17. Any messenger of satanic shame, carry your message to your sender, in the name of Jesus.

18. Lord Jesus, don't allow me to die in shame, in the name of Jesus.

19. Every curse of shame in my life, die, in the name of Jesus.

20. I refuse to be a candidate of shame, in the name of Jesus.

21. Every dream of shame in my life, die, in the name of Jesus.

22. I reject every gift that is assigned to bring shame into my life, in the name of Jesus.

23. Every evil journey that wants to end my life in shame, be terminated, in the name of Jesus.

24. Shame will not celebrate my end, in the name of Jesus.

25. Anointing of shame in my life, die, in the name of Jesus.

26. Evil yoke that wants to end my life in shame, break, in the name of Jesus.

Go back to the words of decree and pass your decree again.

DECREE 39

TO DESTROY DEATH TRAPS

(*Study* 1 Corinthians 15)

By the decree of the Almighty, I stand against every spirit of death assigned to waste my life. Let the power of resurrection arise and disgrace every power of death in my life. I command every torment of death in my life to be cast out by fire, in the name of Jesus.

> "So when this corruptible shall have put on incorruption, and this mortal shall have put on immortality, then shall be brought to pass the saying that is written, Death is swallowed up in victory" (1 Corinthians 15:54).

Let the sting of death and powers of the grave loose their grips over my life. I decree against the powers of sin, and I stand against every evil that leads to sin.

> *"O death, where is thy sting? O grave, where is thy victory? The sting of death is sin; and the strength of sin is the law"* (1 Corinthians 15:55-56).

Any spirit of death that is pursuing my life, turn back to your sender. The death that binds people and kills them in the prison shall not come near me. Every instruction given to terminate my life, I decree against you, you must not be carried out. The death that is targeting my life from my father's house shall fail woefully. I decree against the Herod of my generation assigned to kill me at young age.

Blood of Jesus, arise and spare my life from evil determined spirit of death.

> *"Then Herod, when he saw that he was mocked of the wise men, was exceeding wroth, and sent forth, and slew all the children that were in Bethlehem, and in all the coasts thereof, from two years old and under, according to the time which he had diligently enquired of the wise men. Then was fulfilled that which was spoken by Jeremy the prophet, saying, In Rama was there a voice heard, lamentation, and weeping, and great mourning, Rachel weeping for her children, and would not be comforted, because they are not"* (Matthew 2:16-18).

Every wind of death that blew the children of Job to death, which has been assigned to locate my life, be diverted. I command every evil wind approaching me for evil to backfire now by force and locate its senders.

> *"While he was yet speaking, there came also another, and said, Thy sons and thy daughters were eating and drinking wine in their eldest brother's house: And,*

> *behold, there came a great wind from the wilderness, and smote the four corners of the house, and it fell upon the young men, and they are dead; and I only am escaped alone to tell thee"* (Job 1:18-19).

I decree against every evil arrangement of Haman to kill amass in my family to fail woefully and backfire. Every power of death planned anywhere against me shall not stand. O Lord, arise and defend me from every manner of arrows of death. The death that enemies have planned against me shall turn around and kill my enemies.

> *"Then was Nebuchadnezzar full of fury, and the form of his visage was changed against Shadrach, Meshach, and Abednego: therefore he spake, and commanded that they should heat the furnace one seven times more than it was wont to be heated. And he commanded the most mighty men that were in his army to bind Shadrach, Meshach, and Abednego, and to cast them into the burning fiery furnace. Then these men were bound in their coats, their hosen, and their hats, and their other garments, and were cast into the midst of the burning fiery furnace. Therefore because the king's commandment was urgent, and the furnace exceeding hot, the flame of the fire slew those men that took up Shadrach, Meshach, and Abednego"* (Daniel 3:19-22).

Let fires of death loose their hold over my destiny. The weapons of death in the battlefield will not have power over me. No matter how the enemies want to kill me, I decree that they shall fail. I refuse by the decree of God that I shall die in the hand of my enemies.

> *"King spake and said to Daniel, O Daniel, servant of the living God, is thy God, whom thou continually, able*

to deliver thee from the lions? Then said Daniel unto the king, O king, live for ever. My God hath sent his angel, and hath shut the lions' mouths, that they have not hurt me: forasmuch as before him innocency was found in me; and also before thee, O king, have I done no hurt. Then was the king exceeding glad for him, and commanded that they should take Daniel up out of the den. So Daniel was taken up out of the den, and no manner of hurt was found upon him, because he believed in his God. And the king commanded, and they brought those men which had accused Daniel, and they cast them into the den of lions, them, their children, and their wives; and the lions had the mastery of them, and brake all their bones in pieces or ever they came at the bottom of the den" (Daniel 6: 20-24).

Every lion-like spirit of death, loose your hold over my life, in the name of Jesus.

DECREES TO DESTROY DEATH TRAPS

1. Any power assigned to destroy good things of my life, receive destruction, in the name of Jesus.

2. O Lord, arise in Your anger and kill my killers, in the name of Jesus.

3. By the anointing of the Holy Ghost, I destroy all my destroyers, in the name of Jesus.

4. Any witchcraft sickness that is ready to kill me, kill your owner first, in the name of Jesus.

5. Any generational curse upon my life that is about to waste me, be wasted, in the name of Jesus.

6. O Lord, put off the switch of death hovering over my life, in the name of Jesus.

7. Blood of Jesus, confront and conquer death verdicts in my life, in the name of Jesus.

8. Blood of Jesus, speak death to satanic death in my life, in the name of Jesus.

9. Every mark of death upon my life, you are finished, die by fire, in the name of Jesus.

10. Every angel of death looking for me, be blinded, in the name of Jesus.

11. Lord Jesus, take me away from the grave, in the name of Jesus.

12. O Lord, remove my life from death register, in the name of Jesus.

13. Let the strongman of death in my life be destroyed now, in the name of Jesus.

14. Any demon that is tormenting me with death, be tormented unto death, in the name of Jesus.

15. Fire of God, burn every trace of death in my life to ashes, in the name of Jesus.

16. Death, run away from every good thing that I do in life, in the name of Jesus.

17. The shameful death that killed my parents or anyone I know will not kill me, in the name of Jesus.

18. You my death, die and die again, in the name of Jesus.

19. Any power that wants to wake up my death, die also, in the name of Jesus.

20. Death shall no more trouble me, in the name of Jesus.

21. Let the judgmental fire of God deliver me from death and hell, in the name of Jesus.

22. Every yoke of death upon my life, die by fire, in the name of Jesus.

23. I shall not die but live for my God, in the name of Jesus.

Go back to the words of decree and pass your decree again.

DECREE 40

FOR OPENED DOORS

"For a great door and effectual is opened unto me, and there are many adversaries" (1 Corinthians 16:9).

By the flaming sword of the Holy Spirit, I command every strongman in my life to die. Let everything about me receive divine blessings and great opened doors. Any power that will oppose God's opened doors in my life this year shall die. I decree that the forces of heaven shall stand in the four corners of the earth to usher me into every divine doors opened for my destiny. Let the host of heaven destroy any great door locked up against my life.

I decree against the powers of darkness standing in the front doors that God has opened for me. Let all the host of hell that is standing against my life be scattered, in the name of Jesus. I stand against every demonic alliance that are fighting against my opened doors. Heavenly soldiers, arise in your anger and break every door of prosperity locked against me by every household enemy.

"Behold, I will make them of the synagogue of Satan, which say they are Jews, and are not, but do lie; behold, I will make them to come and worship before thy feet, and to know that I have loved thee" (Revelation 3:9).

I command my heavens to open and let the windows of heavens be opened to me by force. Let angels of God from the third heaven pour great blessings of God into my life. By the power in the Word of God, I decree against every demonic opposition to my opened doors. Let the thunder fire of God from the throne of God come forth and open the doors of every good thing locked up against me. Blood of Jesus, flow into the foundation of my life and open all the doors that my ancestors locked up through sin and idolatry. Any evil in my personal life that has been the cause of locked doors in my life, die by the blood of Jesus.

> *"And when I saw him, I fell at his feet as dead. And he laid his right hand upon me, saying unto me, Fear not; I am the first and the last: I am he that liveth, and was dead; and, behold, I am alive for evermore, Amen; and have the keys of hell and of death"* (<u>Revelation 1:17-18</u>).

Every intimidating wall of Jericho standing against my prosperity, collapse by force, in the name of Jesus. Every demonic padlock against my life, break to pieces and burn to ashes. I arise in power and I enter into every manner of the doors of blessings by force. I walk into my prosperity, divine mercy, financial breakthroughs and unmerited favors.

By this time tomorrow, I shall be announced by people that matters worldwide. It shall be impossible for the enemy to stand against me from today, anywhere I go. By this opened door, lack will die forever in my life. I decree for abundant wealth from the third heaven. Wealth, you must honor God in my life forever.

By the power in the Word of God through these open doors, I shall never be poor again or want any good thing. The wealth of the Gentiles shall be my portion forever. Every satanic storehouse shall be opened for me by force at the mention of the name of Jesus. Every evil head standing against my open doors, I cut you off; fall from your neck.

> *"Lift up your heads, O ye gates; and be ye lift up, ye everlasting doors; and the King of glory shall come in. Who is this King of glory? The LORD strong and mighty, the LORD mighty in battle. Lift up your heads, O ye gates; even lift them up, ye everlasting doors; and the King of glory shall come in"* (Psalms 24:7-9).

I command the gates of blessings to begin to open for my sake now. Let everlasting doors locked up against my generation start opening right now. I release soldiers from the third heaven to knock, break and open every good door locked up against me by the power of the king of glory.

DECREES FOR OPEN DOORS

1. Father Lord, give me divine opened doors that will make me great, in the name of Jesus.

2. Lord Jesus, arise and open great doors for me today, in the name of Jesus.

3. Heavenly Father, break every yoke of poverty in my life, in the name of Jesus.

4. Every enemy of my open doors, be disgraced, in the name of Jesus.

5. Any evil trap assigned to catch me, catch your owner, in the name of Jesus.

6. Every enemy of my divine harvest, fall down and die, in the name of Jesus.

7. Any wall of Jericho standing against my breakthrough, collapse by fire, in the name of Jesus.

8. Let my heavens open by fire and let my miracle appear, in the name of Jesus.

9. Every problem designed to close the doors of my blessings, disappear by fire, in the name of Jesus.

10. Father Lord, let my life attract divine favor, in the name of Jesus.

11. Gates of miracles, open for my sake in every city of this world, in the name of Jesus.

12. Every serpent blocking my breakthrough, I cut off your head by fire, in the name of Jesus.

13. Every appointment with poverty in my life, be broken by fire, in the name of Jesus.

14. Any satanic agent blocking my way to greatness, fall down and die, in the name of Jesus.

15. Let the armies from heaven force the doors of greatness open by force, in the name of Jesus.

16. Every satanic wall, blocking my way to success, collapse by thunder, in the name of Jesus.

17. Every visible and invisible hindrance against my life, appear, in the name of Jesus.

18. Holy Ghost fire, burn every satanic sacrifice against me to ashes, in the name of Jesus.

19. Blood of Jesus, open great doors for me, in the name of Jesus.

20. Every satanic surveillance that has been mounted against my breakthrough, disappear, in the name of Jesus.

21. Let the power of God destroy every evil weapon blocking my way to God, in the name of Jesus.

22. Any evil barricade against my promotion, be roasted by fire, in the name of Jesus.

23. Every problem designed to terminate my journey with God, die, in the name of Jesus.

24. Every evil agenda working against my life, die, in the name of Jesus.

25. Every cloud of darkness that has caged me, clear away, in the name of Jesus.

26. My miracles, suspended in the air, come down, in the name of Jesus.

Go back to the words of decree and pass your decree again.

THANK YOU SO MUCH

Beloved, I hope you enjoyed this book as much as I believe God has touched your heart today. I cannot thank you enough for your continued support for this prayer ministry.

I appreciate you so much for spending time to read this wonderful prayer book, and if you have an extra second, I would love to hear what you think about this book.

Please, do share a rereview of this book on Amazon and share your testimonies with me by sending an email to me at prayermadu@yahoo.com, also in Facebook at www.facebook.com/prayermadueke. I invite you to my website at *www.prayermadueke.com* to view many other books I have written on various issues of life, especially on marriage, family, sexual problems and money.

I will be delighted to partner with you also in organized crusades, ceremonies, marriages and marriage seminars, special events, church ministration and fellowship for the advancement of God's kingdom here on earth.

Thank you again, and I wish you nothing less than success in life. God bless you.

Prayer M. Madueke
CHRISTIAN AUTHOR

BOOKS BY PRAYER M. MADUEKE

- 100 Days Prayers to Wake Up Your Lazarus
- 15 Deliverance Steps to Everlasting Life
- 21/40 Nights of Decrees and Your Enemies Will Surrender
- 35 Deliverance Steps to Everlasting Rest
- 35 Special Dangerous Decrees
- 40 Prayer Giants
- Agbogugu Liberation and Solemn Assembly
- Alone with God (Complete Version)
- Americans, May I Have Your Attention Please
- Avoid Academic Defeats
- Because You Are Living Abroad
- Biafra of My Dream
- Breaking Evil Yokes
- Call to Help the Igbo Nation
- Call to Renew Covenant
- Community Liberation and Solemn Assembly
- Confront and Conquer Your Enemy
- Contemporary Politicians' Prayers for Nation Building
- Corpers, May I Have Your Attention Please
- Crossing the Hurdles
- Dealing with Established Problem
- Dealing with Institutional Altars

- *Deliverance by the Worthy Lamb*
- *Deliverance from Academic Defeats*
- *Deliverance from All Kinds of Problem*
- *Deliverance Letters – 1*
- *Deliverance Letters – 2*
- *Eastern Ministers Prayer Meeting*
- *Evil Summon*
- *Fall and Rise of the Igbo Nation*
- *Foundation Exposed (Part 1)*
- *Foundations Exposed (Part 2)*
- *Gay Crusade in Africa (Tufiakwa)*
- *General Prayers for Nation Building: Prayers for Nation Building Vol. 3 (Volume 3)*
- *Healing Covenant*
- *Igbo Businessmen Prayer Network*
- *International Women's Prayer Network*
- *Ministers Empowerment Prayer Network*
- *More Kingdoms to Conquer*
- *Organized Student in a Disorganized School*
- *Pray for a New Nigeria*
- *Pray for an Organized Nigeria*
- *Pray for Eastern Regional Leaders*
- *Pray for Jamaica*
- *Pray for Trump, America, Israel and Yourself*

- *Pray for Your Country*
- *Pray for Your Pastor and Yourself*
- *Prayer Campaign for a Better Ghana*
- *Prayer Campaign for a Better Kenya*
- *Prayer Campaign for Nigeria*
- *Prayer Campaign for Uganda*
- *Prayer Retreat*
- *Prayer Riots to Overthrow Divorce*
- *Prayers Against All Manner of Sickness and Disease*
- *Prayers Against Premature Death*
- *Prayers Against Satanic Oppression*
- *Prayers for a Happy Married Life*
- *Prayers for a Job Interview*
- *Prayers for Academic Success*
- *Prayers for an Excellent Job*
- *Prayers for Breakthrough in Your Business*
- *Prayers for Children and Youths*
- *Prayers for Christmas*
- *Prayers for College and University Students*
- *Prayers for Conception and Power to Retain*
- *Prayers for Deliverance*
- *Prayers for Fertility in Your Marriage*
- *Prayers for Financial Breakthrough*
- *Prayers for Good Health*

- *Prayers for Healthy Living and Long life*
- *Prayers for Marriage and Family*
- *Prayers for Marriages in Distress*
- *Prayers for Modern-Day Politics and Politicians*
- *Prayers for Nation Building*
- *Prayers for Newly Married Couple*
- *Prayers for Overcoming Attitude Problem*
- *Prayers for Political Excellence and Veteran Politicians (Prayers for Nation Building Book 2)*
- *Prayers for Pregnant Women*
- *Prayers for Restoration of Peace in Marriage*
- *Prayers for Sound Sleep and Rest*
- *Prayers for Success in Examination*
- *Prayers for Successful Career*
- *Prayers for Widows and Orphans*
- *Prayers for Your Children's Deliverance*
- *Prayers for Your Wedding*
- *Prayers to Buy a Home and Settle Down*
- *Prayers to Conceive and Bear Children*
- *Prayers to Deliver Your Child Safely*
- *Prayers to End a Prolonged Pregnancy*
- *Prayers to Enjoy Your Wealth and Riches*
- *Prayers to Experience Love in Your Marriage*
- *Prayers to Get Married Happily*

- *Prayers to Heal Broken Relationship*
- *Prayers to Keep Your Marriage Out of Trouble*
- *Prayers to Live an Excellent Life*
- *Prayers to Live and End Your Life Well*
- *Prayers to Marry Without Delay*
- *Prayers to Overcome an Evil Habit*
- *Prayers to Overcome Attitude Problems*
- *Prayers to Overcome Miscarriage*
- *Prayers to Pray During Courtship*
- *Prayers to Pray During Honeymoon*
- *Prayers to Preserve Your Marriage*
- *Prayers to Prevent Separation of Couples*
- *Prayers to Progress in Your Career*
- *Prayers to Raise Godly Children*
- *Prayers to Receive Financial Miracle*
- *Prayers to Retain Your Pregnancy*
- *Prayers to Triumph Over Divorce*
- *Queen of Heaven: Wife of Satan*
- *School for Children Teachers*
- *School for Church Workers*
- *School for the Igbo Hebrew Nation*
- *School for Women of Purpose: Women*
- *School for Youths and Students*
- *School of Deliverance with Eternity in View*

- *School of Prayer*
- *School of Ministry for Ministers in Ministry*
- *Special Prayers in His Presence*
- *Tears in Prison: Prisoners of Hope*
- *The First Deliverance*
- *The Operation of the Woman That Sit Upon Many Waters*
- *The Philosophy of Deliverance*
- *The Reality of Spirit Marriage*
- *The Sword of New Testament Deliverance*
- *The Vision and Preparation for the Igbo Hebrew Nation Walk with God*
- *Two Prosperities*
- *Upon All These Prayers*
- *Veteran Politicians' Prayers for Nation Building*
- *Welcome to Campus*
- *When Evil Altars Are Multiplied*
- *When I Grow Up Visions*
- *You Are a Man's Wife*
- *Your Dream Directory*
- *Youths, May I Have Your Attention Please?*

Printed in Great Britain
by Amazon